Changing Careers

Steps to Success

Changing Careers

Steps to Success

Lola Sikula

Fullerton College

Brooks/Cole Publishing Company
Pacific Grove, CA

ITP™ The trademark ITP is used under license.

Brooks/Cole Publishing Company
A Division of Wadsworth, Inc.

Printed in the United States of America

10 9 8 7 6 5 4 3 2 1

Library of Congress Cataloging-in-Publication Data

Sikula, Lola, [date]
Changing careers : steps to success / Lola Sikula.
p. cm.
Includes bibliographical references and index.
ISBN 0-534-20766-9
1. Career changes—Handbooks, manuals, etc. 2. Résumés (Employment)—Handbooks, manuals, etc. 3. Vocational guidance—Handbooks, manuals, etc. I. Title.
HF5384.S57 1993
650.14—dc20 93-19491
CIP

Sponsoring Editor: *Claire Verduin*
Editorial Associate: *Gay C. Bond*
Production Editor: *Nancy L. Shammas*
Manuscript Editor: *Laurie Vaughn*
Permissions Editor: *Karen Wootten*
Interior Design: *Katherine Minerva*
Cover Design: *Karen Marquardt*
Art Coordinator: *Susan Haberkorn*
Typesetting: *Bookends Typesetting*
Printing and Binding: *Malloy Lithographing, Inc.*

To my brother,
Jeffery Peter Larson,
. . . who decided it was never too late to start over.

Brief Contents

Contents

Preface

The decade of the 1990s is teeming with change. Numerous economic and political changes, both domestic and foreign, have had a direct impact on the American workplace. These changes, as well as personal life transitions, are prompting many people to reconsider their present careers and to seek new and different options. This book is intended as a guidebook for people who are facing one of life's major transitions—a career change. The book will take you step by step through this transition.

Use this book if your job is disappearing or disappointing. Use it if you have suddenly found yourself out of work due to company reorganization or if you have been terminated. Use it if you are returning to the labor market after an absence of several years and feel you are in either the "over" syndrome (overexperienced, overaged, overpriced), or the "under" syndrome (underexperienced, underaged, underpaid). Use this book if the relocation of your spouse's job has caused you to change jobs or if you are considering a retirement career.

You are also invited to use this book if you are presently experiencing one or more of life's most traumatic events, including divorce, death of a spouse or close family member, business failure, or some other type of financial difficulty. These events often prompt people to change direction and careers. This book will equip you with the coping skills to adapt to and work through the change. The premise of this book is that although these crises are painful, they represent new opportunities and can become turning points in your life.

I am deeply indebted to the hundreds of men and women I have counseled over the past 18 years during my tenure at Fullerton College, as well as in my private practice. The book contains numerous examples drawn from real situations. I have altered some of the details in the examples to preserve the anonymity of these people, but I have not altered the essence of their experiences.

Special acknowledgment and appreciation goes to Claire Verduin, Editor, Brooks/Cole Publishing Company. I am also truly indebted to the entire production and marketing team: Nancy Shammas, Production Editor; Karen Wootten, Permissions Editor; Laurie Vaughn, Copyeditor; Katherine Minerva, Designer; Susan Haberkorn, Art Coordinator; and Connie Jirovsky, Marketing Manager. A very special thanks goes to the academic reviewer, my colleague Robert A. Wood from Cypress College. Last but not least, I thank my husband John Sikula, Dean of the College of Education at California State University, Long Beach, who assisted me in editing the manuscript.

Good luck, relax, and enjoy the journey!

Lola Sikula

Introduction

There still seems to be a myth about what constitutes success in this country. It used to be that you decided at a relatively early age what type of work you wanted to do; obtained the necessary schooling for that occupation; and stayed with one company or organization, rose to the highest possible rank, and then retired.

Today, to an upwardly mobile work force, change seems commonplace. It has been estimated that the average person today will change careers—not jobs—three to five times in a lifetime. This statistic too may be changing, because not all career changes are voluntary. As evidenced by a recent downturn in the national economy, thousands of workers at all levels have been forced out of work.

Change . . . for some, the mere word evokes a nervous response. For others, it is the natural path one must take to achieve a goal. Cyndi is a good example of the latter.

After graduating with a B.A. degree with double majors in child development and communications and a minor in English, Cyndi worked at a network television station for six months as a switcher operator. (A switcher is the television director's control panel for all television cameras in operation.) She had hoped to somehow enter the television field as a writer for children's programs, but that did not occur. Later, a friend of Cyndi's told her about a proofreading position at Sears, Roebuck & Co. Cyndi gambled that this job would lead her into the field of advertising—and it did. Soon she was promoted to a position she had created: the West Coast advertising coordinator.

Eventually, a major reorganization at Sears took place, and Cyndi was out. She then found a job as a technical editor at a publications house where she learned how to use the various military standards and government specifications for government proposals as well as all the terminology used in commercial and aerospace environments. Cyndi stayed with this publications house for one and one-half years, then moved on to another, larger publications house, where over the next three years, she was assigned as a contract consultant to various aerospace companies. Because the prosperity of these companies was short-lived and budgets were reduced, soon Cyndi was out job-hunting again. She then interviewed with a major manufacturer of computer graphics peripherals, where she hired on as a technical editor. Again, she was able to use her previous work experiences and skills and further on-the-job training to become fluent in her company's documentation quality standards. As evidence of her current success, the company and several professional organizations have presented Cyndi with various awards for her editing. She is still with the company.

As you can see by the preceding example, not all career changes are linear; some follow more of a spiral pattern. In this text you will be guided through steps in a logical fashion. But the time it will take for any specific change to come to fruition is highly individualistic and difficult to predict.

♦ Who Should Use This Book?

This book has been written for those facing a career transition. Some of you may have been terminated or laid off. Others may be underemployed, be experiencing job burnout, or simply be misplaced in the wrong job. Still others may be going back to work after several years' absence from the work force or may have to change jobs because a spouse has been relocated. All of you probably have something in common—you are facing an important transition in your life.

Changing careers is uncomfortable and stressful. Going through the process alone without a guide can indeed be intimidating; it is always comforting to know that others have gone before you and succeeded. This book is intended to be your guide. It combines the strategies I have taught to hundreds of men and women over two decades as a college instructor, counselor, and private consultant. The strategies really do work. Let me be your guide as I take you through the steps involved in making this important transition.

♦ What Is It All About?

Chapter One begins to move you toward transition by identifying who changes careers and by examining the various life stages and the changes inherent in each. We will examine the changing times and how we are influenced by socioeconomic factors. We will also look at futurism as a topic to consider when preparing for realistic jobs in an age of automation and economic uncertainty.

Chapter Two is dedicated to mobilizing a support system. "Rome was not built in a day!" People tend to become restless and frustrated during career transition. The purpose of this chapter is to help you develop and maintain a positive mental attitude. You will be encouraged to engage the assistance of others by developing a network of appropriate relationships. A strong support network can help you cope with the difficulties involved in changing careers.

Chapter Three allows you to take a good look at managing yourself and your life during transition. Fear and anxiety are understandable emotions in any type of change. This chapter will give you methods of identifying and coping with stress as well as of monitoring the way you spend your time. Total "wellness" will be emphasized as you take into account the importance of proper nutrition and exercise in the transition process.

Chapters Four and Five start the process with self-assessment. You will examine in depth your interests, skills, temperament, and values. Your values will lead you directly to decision making and will allow you to make choices based on how you choose to lead your life. All the exercises in Chapters Four and Five have been used extensively in my "Changing Careers" classes. These four elements form the basic framework for who you are.

Unless you know yourself thoroughly, you cannot make well-thought-out choices. The perfect career match fits your interests, skills, temperament, and values. Is this possible, you ask? Of course it is! Also, changing careers need not be frustrating and stressful. Actually, it will be quite enjoyable. What person is not interested in himself or herself? In reading this book, you will focus only on yourself, not on what another person wants for you. The concepts covered in the self-assessment chapters will also become tools you can use to solve other problems in your life.

Chapter Six will lead you through some tried-and-true research methods. It has been satisfying to take hundreds of people through a process that really works. Information is gathered in two ways: by using printed material and by talking to others. Step-by-step guidance will be given as to where to find career information and how to use these data. Perhaps the most valuable information you collect will be that which you gather from talking to persons who are already doing the kind of work you want to do. So much has been written about informational interviewing that the subject will not be repeated here other than to offer testimony that it does work. Some special hints will be given to "fortify" those who feel a little timid in this process.

Chapter Seven will begin with setting goals and objectives. What do you want from a career? From life? This may be a time for repositioning, of evaluating where you have been and where you want to go. You will also be prompted to begin this process with a positive mindset.

This chapter gets you started with a plan of action. You are now going to take the data and use them to make decisions. Perhaps you will opt for self-employment; Chapter Seven helps you examine this option. It will lead you through some preliminary points to consider in planning a business of your own.

Chapter Eight is concerned with marketing yourself through résumés and cover letters. After you have a clear picture of yourself and the job you want, how do you get it? The first step in this marketing process is to sell yourself on paper to those who have the power to hire you. For most of you this will mean writing a functional résumé—one that sells you on the basis of what you have accomplished, what you do best, and what you can do for the prospective employer. Here is where your transferable skills come into play. All those wonderful things you found out about yourself in Chapter Four can now be brought out fully in the form of a résumé that really sells you.

Sound too easy to be true? It is not only quite easy, but also very possible. You will find annotated examples of résumés that others have used successfully to change careers. Their names, however, have been changed.

Chapter Nine contains a review of the steps of interviewing. Included in this chapter is a rationale of why certain questions are asked, and suggestions are provided on how to prepare yourself for an interview. You will be able to formulate your own responses to questions that are frequently asked during an interview. The section on stress-oriented interviews gives ideas on how to respond to some of the more difficult questions. This chapter contains clear guidelines and practice exercises that should make your next and *last* interview very successful.

Finally, for your convenience, the appendices at the end of the book include a vocational history questionnaire, a financial planning guide, and a source list for supplemental reading. A bibliography and a resource list are also provided. Now, on with the journey!

1 Preparing for Change

"The hardest thing to see is what is in front of your eyes." 

Goethe

People develop continuously throughout life. Each person goes through various life stages, but the sequence and intensity of the changes may vary. You should understand that a career change is an actual change of occupation rather than a job upgrade or upward mobility within the same line of work. After considering your reasons for change, some of you may find that you need to change your working conditions, not your career. Or, after examining current trends in the labor market, you may find that your career change needs to take place in steps over a period of time. The first step may lead to an entry-level position in a new field and from there you can look at additional possibilities and plan your next strategy. In this chapter you will be asked to consider all the ramifications of making a career change.

After reading this chapter you should understand the following:

- That you can expect to find yourself in a particular life stage that can affect the way you view change in general
- That people develop continuously throughout life
- That a career change is an actual change of occupation rather than a job upgrade or upward mobility within the same line of work

- That a number of occupational trends will affect your career transition during the next decade

You should be able to do the following:

- Identify the life stage you now occupy
- Define what is meant by a career change
- Understand your reasons for changing careers
- Determine how some of the prevailing occupational trends may affect your career transition

This book is about transition and change. Although its primary focus is career transition, the process of career transition happens in conjunction with other changes in your life. Thus, this book addresses not just a job search but also a self-search: What are your values and interests? What needs or impulses are affecting you and nudging (or shoving!) you toward career and life changes? How will you go about making these changes, considering your busy schedule, your responsibilities, and your fears?

This book is not designed for college freshmen deciding on a first-time career (although it would certainly be useful to those individuals). Instead, it is designed for people who have already been active in the work world for some time and who now find themselves, for any number of reasons, ready for a change.

For those of you who have been homemakers and are now seeking employment outside the home, make no mistake about it: You are changing careers because your previous job in the home was indeed a career. One reentry woman summed it up this way:

> I am a woman who has worn many hats. I have been a daughter, granddaughter, aunt, niece, cousin, wife for 22 years, mother of nine children for the past 35 years, self-employed head of a day care business, student, college graduate, sales representative, community volunteer, grandmother to nine children, neighbor, and friend.

This book will address the special needs of all who are in career transition. People find themselves in career transition for many reasons. Perhaps you have found yourself the victim of a company reorganization, a "reduction in force," or a plant closure. As a former homemaker, necessity or your own desires may be pushing you toward change. Maybe you are growing bored with your current job and see little hope of finding an interesting position in your present field. Perhaps you are working in a job that does not reward you adequately, and you want to begin working toward a more satisfying career.

These reasons and many others bring people into career classes where they can tune in to other people's experiences and learn more about themselves and the world of work.

♦ The First Steps

Whatever your circumstances, it is up to you to make the fullest use of this text and your learning environment so you will be better prepared to make your choices and changes. Most of you will already have experienced one or more of life's many positive transitions—moving away from your parental home, going to college, getting your first job, getting married, and having a family. When you make positive life transitions you are more likely to perceive other life transitions, such as a career change, as a challenge rather than as something to fear.

Facing Challenges

Every transition begins with an ending. Whether you are embarking on a career or life change due to choice or to forced circumstances, it is necessary to begin looking forward and to face the challenge that lies before you. For example, perhaps you are recently divorced or have recently been laid off. It is crucial that, to as great a degree as possible, you now put the negative aspect of this transition behind you.

Facing the future is not always easy. You may feel that your identity is linked to your previous job or to your marriage; you may miss former co-workers or fear leaving your current job. Perhaps you feel anxiety about returning to school or about leaving your children with baby-sitters. To help resolve these doubts and maintain a positive attitude, think of this time as a neutral zone—a space of time in which you sort your thoughts and collect the information necessary to make sound decisions. As one single parent stated:

> In the course of my many years as a single parent, I have made so many decisions; I feel I have been president of a major corporation, but with one drawback—no pension or retirement plans to see me through my old age.

Resist the impulse to make snap decisions or to panic. Instead, think of this as a time to lean on others for help, to establish ground rules for the coming months regarding your time and your goals.

Getting Support

You may feel that this transition period is too difficult to be managed, that your unique situation is by far the worst possible one, and that others do not understand how difficult your road is. Indeed, those in career transition may be out of work, yet still have all their monetary obligations. Others may have a time-consuming job and family responsibilities and have to squeeze in schooling or hunting for a new job. Although this book cannot address all the problems and questions that arise during a time of transition, help is available through a number of channels. Whether you need financial help, emotional support, practical advice, or some other form of assistance, the first step is to find out what types of help are available. For example, you may wish to join a support group made up of people in situations similar to yours. If so, your counselor or advisor should be able to direct you to such an organization or to a list of such groups. Remember these general guidelines:

- Take comfort in the fact that those around you are in situations similar to yours and can offer you advice and help. Take advantage of your classroom situation to meet others, to learn, and to network.
- Seek out the advice of career counselors, academic advisors, and other such individuals; their job is to assist people in your position.
- If you are between jobs, consider looking for temporary or part-time employment.
- Remember that the sooner you begin making the necessary changes, the sooner you will complete them.

♦ Adults' Changing Needs and Roles

It is natural for adults to have changing needs and changing roles, although this has only recently become a topic of study for psychologists and others. Many people facing career transition believe they are the "odd person out." You may have the mistaken belief that other people your age are settled and happy and do not question their choices or consider making changes. In fact, the adult-development theorists Erikson (1963) and Gould (1978) offer considerable evidence that people change continuously throughout life. It is important for you to evaluate where you are in your development and to analyze some of the forces within you that may be calling for change.

The following is a summary of the life stages that most adults go through to some degree. Please remember that the descriptions and time periods are general. Everyone goes through various life stages, but the sequence and intensity of the changes may vary greatly from person to person.

Ages 20 to 30

This period involves much testing of skills and the establishment of individual independence and identity. Peer groups are important as the individual searches for personal identity. During this stage, people tend to reach out toward others in an attempt to develop intimacy in relationships. In some cases, close friendships meet this need. This period is usually marked by the end of formal education and the beginning of full-time work. The individual may hold a variety of jobs as he or she tests working environments and job skills. Having to start at the bottom of the ladder in many organizations and the slow movement into areas of increased responsibility can be sources of frustration. Many individuals have a need to move quickly and may not be accepting of older people and the establishment.

Family skills are tested during this time, often through a marriage relationship and the effort it takes to make such a relationship work. In many cases, individuals are unable to maintain a positive relationship, which can lead to frustration and self-doubt.

In summary, this period is one of rapid growth and development. In many ways this is a time in which opportunities seem great—so great that the person may be frustrated with the rate at which some goals are achieved. During this stage, the individual tests, learns, and develops new skills and identity as an adult.

Ages 30 to 40

This period may be marked by a reevaluation of life's purpose. Individuals may question early decisions they made regarding self, career, and family. Recognition has been granted for accomplishments on the job, and the individual has the satisfaction of making significant contributions in the work setting. However, more marriages end in divorce in this period than in any other. Women who have been working in the home or in a job that offers little challenge may want to change and find a new job or career.

During this time, individuals are reminded that there is a life process to be understood. Their physical strength and capabilities may not be the same as before. They feel a need to define success and to feel successful. Many times success is displayed in the form of material things—in "keeping up with the Joneses." This age range has been a favorite target of the media, and the terms *yuppie* and *baby boomer* are frequently attached to these individuals. Much advertising is also targeted to this group.

This is indeed the most dynamic of all life periods. It begins with relative youth and ends with middle age. Individuals confront more issues during this period than any other, and the decisions made at this stage tend to determine an individual's life-style for years to come.

Ages 40 to 50

Individuals in this period begin to face the challenge of midlife. For some, this is a time to reflect on what could have or should have been done. During this stage, people often feel that time is running out. Time becomes more important as individuals realize they may not be as free to make the same decisions they made in their 20s or 30s. Often, a reevaluation of goals and objectives occurs. There may be less opportunity to move up the ladder and fewer possibilities of moving from one job to another. This period is also marked by children's leaving home, and a large void may need to be filled. Further, this is a time when some people face their own mortality as they experience their parents' deaths.

Although the early forties can be a time of upheaval, the middle to late forties can be a period of settling down. The individual may be more willing to settle, less driven, and more willing to relax. Leisure time becomes more important. Reaching out for new friendships may be coupled with declining health, an unhappy marriage, or fear of being passed up for promotion.

Ages 50 to 60

People typically go through this stage in one of two ways. One approach is to view the period with discouragement, withdrawal, and resignation, and the aging process with great negativity and fear. The other approach is to see this period as an opportunity to try new things and to establish new friendships, unencumbered by some of the demands and responsibilities of earlier years.

This period is marked by a mellowing process in which a softening of feelings and relationships occurs and more emphasis is placed on the joys of everyday living. At this time, a person typically pays increased attention to preretirement planning.

This period can be marked by new challenges. Some individuals, challenged by the stimulation of beginning something new, may enter a new career. Retirement offers may also be made at this time. However, corporations often value the wisdom and experience offered by members of this group. The majority of upper management of the Fortune 500 companies are in this age range. Indeed, as we progress into the 1990s we will find more people in this age group actively participating in the labor market.

Ages 60 and Up

Most people are faced with retirement during this period, and their attitudes toward retirement color their reactions to this stage of life. Some may perceive retirement as a way of being told they are no longer useful, and they may find themselves with large blocks of unfilled time. Others see this time as an opportunity to try new things and to spend more time on activities for which they had little time in the past. The physical deterioration of the aging process must be faced during this period, and a person may need to adjust to the loss of his or her spouse and close friends.

Although professionally this is usually a time of winding down, it can also be a time of high productivity. A look at the ages of the world leaders will attest to this. There is also the possibility of entering meaningful work in an area of interest for which financial gain is not a primary goal. This activity may take the form of volunteer work. People who are prepared for this period can approach it as one of freedom, opportunity, and pleasure.

In light of what researchers have discovered about the ongoing nature of life changes, it becomes crucial for you to examine your attitude toward change. It is far healthier to take change in stride and to recognize its positive, challenging aspects than to fear it or attempt to avoid it. As you proceed through this book, take time to examine your attitudes and values. By learning more about yourself, you will be better equipped to learn more about the world and your evolving place in it.

♦ Understanding Change

We are living in an age when you, as a career changer, will face new and important challenges and must ask yourself these questions: Am I dissatisfied with my career or only with my job? Could I find satisfaction in a related job within the same field? If I retrain for a new career, will there be a job waiting for me when I finish? How will the current state of the economy affect my chances of finding a job?

You have probably asked yourself all these questions at one time or another. There are no easy, pat answers. The marketplace for workers is constantly changing, so much so that an entire chapter could be devoted solely to answering these questions.

Here the effect of the economy on occupations and career choice will be addressed. Although economists disagree on what lies ahead in the economy, we can learn from what some of the analysts tell us.

Occupational Trends

Several trends will affect you as you change careers. Consider some of the facts described by researchers John Naisbitt and Patricia Aburdene (1990).

- The skill requirements of jobs are growing faster than the skill levels of both labor and management.
- Women and minorities will constitute 68 percent of the total number of new workers between 1988 and 2000.
- Many people will work from their homes. Estimates predict there will be as many as 40 million home-based enterprises by the year 2000.
- By the year 2000, 85 percent of Americans will work in a company of 200 or fewer employees.
- Twenty-one million new jobs generated by the year 2000 will be in the service sector.
- Large companies will continue to cut out layers of middle management. Outside contractors will provide services once taken care of in-house.
- Small teams of people, not whole departments, will meet to solve problems.
- A global economic boom is developing from such practices as free trade and telecommunications between nations.
- Free-market policies are being advanced throughout the socialist part of the world.
- The following industries will provide the greatest number of jobs:

  Health care services (hospitals, nursing, ambulatory care)
  Hospitality
  Personal services
  Entertainment
  Environment (pollution control, recycling, hazardous-waste disposal)

According to the latest projections from the Bureau of Labor Statistics, the American labor force—and therefore the American economy—will grow more slowly during the next 15 years than it has in the past (*Occupational Outlook Quarterly,* 1992).

In today's competitive marketplace, you need to know which occupations will be providing the most jobs. Because projections are subject to change, only an attempt has been made to give you an overall view of the job outlook. This should be supplemented with projections of the local geographic labor market. Chapter Six provides you with sources of occupational information.

Think about these trends and the changes occurring in the world around you. To sum it up, make occupational projections part of your career change process, but not all of it. While you keep in mind the effect these occupational trends may have on your transition process, you might also ask yourself, "Should I change my job rather than my career?" Let us discuss that next.

Career Change versus Job Change

Career change is an actual change of occupation rather than a job upgrade or upward mobility within the same line of work. For example, a move from nurse to director of nursing or from computer programmer to systems analyst, is not a career change; a move from computer programming to nursing is a career change.

Career change may involve additional training or schooling, but this is not always the case. One purpose of this book is to teach you to identify and transfer the skills you have developed in your past work experience. The most important aspect of career transition is careful assessment both of yourself—your interests, your values, your skills—and of the work world—what is available, what a job really entails, and who can help you get started in a new career.

It is natural that questions and concerns accompany the process of change. In fact, anyone considering a career change should ask the following questions as the first step of self-assessment.

1. Am I dissatisfied with my career or only with my job? Could I find satisfaction in a related job within the same field?
2. Are working conditions the motivating factor for a change?
3. If so, could I change my environment or my attitude toward it, or is the only resolution a career switch?
4. Do I wish to express certain values on the job that I can't express in my present occupation?
5. Do I feel as though I could use more of my abilities and skills in another occupation?
6. Do I have an understanding of my personality and the type of environment in which I prefer working?
7. Do I know where my interests lie? What do I know about my vocational interests?
8. Have I taken inventory of my skills, and do I know what my marketable functional skills are?
9. Have I acquired skills that I don't have the opportunity to use in my present occupation even though I'd like to?
10. Am I willing to make sacrifices to begin a new occupation—such as taking a salary cut? Are the people who are dependent upon me also willing?
11. Will additional training or schooling be necessary for me to enter my newly chosen occupation?
12. Will my functional skills transfer to the occupation I choose, or must I develop new skills?
13. Do I have alternative plans, or are "all my eggs in one basket"?
14. Are there any ways I can try out a new career without quitting my full-time job?

15. Exactly what will I be giving up and what will I be gaining to change careers?
16. How important are the benefits—seniority, retirement fund, profit sharing, and so on—to my welfare in both the short run and the long run? Have I done pen-and-pencil figuring, or only daydreaming?
17. Is there help available in my community to ease my career change or to help me achieve my goal?
18. Do I feel that I have the patience to spend the time in an entry-level position to achieve my goal?
19. What small preparations can I begin today to help with my career switch? Have I made a list of short-, medium-, and long-range goals and minigoals?
20. How willing am I to take risks, such as that of not being happy in a new occupation? Would I be willing to make another switch if that happens? (Adapted from *Occupational Outlook Quarterly*, 1981, p. 6)

This book will help you answer many of these questions. By informing yourself and following specific steps, you will control the process of change instead of it having power over you. You may feel that in the past you made job and career decisions randomly, or at least without learning enough about the available options. Or you may feel that you made choices based on necessity rather than interest. Many people simply "find" themselves in a job. As one midlife career changer explained:

> Upon graduation from high school I was hired as a temporary worker by Sears. After working for about three hours the first day, I was called out of the room where about three of us were working. I was offered and accepted a full-time permanent position in the credit department. I never really knew why I was chosen over the others, but I think it was because I was the only temporary that had come to work dressed in business attire.

At the time, this person probably felt very fortunate. Others may have believed she was "in the right place at the right time." As the years passed and she stayed on in the credit department, however, she eventually felt cheated because she had never actually *chosen* her career path—instead, it had been thrust upon her.

♦ Summary

Now on to what lies ahead. Think about your own job or career pattern. Have you set goals, made decisions, set a path for yourself and followed it? Or have you bounced from job to job or remained in one position, only to now find yourself seeking control over your career path? The steps offered in this text will help you establish that control.

♦ EXERCISES

Now it is time to examine your own background and patterns of career development. The first exercise will help you identify significant life events that have contributed to your choice of a particular career path. The second exercise focuses on your present life stage. Next, you will describe your work history and the career paths that led to your present position.

♦ EXERCISE 1.1 Life Line

Begin by taking a "trip down memory lane," and try to recall significant emotional events in your life. Try to remember special events, certain people who had an influence on your life, changes in jobs, moves, or special skills you have acquired. Make a list according to age categories.

To Age 10

1. ______________________________
2. ______________________________
3. ______________________________
4. ______________________________
5. ______________________________

Ages 11–20

1. ______________________________
2. ______________________________
3. ______________________________
4. ______________________________
5. ______________________________

Ages 21–30

1. ______________________________
2. ______________________________

3. ______________________________
4. ______________________________
5. ______________________________

Ages 31–40

1. ______________________________
2. ______________________________
3. ______________________________
4. ______________________________
5. ______________________________

Ages 41–50

1. ______________________________
2. ______________________________
3. ______________________________
4. ______________________________
5. ______________________________

Ages 51–60

1. ______________________________
2. ______________________________
3. ______________________________
4. ______________________________
5. ______________________________

Ages 61 +

1. ______________________________
2. ______________________________
3. ______________________________
4. ______________________________
5. ______________________________

Now plot these events on a graph, using the name or number of the event. Consider the following example, plotted in Figure 1.1.

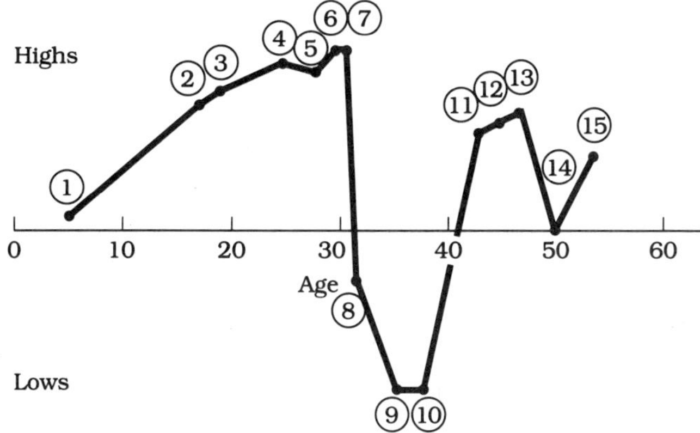

Figure 1.1 Sample life line

1. Moved from Idaho to California
2. Graduated from high school and was voted "most likely to succeed"
3. Married the high school student-body president
4. Four daughters born over the next ten years
5. Began a licensed child care business out of the home
6. Obtained an associate of arts degree
7. Five more children born over the next ten years
8. Husband's business failed
9. Eighth child (only boy) left paralyzed by auto accident
10. Husband left and filed for divorce
11. Landed a professional sales position
12. Met significant other and had a great six-and-one-half-year relationship
13. Graduated with a bachelor of arts degree in communications
14. Relationship with significant other ended with his death
15. Began to explore further options and career enrichment

As another example, you might want to consider the author's life line, plotted in Figure 1.2.

1. Lived away from family from the second through the fifth grades
2. Valedictorian of high school graduating class
3. Graduated with a B.S. degree
4. Graduate school in Colorado
5. Moved to California and began first "career" position
6. Married
7. Completed first master's degree
8. Birth of children
9. Completed second master's degree

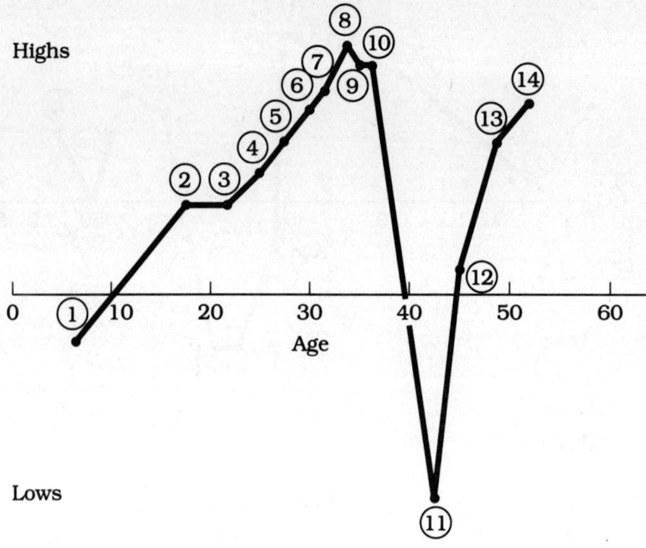

Figure 1.2 Author's life line

10. Began college teaching career
11. Divorced
12. First book was published
13. As a single parent, raised two children from ages nine and ten through adulthood
14. Remarried

♦ EXERCISE 1.2 Life Stages

Write two to three paragraphs discussing the life stage in which you presently find yourself. Use this as an opportunity to honestly assess your current stage. You need not recount your entire autobiography, just sum up your current situation without giving the background.

♦ EXERCISE 1.3 Autobiography

Write a short autobiographical sketch (one or two pages) describing your work history and the career paths leading to your present position. Include any personal data you feel would be appropriate.

♦ EXERCISE 1.4 What You Intend to Accomplish in This Class

In one paragraph, summarize what you intend to accomplish in this class. Try to stay away from using the word *hope*. Instead, say "I will," "I intend," or "I plan." In the next chapter you will learn more about goal setting, but use this opportunity to begin formulating your goals.

♦ Notes

ERIKSON, E. H. (1963). *Childhood and society* (2nd ed.). New York: Norton.

GOULD, R. L. (1978). *Transformations: Growth and change in adult life*. New York: Simon & Schuster.

NAISBITT, J., & ABURDENE, P. (1990). *Megatrends 2000*. New York: Morrow.

U.S. DEPARTMENT OF LABOR, BUREAU OF LABOR STATISTICS (Spring, 1981). *Occupational Outlook Quarterly*. Washington, D.C.: U.S. Government Printing Office.

U.S. DEPARTMENT OF LABOR, BUREAU OF LABOR STATISTICS (Spring, 1992). *Occupational Outlook Quarterly*. Washington, D.C.: U.S. Government Printing Office.

2 Moving Toward Change: Mobilizing Support

"The greatest discovery in our generation is that human beings, by changing the inner attitudes of their minds, can change the outer aspects of their lives."

William James

Before you proceed through the steps necessary for changing careers, it is important that you examine both your attitudes toward change and the events that have influenced your decision to make a change. You may need to develop some coping skills or use special support services to help you get through the tougher times of the transition. This is a time to call upon a variety of resources and to mobilize a support system to the fullest extent. Through this added support, you will come to realize all your true strengths and abilities and be able to move on to another phase in your life.

After reading this chapter, you should understand the following:

- that your attitudes and beliefs may affect how you view change
- how to develop a positive mental attitude
- the importance of a support system to the career-change process
- how to identify and to activate your own support network

You should be able to do the following:

- identify your present belief system to determine whether it enables or inhibits your progress

- apply the techniques presented in this chapter to develop a positive mental attitude
- identify and activate a positive support network similar to those suggested in this chapter

As you move forward with a career change, you may want to examine how you approach this transition. You will need to look at your attitude toward change. It may be helpful to develop a more positive mental attitude and to learn new coping skills to use during the tougher times of the transition. Ultimately you will lay the groundwork for the new field of endeavor that lies ahead of you.

♦ Examining Your Belief System

Our belief system is established by early adolescence. The experiences of early childhood, as well as the messages given us by our parents, remain with us throughout most of our adult lives. Does this mean we cannot change our belief system? Absolutely not! If we truly believed that, none of us would ever make a change. Even though your attitudes and belief systems were formed when you were a child, it is important that you take steps to change and to improve them. You must examine any emotional "baggage" you may be carrying that will affect your decision-making process in this time of career change. For example, if the parental statement "Do as I say" is reinforced throughout childhood, it can later be interpreted as "Don't use your own initiative—wait until someone tells you what to do."

Further, beliefs tend to be self-reinforcing. Consider the following hypothetical situation. You don't particularly care for math and you keep reminding yourself that you dislike math. What happens? You don't do well in mathematics courses. If you change your belief system even slightly, to "I don't exactly love math, but I'm beginning to see some of the utilitarian aspects of it," you will note that just your change in *attitude* toward the subject will help improve your performance.

Attitudes

Attitudes affect nearly everything we do and say, and they have an amazing impact on our ability to succeed, to get along with others, and to be happy. Attitudes are powerful because they create behavior—both good and bad. Thoughts can also be self-fulfilling. If you believe a certain thing is going to happen, the chances are very good that it will.

For example, if you believe you're too old to change careers, then your behavior will probably match your attitudes, and you could come across as complacent and devoid of fresh ideas. On the other hand, if you believe an employer would be lucky to find someone as highly skilled as you are, then your attitude is more likely to be positive. Soon people will start to notice you and not your age. Our attitudes make up our belief system.

Changing your attitudes and beliefs can be difficult, and a certain amount of risk is involved. If you believe it may be safer to remain neutral rather than to change, then your belief system will probably win out. This explains why people stay in situations in which they are uncomfortable. For example, consider this career changer:

Angela had been working in a data entry position in an aerospace firm for over ten years, even though she found her job to be routine and boring. She remained in the position because it was "secure," and she was afraid she would never find another job. Then, without prior notice she was laid off. After the initial numbness and disbelief, she began slowly to work through the transition process. Four months later, she could look back on the experience as "the best thing that could have happened to me."

Stay in touch with any hidden messages that may be controlling you during your time of change, and work on getting rid of any negative beliefs. This is also a good time to work on being more assertive. Changing your career can involve some risk; therefore, you must take control of your actions and not let fear overpower you.

♦ Positive and Negative Self-Talk

In his book *Humanistic Psychotherapy: The Rational–Emotive Approach* (1973), psychologist Albert Ellis refers to an "A-B-C cycle of behavior." The cycle begins when an event takes place that may or may not have anything to do with us. For example, due to a company merger and restructuring, Joe, age 55, is told that his services are no longer required by the company. Let us refer to this as event A, which incidentally may or may not have anything to do with Joe. Then there is Joe's response, C, to that event. Between the two lies B, which is what Joe says to himself and how he sees and defines the situation, which in turn determines his response. Either Joe can see this situation as totally his problem and think that his ineptness caused his early retirement, or Joe can tell himself that he could not have prevented the event but was merely a victim of circumstance. Our perception of an event, or our appraisal of situations, is a key determinant in our mental well-being.

Positive Thinking

Self-esteem and positive thinking go hand in hand. You may want to address these issues as you go through transition. Colleges and universities have excellent courses and workshops that could assist you in learning to think positively. In addition, you may want to do a little reading on the subject. There are many popular books on possibility thinking, motivation, and self-help. They range from Maxwell Maltz's classic, *Psycho-Cybernetics* (1960), to Norman Vincent Peale's *Power of Positive Thinking* (1987), to the more recent *Wishcraft: How to Get What You Really Want* by Barbara Sher (1983). One of the finest books on assertiveness is *Your Perfect Right* by Robert E. Alberti and Michael L. Emmons (1990).

Negative Self-Talk

Even though we may appear silent to others, we are constantly having conversations with ourselves. It is what we say in these conversations that makes all the difference; there are such things as positive and negative self-talk. Suppose you are getting ready for that all-important job interview. Within your mind you could be saying, "I probably don't have the qualifications for this job," or "I'm going to get nervous and tongue-tied." This would be negative self-talk. The following are common forms of negative self-talk.

Wrong assumptions. "There are just too many teachers; I will never find a teaching job." Just because your best friend had a hard time finding a job doesn't necessarily mean you will run into the same difficulties. Or just because the field is somewhat competitive doesn't mean that you shouldn't pursue it. A preconceived notion of an outcome to a situation can prevent you from even trying to pursue it.

Shoulds. "I should have had a job by now." Instead of spurring you to act positively, "shoulds" do the reverse. Others will place enough shoulds on you; you do not have to add to them. By telling yourself what you ought to be doing, you are actually setting yourself up for ways of removing yourself from the situation. You can create anxiety by telling yourself what you ought to be doing.

Self-criticism. "I blow every interview because I talk too much." Usually your criticism of yourself is far harsher than others' criticism of you. You could work more on interviewing technique, but if you keep criticizing yourself you may never take the positive steps necessary for change.

Self-blame. "If only I had left my last job sooner, then I wouldn't be in this mess." Blaming yourself for situations out of your control will not help the present situation. "If only's" are part of the past. Let go of them.

Negative expectations. "I might have trouble getting along with the next boss, too." Our imaginations can run away with us. Not only have you created stress by assuming that bad things will happen to you, but you have also set off the "worry" pattern, which can create a problem where one does not exist.

To create a positive mindset, you must work on removing all negative self-talk. Learn to replace it with positive statements, or affirmations. (At this point you may want to complete Exercise 2.1 at the end of this chapter.)

Affirmations

Affirmations are positive statements that counteract negative beliefs and expectations and motivate us in new directions. You can use affirmations to replace a negative attitude with a positive thought. To use affirmations, first determine what you want and then describe yourself as already having it. For example, if you decide you want a satisfying career, you might write; "I, Mike Thomas, have a satisfying career. I am respected by my colleagues, and I look forward to going to work every day."

However, a word of caution is in order here. Affirmations are effective only if used properly. For example, repeating to yourself, "I will win the lottery this week" is unlikely to be effective. Affirmations are not attempts to apply magic to the world around us, and they cannot create the impossible. Instead, affirmations are attempts to modify the negative belief system that creates doubt and frustration and keeps us from getting what we really want.

Here are some simple rules to make your affirmations effective:

1. Before you begin, place yourself in a receptive state of mind. You can do this by placing yourself in a deep state of relaxation.
2. Keep your affirmations short, clear, and specific.
3. Phrase affirmations positively. Avoid such negatives as *should, can't, don't,* or *stop.* Instead, state what you actually want to think, feel, and do.
4. Phrase affirmations in the present tense.
5. Write down your affirmations and place them where you can refer to them during the day.

Consider some of the following affirmations:

- It's OK to get what I want.
- I deserve to be successful.
- I can ask others for help.
- I love and appreciate myself.
- I now let go of all accumulated fears, guilt, and grudges. I am free and clear!
- I don't have to try to please others. I am likable the way I am.
- My work supports my creativity and initiative.
- The universe always provides.

Spend a few moments several times a day slowly repeating your affirmations to yourself. As you repeat them, try to imagine how the change really feels. Actually see yourself change. Use these affirmations when you are anxious or feel stressed; they will become reminders of your potential and commitment to change. (Refer to Exercise 2.2.)

♦ Identifying Support Systems

Throughout the process of changing careers, engaging the help of others will become increasingly important. For some of you, this will be an entirely new experience. Perhaps you have been taught that you must "do for yourself" or that it is morally wrong to "use" people. Keep in mind that you are not being encouraged to "use" people in the negative sense of the word. Rather, you are being encouraged to develop a support system—a network of personal relationships that will provide you with encouragement, emotional help, and support.

Perhaps you recall the phrase "no man is an island." You will come to know the real meaning of this phrase as you progress through your change process. We all live within a network of relationships with family, friends, co-workers, service professionals, and acquaintances. We depend on others not only for goods and services, but also for our feelings of self-worth. When you are under pressure and experience stress, you naturally gravitate to your loved ones for support and encouragement; you rarely handle difficulties alone.

People who must change careers due to geographic relocation often experience disruption in the relations they had previously formed. Our society's geographic mobility (which often is necessary for career advances) keeps us from forming lasting relationships. What has developed instead is a strong sense of individuality and competitiveness that keeps us from seeking help of any kind.

The process of developing a support group is called *networking*. Networking will be discussed further in Chapter Six; however, in this chapter it will refer to your emotional well-being. Therefore, you need to examine your own personal support network. In Chapter Six, "Exploring Your Options," you will be provided with a list of sources that you can use to put you in touch with persons in a position to hire you. Those same persons in positions to hire you may also offer great support to you throughout your career change.

Types of Support Systems

There are four major types of support systems:

1. *Family and significant others.* This group includes both your immediate family and your extended family.
2. *Friends and community contacts.* These people figure strongly in your social life and involvement in leisure activities. They are the people you see every day. Perhaps they live next door, or their children go to the same school or play on the same soccer team.
3. *Work associates.* These are the people with whom you work and to whom you could comfortably go for work-related advice. Often, these associates are mentors or others who are concerned about your career development.
4. *Service professionals.* These include counselors, psychologists, psychiatrists, social workers, and members of the clergy. In addition, there are numerous paraprofessionals who can be very supportive and encouraging. You might also want to look into nonprofit organizations that have job placement as their main goal. One such group is Forty Plus, a national nonprofit organization that works with displaced workers over 40 years of age (see Appendix D).

Before you can use your network effectively, you must be willing to share feelings. For some people, this may be the most difficult part of networking because it requires that you become somewhat vulnerable. Building support systems also demands a certain amount of assertiveness in being able to ask for help.

During your career change, you will need different kinds of support from different people. For example, one person might be a good listener and sounding board. Another may be goal-oriented and encourage you to take risks. Still another may seem to always "know somebody who knows somebody" and can offer you many contacts.

Functions of Support Systems

These support groups serve many varied functions. Here are just a few of them.

- *Referral:* providing you with names of persons or sources of support
- *Role models:* providing you with proof that "it can be done"
- *Motivation:* keeping you on target and in sight of your goal
- *Nurturance:* keeping you in touch; offering friendship
- *Mentoring:* providing you with a respect for your skills and accomplishments; keeping you focused

It will probably come as no surprise that your most important support group is your family or those closest to you. When a family member is out of work or in the midst of transition, it becomes important to respect his or her individuality. For example, family members must recognize that parents are not just mothers and fathers and "doers for children," but individuals and persons in their own right who need to be treated as such.

(At this point, you may want to complete Exercises 2.3 and 2.4 at the end of this chapter.)

Using Professional Services

Some of you may feel the need to consult a psychotherapist, psychologist, or other mental health professional as you go through your career change. This is particularly true if you are also going through a divorce or separation, are experiencing anxiety, or are dealing with old issues that this process may have triggered. Change, whether self-initiated or involuntary, does not in itself necessitate the need for counseling. What it does require is a clear decision and the motivation to take risks and to develop new skills. A wide range of possibilities awaits you; use these possibilities to the very best of your ability.

As mentioned earlier in this chapter, you may also want to find out about other types of classes and workshops available at the college or university you are attending. Look for workshops on building self-esteem, developing human potential, and assertiveness training. Any of these workshops would enhance the process of changing careers.

People with disabilities have many special needs and concerns related to changing careers—so many, in fact, that an entire book could be devoted solely to such issues. Therefore, it is suggested that they contact a vocational rehabilitation center in their area. If they are returning to school for retraining, they should contact the disabled student center of their local college or university.

Although personal financial planning is outside the scope of this book, it becomes such an important issue when changing careers that we would be somewhat remiss if we didn't at least address the issue. At this point it would be wise to seek the advice of a financial planning professional. In addition, Appendix B contains a financial planning guide that may be useful to you at this time.

♦ Summary

In this chapter you examined your belief system and learned that certain attitudes can actually inhibit your progress. You worked on developing a more positive mindset and discovered that you don't have to "go it alone" as you embark upon your career transition. You also learned about the four major types of support networks, namely (1) family and significant others, (2) friendships and community contacts, (3) work associates, and (4) service professionals. These support groups function as sources of (1) referral, (2) role models, (3) motivation, (4) nurturance, and (5) mentoring.

Before you go any further with your career change, take a good look at yourself and where you are right now, and elicit the help and support of others. The exercises in this chapter are meant to be guidelines that will assist you *throughout* the process.

♦ EXERCISES

The following exercises will help you examine your belief system and identify your support system. You may want to return to them from time to time as you complete this course.

♦ EXERCISE 2.1 Your Attitudes about Life

First, think about your past and list some of the prevalent attitudes you have held. Turn back to page 24. Have you held any wrong assumptions? How about "can'ts," "shoulds," or negative expectations? List as many as you can. Then write another sentence to replace the negative self-talk with a positive statement.

Negative Self-Talk

(Example: "I'll never find another job in this economy.")

1. ______________________________

2. ______________________________

3. ______________________________
4. ______________________________
5. ______________________________
6. ______________________________
7. ______________________________
8. ______________________________
9. ______________________________
10. ______________________________

Positive Self-Talk

(Example: "There is always room for another good engineer.")

1. ______________________________
2. ______________________________
3. ______________________________
4. ______________________________
5. ______________________________
6. ______________________________
7. ______________________________
8. ______________________________
9. ______________________________
10. ______________________________

♦ EXERCISE 2.2 Affirmations

Write at least ten affirmations that will modify some of the negative things you think to yourself. Create affirmations that are meaningful and important to you in your life right now. For example, if you are embarking on a change in careers, you might want to refer back to those affirmations listed on page 26.

Now write your own. (Example: "I will do well in the interview today.")

1. ______________________________
2. ______________________________

3. ______________________________

4. ______________________________

5. ______________________________

6. ______________________________

7. ______________________________

8. ______________________________

9. ______________________________

10. ______________________________

♦ EXERCISE 2.3 Identifying Your Support Needs

Several kinds of needs may surface as you go through a transition. The following chart contains six types of needs common to persons changing careers. Write down as many people as possible who could help you in each of these areas.

Educational	*Physical*	*Emotional*	*Financial*	*Spiritual*	*Legal*
Career counselor	Physician	Family Friends Professional counselor	Accountant	Pastor Priest Rabbi	Lawyer

♦ EXERCISE 2.4 Your Support System

After you have determined your needs in Exercise 2.3, identify at least six people who could help you in each of the six areas of support you need. These people could be friends, relatives, neighbors, co-workers, teachers, or service professionals. On a separate piece of paper, write one person's name in each of six boxes. Then, in each box, describe briefly how the person listed could provide support. What do you need from each of them to support your goal? Use a different sheet for each need, and try to list a different set of support personnel for each. (It is possible, however, that a person can provide support in more than one area.)

The following is an example of a support system that meets a person's emotional needs.

My emotional support system

Mary (wife)	*Joe (co-worker)*	*Max (brother)*
Caring Understanding Sharing of feelings	Guidance Support Partner for racquetball	Contacts from his work Family support
Robert (friend)	*John (neighbor)*	*Dr. Smith (psychotherapist)*
Contacts Networking Good company	Networking Friend	Professional counseling

♦ EXERCISE 2.5 Family Management Inventory

If your career change requires you to return to school, work two jobs, or take on any other new or added responsibility, or requires your spouse to return to work, examine the impact of this decision on your family, using the following inventory.

1. Financial Concerns

Ensuring continuity of financial support for the family is a major consideration in implementing a career change. Going back to school, taking a lower-paying but more growth-producing job, moving from full-time to part-time work, starting your own business, and many other career decisions can cause financial problems.

Here is a checklist of possible ways to cope with financial problems in the family.

___ Family reduces expenditures in major ways.
___ Family borrows on assets (home, insurance).
___ Spouse goes to work full-time.
___ Family borrows from close friends or relatives.
___ Family takes advantage of benefits available for training or education (GI Bill, scholarships, low-payback loans).

2. Child Care

The ages of your children and their ability to manage on their own may play a part in your career transition. Planning should account for both everyday responsibilities and emergencies. Child care options to consider include the following:

- ____ An elementary school with a latchkey program
- ____ A day care center to care for the children all day
- ____ A housekeeper hired to care for the children, clean, and cook
- ____ A responsible teenager who can tend the children
- ____ A relative or friend to care for the children
- ____ A nursery school
- ____ A caring adult to tend the children in your home
- ____ Summer day care or full-care camps
- ____ Job sharing (if your company promotes such a benefit)
- ____ A work schedule that allows you to leave if an emergency arises
- ____ A work schedule where one parent can be home with the children after school

3. *Spouse's Cooperation*

The amount of cooperation you have from your spouse will directly affect your transition. Consider the following facts and place a check by those that may apply to you.

- ____ Spouse's willingness to return to work
- ____ Cooperation with household chores and parenting duties
- ____ Emotional support
- ____ Financial planning to adjust household budget
- ____ Reduction of nonessential expenditures

4. *Household Maintenance*

Some changes may have to be made in the way you manage your household. Here are some suggestions. Place a check by those that apply to your situation.

- ____ Involve all family members in cooking, cleaning, and other chores without special compensation.
- ____ Involve older family members in household tasks with special compensation.
- ____ Simplify chores by using time-saving methods (for example, purchasing nonperishable items in bulk once a month).

5. *Volunteer Activities*

Some sacrifices will have to be made in terms of how you spend your free time. Check off the changes you can make.

- ____ Concentrate only on those activities most meaningful to you.
- ____ Learn to say NO!

SOURCE: Adapted from *Career Actualization and Life Planning*, pp. 170–171, by D. H. Blocher, 1989, Denver: Love Publishing. Reprinted with permission.

♦ EXERCISE 2.6 Self-Assessment: The Strength of Your Support Networks

This exercise assesses the quality and level of support in your life in three major areas: family, friends, and work. After each statement place a check in the column that best describes how true each statement is for you now.

Family support

	3 *Very True*	2 *Somewhat True*	1 *Slightly True*	0 *Not True*
1. I feel I can ask the people in my family for help when I need it.				
2. I feel I am honest with the people in my family, and they are honest with me.				
3. The quality of time I spend with my family is high.				
4. I feel accepted and loved by my family.				
5. I am able to give what I would like to my family.				
6. My family understands me when I am upset.				
7. My family expresses caring and affection to me.				
8. I feel close and in touch with my family.				
9. My family responds to my feelings, such as sorrow, anger, or love.				
10. My family gives me as much as I give them.				

A score of 20 or more indicates that you feel a high level of support from your family network.

Friendship support

	3 *Very True*	2 *Somewhat True*	1 *Slightly True*	0 *Not True*
1. I find it hard to ask for what I want.				
2. I find it difficult to share my feelings with other people.				
3. I am often lonely and alone.				
4. I usually don't feel close to other people.				

(continued)

	3 Very True	2 Somewhat True	1 Slightly True	0 Not True
5. I usually can't find people to spend time with me.				
6. I am not able to give what I would like to others.				
7. I find it hard to touch other people.				
8. Few people know me very well.				
9. There are few people I can really trust.				
10. Other people rarely hug or touch me.				
11. I have few friends or people to whom I am close.				
12. I don't like to spend time with other people.				
13. I don't expect much from people.				
14. I find it hard to ask others for help.				
15. People rarely help me.				
16. People don't want to get to know me.				
17. I feel distant and apart from other people.				
18. I don't feel cared for or valued by others.				
19. I usually place others' needs above my own.				
20. I feel I am basically on my own.				

Note that these statements are phrased in negative terms. In this case, the higher your score, the less supportive your network of friends. A score above 25 indicates that your personal support system may have weaknesses and that you need to take steps to increase the depth of these relationships or create new relationships.

Work Support

	3 Very True	2 Somewhat True	1 Slightly True	0 Not True
1. There are people I can talk to informally each day.				
2. The climate of my workplace is pleasant and comfortable.				
3. The people around me care about me as a person.				
4. I feel my abilities are valued by others at work.				

(continued)

	3 Very True	2 Somewhat True	1 Slightly True	0 Not True
5. Information is shared freely among people who should know things.				
6. When people are upset about something at work, it is usually talked about.				
7. I can ask for guidance and help from my superiors.				
8. I feel I can question and negotiate with supervisors about work assignments.				
9. I am clear about what I am to do and what others expect from me.				
10. Many things about work are pleasant and enjoyable.				
11. There are outlets to help me handle the frustrations and irritations of my work.				
12. People are given what they need to complete the tasks they are assigned.				
13. People at work are more concerned about getting things done than about competing among themselves.				
14. When I run into trouble, there are co-workers I can seek out for help.				
15. When I can't do something on my own, I can take my problems to others, and they will help me.				

Like the family support inventory, this assessment consists of positive statements. A score higher than 20 indicates a supportive work network. If your score is below 20, work on strengthening your network.

SOURCE: Adapted with permission from *From Burnout to Balance* by Dennis T. Jaffe and Cynthia D. Scott (1984).

♦ Notes

BLOCHER, D. H. (1989). *Career actualization and life planning.* Denver, CO: Love.

JAFFE, D. T. & SCOTT, C. D. (1984). *From burnout to balance: A workbook for peak performance and self-renewal.* New York: McGraw-Hill.

♦ Further Reading

ALBERTI, R. E. & EMMONS, M. L. (1990). *Your perfect right: A guide to assertive living*, 6th ed. San Luis Obispo, CA: Impact.

ELLIS, A. (1973). *Humanistic psychotherapy: The rational-emotive approach.* New York: The Julian Press.

MALTZ, M. (1960). *Psycho-cybernetics.* Englewood Cliffs, NJ: Prentice-Hall.

PEALE, N. V. (1987). *The power of positive thinking: Fifth anniversary edition.* New York: Fawcett.

SHER, B. (1983). *Wishcraft: How to get what you really want.* New York: Ballantine Books.

3 Managing Yourself and Your Life

"Worry is wasting today's time to clutter up tomorrow's opportunities with yesterday's troubles."

—*Anonymous*

How you manage yourself and your life during the career change can directly affect the outcome. It can mean the difference between a smoothly functioning, well-thought-out plan and a plan fraught with anxiety and stress. As you go through the process of changing careers, you will have more demands on your time than ever before. And yes, occasionally you may even experience some stress. Eating well and getting plenty of rest and exercise are good prescriptions for anyone at any time, but they are especially important during a career change. You will be encouraged to do all these things during your period of transition.

After reading this chapter you should understand the following:

- The basic principles of good time management
- How to manage the stress in your life
- The importance of proper diet and exercise for healthful living during your transition period

You should be able to do the following:

- Identify ways of improving how you manage your time
- Apply stress management techniques

- Incorporate principles of good nutrition and proper exercise into your everyday living

♦ Managing Your Time

Managing your time well during career transition will help you accomplish more and will reduce anxiety. During a career change you find you must juggle many more tasks than before in the same amount of time. Time management is quite simple in theory, but it requires practice and consistency. For starters, you must monitor how you manage your time so you can be assured that your career change will go as smoothly as possible.

At this point, complete the time management rating (Exercise 3.1) at the end of this chapter. If your score indicates that you manage your time poorly or that there are areas where you can improve, take some time to reflect on what you actually do with your time.

Symptoms of Poor Time Management

Poor time management can lead to burnout and stress. One way to determine how you manage your time is to check yourself against the following statements. Perhaps you can see yourself in one or more of the following situations.

- Your family and friends complain that you no longer have any time for them—you always seem "so busy!"
- You have missed a couple of important deadlines at your work, and the boss has started to notice it.
- You are always rushing to get things done by the end of the day.
- You seem to have little or no time to read for pleasure anymore. You haven't read a novel in two years.
- You are beginning to feel overwhelmed by all the things you have to do at work and at home.
- You are beginning to snap at people—sometimes for little or no reason.

Principles of Time Management

Alan Lakein (1973), author of *How to Get Control of Your Time and Your Life*, has outlined four basic but powerful principles of time management: prioritizing, avoiding procrastination, delegating, and handling interruptions.

Prioritizing. Prioritizing simply means doing the most important tasks first. For career changers, this may mean putting the tasks involved in the career change in first position. How important is each task in relation to your goal? You will find you can categorize your activities into two major areas: high-payoff activities and low-payoff activities. Here are some characteristics of each.

HIGH-PAYOFF ACTIVITIES	*LOW-PAYOFF ACTIVITIES*
Usually not repetitive	Easy to accomplish
May take a long time to accomplish	Comfortable and safe to do
Usually require large blocks of time to organize and substantial amounts of followup and coordination	Routine, predictable tasks
Frequently difficult and carry some risk of failure	Contribute little to the achievement of one's goals
Usually contribute significantly to the achievement of one's goals	Final results are easy to measure

Take some time to examine which activities are low-payoff for you and which are high-payoff. Stay with the high-payoff activities as you proceed toward your goal.

Avoiding procrastination. One of the biggest problems in managing time is *procrastination*. Entire books have been written on this subject. However, there are some specific ways of avoiding this tendency.

- Make a prioritized action list daily.
- When preparing the action list, refer to long-range goals.
- If your top daily priority is overwhelming, divide it into chunks.
- Reward yourself for getting each chunk done.
- Anticipate interruptions that could divert you from your priorities.
- Plan interruptions away from priority time.
- Select the best time of day for the type of work required.
- Do the most distasteful tasks first.
- Commit to a deadline.
- Enlist the help of other people to remind you of your priorities.

Delegating. Delegating effectively increases your efficiency. The process of delegating involves the following steps:

1. Identifying tasks you alone do not have to do
2. Finding the best person to whom you could delegate a specific task

3. Making clear to the person what he or she must do to accomplish the task
4. Keeping track of the person's progress

Create a positive attitude toward delegating. Avoid the trap that most people fall into: "If I don't do it myself, it won't get done exactly as I would do it." That's right, it will not be done *exactly* as you would have done it, but there is more than one way to get things done.

Handling interruptions. There are several ways you can handle interruptions. Here are some of them.

- *Schedule interruptions.* Schedule blocks of time when you *can* be interrupted. For example, you may want to set aside an hour or two per week to obtain feedback or listen to complaints.
- *Train others to serve as resources.* Then, when you are busy, people will not always come to you. You can use call forwarding to redirect phone calls.
- *Consider your office or work arrangement.* If you are easily accessible, you could encourage socializing. At home, have a special place in which to do your studying or "after-hours" work.
- *Return calls when it is most convenient for you.* Get in the habit of telling people, "The best times to call me are. . . ." Obtain information from people in advance so you can save time on the phone.

If you find you are constantly interrupted by the telephone, use the direct approach—with a dash of diplomacy. The following is an example.

> I'm glad you called, Bill. Catching up on the news with you is always a lift. If I had my way, I'd put my feet up and talk with you and forget this stack of work. But I think I had better keep plowing through. I'm glad you called and had a minute to touch base.

Refer often to the following time-honored words of wisdom:

NOW NEVER WAITS

What happens to unused nows?
They turn into unusable thens.

JUST FOR TODAY

I will live through the next 12 hours and not tackle all my life's problems at once.

JUST FOR TODAY

In one thing I know I am equal with others—*time.* All of us draw the same salary in seconds, minutes, and hours.

JUST FOR TODAY

I refuse to spend time worrying about what might happen. I usually do not. I am going to spend my time making things happen.

JUST FOR TODAY

I will stop saying, "If I had time. . . . " I know I never will "find time" for anything. If I want time, I must make it.

JUST FOR TODAY

I will improve my mind. I will learn something useful. I will read something that requires effort, thought, and concentration.

JUST FOR TODAY

I will be agreeable. I will look my best, speak in a well-modulated voice, and be courteous and considerate.

JUST FOR TODAY

I will not find fault with friends, relatives, or colleagues. I will try not to change or improve anyone but myself.

JUST FOR TODAY

I will have a program. I will save myself from two enemies—hurry and indecision.

JUST FOR TODAY

I will exercise my character in three ways:

I will do a good turn and keep it a secret. (If anyone finds out, it won't count.)

I will do two things I don't want to, just for exercise.

I will be unafraid. Especially will I be unafraid to enjoy what is beautiful, and believe that as I give to the world, the world will give to me.

JUST FOR TODAY

I will have a quiet half-hour all by myself to relax. During this half-hour, I will get a better perspective of my life.

JUST FOR TODAY

I will be happy.

(Author unknown)

♦ Managing Stress

You cannot escape all the stresses of life; however, you can learn to manage them. Changing careers can be exciting, but it can also be stressful. Change—positive or negative—involves stress to which you must adjust.

Sources of Stress

You experience stress from three basic sources: (a) your thought processes, (b) your body, and (c) your environment.

Thought processes. This is much like the *negative self-talk* discussed in Chapter Two. How you interpret your experience can cause stress. Dwelling on your worries and problems produces tension in the body, which can take the form of increased distractibility and decreased concentration or sleep disorders.

Body. Improper diet and lack of sleep are physiological sources of stress. Some forms of stress can show up as heightened muscle tension, elevated blood pressure, and rapid heartbeat. Ultimately, this can result in hypertension and other physical ailments.

Environment. Your environment is constantly forcing you to adjust. Your performance rating at work, personal demands, time pressures, traffic conditions, and threats to job security are all threats to your security and self-esteem. Your body reacts to these stressors in ways similar to the "fight or flight" response you inherited from your primitive ancestors. Although a certain amount of this involuntary response is helpful (for example, slamming on the brakes to avoid hitting the car in front of you), heightened or prolonged responses can lead to hypertension and other medical disorders.

Suggestions for Reducing Stress

There are certain things you can do to reduce stress. The following are some suggestions.

- Become aware of the major sources of stress in your life. (To determine the amount of stress you have experienced in the past year, fill out the "Schedule of Recent Experience" in Exercise 3.7.)

- If possible, anticipate life changes and plan for them well in advance.
- Use your support system to the fullest extent.
- Maintain good time management techniques.
- Eat nutritious meals in restful, comfortable surroundings.
- Get plenty of sleep.
- Maintain an exercise program that is appropriate for you.
- Whenever possible, avoid drastic changes in residence or in social and recreational activities when experiencing a period of stress.
- Maintain a healthy balance between work and leisure activities.
- If necessary, learn to be more assertive.
- Practice progressive relaxation techniques.
- Use visualization methods.

Methods of Reducing Stress

Relaxation. You can train yourself to relax, but you must work at it. As with any skill, you must practice to become better at using relaxation techniques. Make a habit of setting aside time to practice. Begin by doing the following exercise daily.

1. In a quiet environment, sit in a comfortable position.
2. Close your eyes.
3. Deeply relax your muscles, beginning at your feet and progressing upward to your face—feet, calves, thighs, lower torso, chest, shoulders, neck, head. Allow these muscles to remain deeply relaxed.
4. Breathe through your nose. Become aware of your breathing. As you breathe out, say the word *one.* In . . . out, with *one.*
5. Continue practicing step 4 for 20 minutes. You may open your eyes to check the time, but do not use an alarm. When you finish, sit quietly for several minutes; at first with your eyes closed, and later with your eyes open.

Visualization. Visualization is the technique of using your imagination to create what you want in your life. Imagination is the ability to create an idea or mental picture in your mind. Used in conjunction with relaxation techniques, visualization is very powerful. One of the best books on visualization is Shakti Gawain's *Creative Visualization* (1983). There are also a number of good audiotapes available on this subject. For your convenience, several sources appear at the end of this chapter.

Proper Nutrition and Exercise

Aging is an inevitable, natural process, but by adopting good habits related to proper nutrition and exercise, people can slow the aging process—within the natural limits set by heredity.

Proper Nutrition

A nutritional program that combines moderation with adequate intake of all essential nutrients can forestall certain diseases and improve the quality of life in later years.

The following guidelines give you some suggestions for making wise dietary choices:

1. *Eat a variety of food daily.* Include these foods every day: fruits and vegetables; whole-grain and enriched breads and cereals and other products made from grains; milk and milk products; meats, fish, poultry, and eggs; and dried peas and beans.
2. *Maintain desirable weight.* Increase physical activity; control overeating by eating slowly, taking smaller portions, and avoiding "seconds"; eat fewer fatty foods and sweets and less sugar. Drink fewer alcoholic beverages, and eat more foods that are low in calories and high in nutrients.
3. *Avoid too much fat, saturated fat, and cholesterol.* Choose low-fat protein sources such as lean meats, fish, poultry, and dry peas and beans; use eggs and organ meats in moderation; limit intake of fats on and in foods; trim fat from meats; broil, bake, or boil—do not fry; limit breaded and deep-fried foods; read food labels for fat contents.
4. *Eat foods with adequate starch and fiber.* Substitute starchy foods for foods high in fats and sugars; select whole-grain breads and cereal, fruits and vegetables, and dried beans and peas to increase fiber and starch intake.
5. *Avoid too much sugar.* Use less sugar, syrup, and honey; reduce concentrated sweets like candy, soft drinks, cookies, and the like; select fresh fruits or fruits canned in light syrup or their own juices; read food labels—sucrose, glucose, dextrose, maltose, lactose, fructose, syrups, and honey are all sugars; eat sugar less often to reduce dental problems.
6. *Avoid too much sodium.* Learn to enjoy the flavors of unsalted foods; flavor foods with herbs, spices, and lemon juice; reduce salt in cooking; add little or no salt at the table; limit salty foods like potato chips, pretzels, salted nuts, popcorn, condiments (soy sauce, steak sauce, and garlic salt), some cheeses, pickled foods and cured meats, and some canned vegetables and soups; read food labels for sodium or salt contents, especially in processed and snack foods; use lower-sodium products when available.

7. *If you drink alcoholic beverages, do so in moderation.* For individuals who drink, limit all alcoholic beverages (including wine, beer, liquors, and so on) to one or two drinks per day. "One drink" means 12 ounces of beer, 3 ounces of wine, or 1½ ounces of distilled spirits. Pregnant women should refrain from the use of alcohol. If you drink, do not drive. *Source: Nutrition and Your Health: Dietary Guidelines for Americans.* U.S. Department of Agriculture and the U.S. Department of Health and Human Services, 1985.

Proper Exercise

Not only is exercise necessary for good health, but it is also one of the simplest and most effective means of stress reduction. Today, very few Americans exercise enough. Now would be a good time to break out of a sedentary life-style (if you are in one) and embark on an exercise program that will keep you fit for life. There are two broad categories of exercise: aerobic exercise and low-intensity exercises.

Aerobic exercise. Popular aerobic exercises are running, jogging, brisk walking, swimming, bicycling, and dancing. The goal of aerobic exercise is to produce a "training effect" that will gradually strengthen your cardiovascular system and increase your stamina. To benefit from aerobic exercise, your heart must beat at 70 percent of its maximum rate for at least 20 minutes. This places moderate stress on your heart, which gradually will improve its efficiency. The maximum heart rate is the fastest speed your heart can beat when you exercise. Table 3.1 shows the estimated heart rates for different age groups.

To determine your heart rate for one minute, simply take your pulse for six seconds and then add a zero to that number.

Table 3.1 Estimated heart rates per minute for average man or woman by age group

		Exercise Level			
Age Group	*Maximum Heart Rate*	*80% Maximum Heart Rate*	*70% Maximum Heart Rate*	*60% Maximum Heart Rate*	*50% Maximum Heart Rate*
18–29	203–191	162–153	142–134	122–115	101–95
30–39	190–181	152–145	133–127	113–108	95–90
40–49	180–171	144–137	126–120	107–102	90–85
50–59	170–161	136–129	119–113	101–96	85–80
60–69	160–151	128–121	112–106	95–90	80–75
70–79	150–141	120–113	105–99	89–84	75–70

Source: Metropolitan Life Insurance Company

Low-intensity exercise. Low-intensity exercise is not as vigorous. However, it does help to increase muscle strength and flexibility and joint mobility. Some examples of low-intensity exercise are walking and gardening.

Other forms of low-intensity exercise designed to increase muscle strength are calisthenics, isometrics, and isotonics.

Calisthenics develop muscle strength and flexibility by combining such exercises as toe-touching, sit-ups, and knee-bends. They are used in combination with aerobic exercise for warming up and cooling down.

In *isometrics*, a muscle's force is pitted against an immovable object. For example, you can hook your fingertips together and pull outward vigorously. Little or no movement occurs, but the muscle develops strength by exerting effort against the resistance.

Isotonics involve the contraction of muscles against a resistant object. Weight lifting is an example of an isotonic exercise.

Be sure to talk to your physician before you begin any exercise program for the first time. When you do begin exercising, be sure you are warming up and cooling down properly. If you use a fitness center, be sure to engage the assistance of a qualified counselor to ensure that you are using the equipment properly. If you are beginning to do aerobic exercise, begin slowly and work up to more difficult routines. Refer to Table 3.1 for the appropriate exercise level for you.

Finally, take time for yourself. Take advantage of life's pleasures—a walk on the beach, a stroll in the park, a phone call to a friend—to get your mind off the immediate pressure. In other words, take time out to "smell the roses."

♦ Summary

Because you will be devoting extra time to your career change, time management becomes extremely important. Not only will you be spending extra time on tasks related to the change, but you may also be juggling them with your present job and numerous outside obligations.

The amount of time it takes you to change careeers will be directly related to the amount of time and energy you devote to it. The results you gain will be in direct proportion to the amount of time spent. Therefore, start by reaffirming that your goal, indeed, is to change careers; then allocate the appropriate amount of time needed to accomplish this.

Work to keep yourself healthy and stress-free during this time of transition. Practice the relaxation techniques outlined in this chapter, and accompany them with appropriate exercise and good eating habits. This is not only a good prescription during your time of transition, but you should also practice it continuously throughout your life to remain healthy.

♦ EXERCISES

The exercises that follow are designed to assist you with the essentials of time management and stress management. Because constraints on your time can change, you may want to come back to these exercises from time to time.

♦ EXERCISE 3.1 Time Management Rating

The following ten questions will help you determine how well or how poorly you now manage your time. After each question, place a check mark under the column that best describes your answer. The number at the top of each column is used for scoring. How well do you manage your time?

	5 *Always*	4 *Often*	3 *Sometimes*	2 *Occasionally*	1 *Seldom*	0 *Never*
1. Do you take on more work than you can handle?						
2. Do you worry about work on vacations?						
3. Do you have trouble remembering?						
4. Are you unable to work because of interruptions?						
5. Do you become uncertain about what to do next?						
6. Do you think too much about small details?						
7. Does time pass slowly for you?						
8. Is your work area messy?						
9. Are your personal records disorganized?						
10. Does time pass quickly for you?						

Add your score according to the numbers at the top of each column.

35–50 You manage your time poorly.
16–34 Your time management skills are average; there are areas in which you can improve.
0–15 You manage your time well.

♦ EXERCISE 3.2 How We Spend Our Time

Workweek

On the left, list up to six activities that take up the most time during the workweek. Then estimate the total time spent on each. Next, fill in the pie chart on the right; start with the largest piece first. (The numbers on the pie chart represent the number of hours in a workweek.)

Hours	*Activities*
_______	______________________________
_______	______________________________
_______	______________________________
_______	______________________________
_______	______________________________
_______	______________________________
_______	Miscellaneous (calculate *after* filling in the pie chart)

40/0

30 10

20

Total week

On the left, estimate the total hours spent on each activity for an entire week. Add other activities you spend significant amounts of time on. Then fill in the pie chart on the right. (The numbers on the pie chart represent the number of hours in a week.)

Hours		*Hours*	
_______	Work	_______	Recreation
_______	Sleep	_______	Hobbies
_______	Travel	_______	Family
_______	Meals	_______	Shopping
_______	Worship	_______	Studying
_______	Reading	_______	
_______	Hygiene	_______	
_______	Chores	_______	Free time (calculate *after* filling in the pie chart)
_______	Television		

168/0

126 42

84

♦ EXERCISE 3.3 Time Chart

Fill in the chart below with a typical week's activities. Analyze where your time is going.

Hours	*Monday*	*Tuesday*	*Wednesday*	*Thursday*	*Friday*	*Saturday*	*Sunday*
6–7							
7–8							
8–9							
9–10							
10–11							
11–12							
12–1							
1–2							
2–3							
3–4							
4–5							
5–6							
6–7							
7–8							
8–9							
9–10							
10–11							
11–12							
12–1							
1–2							
2–3							
3–4							
4–5							
5–6							

♦ EXERCISE 3.4 Setting Priorities

Divide a sheet of paper into two columns. In the left column, list all the major responsibilities of your job. For example, consider the case of a systems analyst whose major responsibilities are (1) performing systems analysis for an accounting package, (2) developing and documenting production schedules, data communications, and remote-bureau instructions for evening-shift operations; (3) training personnel in data entry; (4) organizing systematic control procedures for evening-shift operators; and (5) writing computer programs in BASIC for accounting applications.

Now go to the right column and list all the tasks you do in a "typical" day. You might start at the beginning of the day and account for each block of time. For example, the systems analyst's list might look like this:

RESPONSIBILITIES OF THE JOB	*A TYPICAL DAY*	
1. Performing systems analysis for an accounting package	9:00–10:00	Pick up phone messages, return calls, open mail, and set schedule for the day
2. Developing and documenting production schedules	10:00–12:00	Staff training
	12:00–1:00	Lunch
3. Training personnel	1:00–3:00	Programming activities
4. Organizing control procedures for evening shift operators	3:00–4:00	Meetings, schedule production
5. Writing programs in BASIC for accounting applications	4:00–6:00	Plan activities for the evening-shift operators

Examine the chart you have just completed, and consider which tasks (listed in the right column) are directly related to your major job responsibilities (listed in the left column). Which tasks are time wasters? This is an excellent way to document your time if you feel you are not addressing the major responsibilities of your job because you are asked to do tasks unrelated to your job description.

♦ EXERCISE 3.5 Time Efficiency Curve

The purpose of this exercise is to identify your levels of energy during the work day. Then you can schedule less challenging activities during "low" times.

Using Figure 3.1 as an example, plot your own efficiency curve.

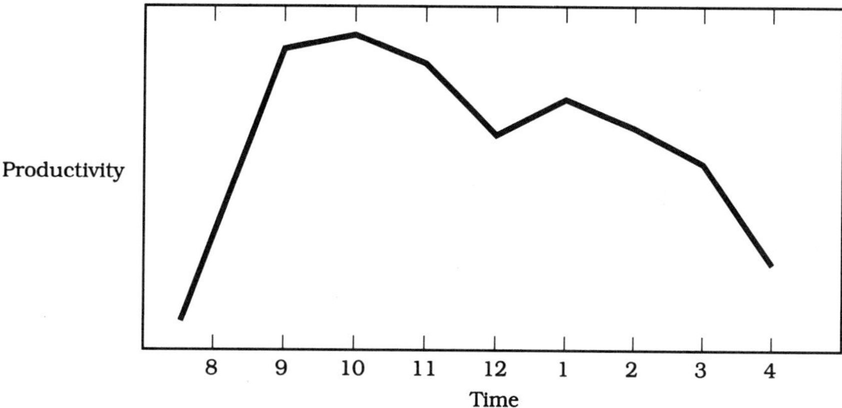

Figure 3.1 A typical efficiency curve

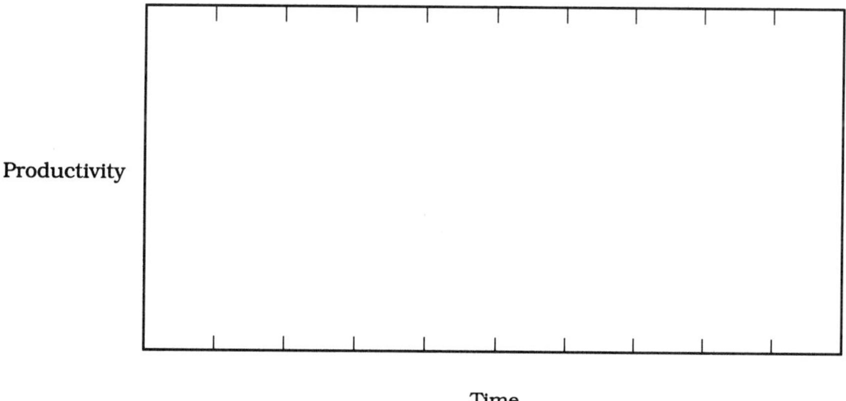

Your efficiency curve

♦ EXERCISE 3.6 Delegating

List 20 jobs that you are responsible for at home or at work or both (for example, banking, paying bills, mowing the lawn, cleaning, shopping, or grading papers). Place an asterisk next to the jobs that you feel *you* must complete. Then circle the jobs that someone else can be paid, assigned, or asked to do. Now you have started the process of delegating.

1. ______________	11. ______________
2. ______________	12. ______________
3. ______________	13. ______________
4. ______________	14. ______________
5. ______________	15. ______________
6. ______________	16. ______________
7. ______________	17. ______________
8. ______________	18. ______________
9. ______________	19. ______________
10. ______________	20. ______________

♦ EXERCISE 3.7 Schedule of Recent Experience

Part A

In the space provided, place the listed mean value in the left column if the event described happened to you within the last two years.

	Place mean value here if event happened to you. Your Score	*Mean Value*
1. A lot more or a lot less trouble with the boss	______	23
2. A major change in sleeping habits (sleeping a lot more or a lot less, or change in part of day when asleep)	______	16
3. A major change in eating habits (a lot more or a lot less food intake, or very different meal hours or surroundings)	______	15
4. A revision of personal habits (dress, manners, associations, etc.)	______	24
5. A major change in your usual type and/or amount of recreation	______	19
6. A major change in your social activities (clubs, dancing, movies, visiting, etc.)	______	18

(continued)

	Place mean value here if event happened to you. Your score	*Mean value*
7. A major change in church activities (a lot more or a lot less than usual)	______	19
8. A major change in number of family get-togethers (a lot more or a lot less than usual)	______	15
9. A major change in financial state (a lot worse off or a lot better off than usual)	______	38
10. In-law troubles	______	29
11. A major change in the number of arguments with spouse (a lot more or a lot fewer than usual regarding child-rearing, personal habits, etc.)	______	35
12. Sexual difficulties	______	39

Part B

In the space provided, indicate the *number of times* each applicable event happened to you within the last two years. Multiply it by the listed mean value to get your score.

	Number of Times	×	*Mean Value*	=	*Your Score*
13. Major personal injury or illness	______		53		______
14. Death of a close family member (other than spouse)	______		63		______
15. Death of spouse	______		100		______
16. Death of a close friend	______		37		______
17. Gaining a new family member (through birth, adoption, older person moving in, etc.)	______		39		______
18. Major change in the health or behavior of a family member	______		44		______
19. Change in residence	______		20		______
20. Detention in jail or other institution	______		63		______
21. Minor violations of the law (traffic tickets, jaywalking, disturbing the peace, etc.)	______		11		______
22. Major business readjustment (merger, reorganization, bankruptcy, etc.)	______		39		______

(continued)

	Number of Times	×	Mean Value	=	Your Score
23. Marriage	________		50		________
24. Divorce	________		73		________
25. Marital separation from spouse	________		65		________
26. Outstanding personal achievement	________		28		________
27. Son or daughter leaving home (marriage, attending college, etc.)	________		29		________
28. Retirement from work	________		45		________
29. Major change in working hours or conditions	________		20		________
30. Major change in responsibilities at work (promotion, demotion, lateral transfer)	________		29		________
31. Being fired from work	________		47		________
32. Major change in living conditions (building a new home, remodeling, deterioration of home or neighborhood)	________		25		________
33. [Spouse] beginning or ceasing work outside the home	________		26		________
34. Taking on a mortgage greater than $100,000 (purchasing a home, business, etc.)	________		31		________
35. Taking on a mortgage or loan of less than $100,000 (purchasing a car, TV, etc.)	________		17		________
36. Foreclosure on a mortgage or loan	________		30		________
37. Vacation	________		13		________
38. Changing to a new school	________		20		________
39. Changing to a different line of work	________		36		________
40. Beginning or ceasing formal schooling	________		26		________
41. Marital reconciliation with mate	________		45		________
42. Pregnancy	________		40		________
				Your Total Score:	________

Scoring

Add the mean values in Part A to your scores in Part B to obtain your total score.

The more change you have experienced recently, the more likely you are to suffer a major illness. Of those with a score of over

300 for the past year, almost 80 percent get ill in the near future; with a score of 150 to 299, about 50 percent get ill in the near future; and with a score of less than 150, only about 30 percent get ill in the near future. So the higher your score, the harder you should work to stay well.

Stress can also be cumulative. Events from two years ago may still be affecting you now. If you think this applies to you, you may want to take this test separately for the events of each of the last two years.

SOURCE: From *Schedule of Recent Experience (SRE). Examiner's Manual* by Thomas H. Holmes, copyright 1981, University of Washington Press. Reprinted with permission of the publisher.

NOTE: This exercise is not meant to alarm you unduly but to make you more aware of your stressors; with this awareness, you can take measures to prevent unnecessary mishaps or illnesses.

♦ Notes

HOLMES, T. (1981). *Schedule of recent experience (SRE). Examiners manual.* Seattle: University of Washington Press.

LAKEIN, A. (1989). *How to get control of your time and your life.* New York: New American Library/Dutton.

U.S. Department of Agriculture & U.S. Department of Health and Human Services (1985). *Nutrition and your health: Dietary guidelines for Americans.* Washington, D.C.: Government Printing Office.

♦ Further Reading

BARNARD, N. (1990). *The power of your plate.* Summerton, TN: Book.

CALE, B. (1979). *The wonderful world of walking.* New York: Morrow.

DAVIS, M., ESHELMAN, E. R., & McKAY, M. (1991). *The relaxation and stress reduction workbook* (4th ed.). Oakland, CA: New Harbinger.

GALLWAY, W. (1979). *The inner game of tennis.* New York: Bantam Books.

GAWAIN, S. (1983). *Creative visualization.* New York: Bantam Books.

HAMILTON, E., WHITNEY, E., & SIZER, F. (1988). *Nutrition: concepts and controversies.* St. Paul, MN: West.

KOWALSKI, R. (1987). *The 8-week cholesterol cure.* New York: Harper & Row.

KUNIN, R. (1980). *Mega-nutrition: The new prescription for maximum health, energy, and longevity.* New York: McGraw-Hill.

LAWRENCE, A., & SCHEID, M. (1990). *Running and racing after 35.* Boston: Little, Brown.

PEARL, B., & MORAN, G. (1986). *Getting stronger.* New York: Random House.

SCHUBERT, J. (1988). *Richard's cycling for fitness.* New York: Ballantine Books.

VEDRAL, J. (1989). *The 12-minute total-body workout.* New York: Warner Books.

4 Taking Inventory

"I am a part of all that I have met."

—*Alfred, Lord Tennyson, "Ulysses"*

Whether you are planning your first career or are on your way to making a career change, you begin with self-assessment. In the self-assessment stage, you will identify your interests, personal qualities, and skills. Self-assessment also includes clarifying your values and making informed decisions. In this chapter, you will learn how to identify your interests and assess your skills. In addition, you will discover that many of your skills are transferable from one career to another.

After reading this chapter you should understand the following:

- That successful career planning begins with self-assessment
- The concept of transferable skills
- How you can identify your interests

You should be able to do the following:

- Identify your interests in terms of personality types and environments
- Determine which of your skills are transferable from one job to another
- Identify your skills according to working conditions and roles

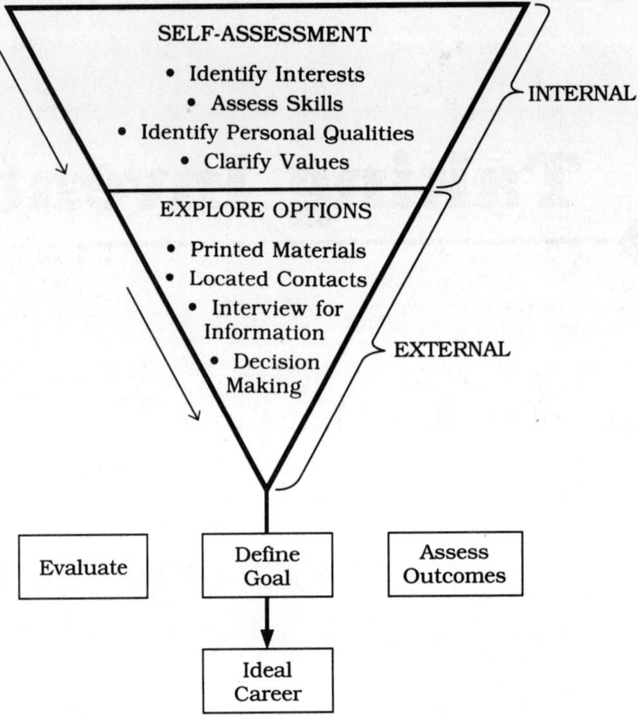

Figure 4.1 Career change model

The career change process involves several steps (see Figure 4.1). Admittedly you can be successful without going through the steps, but the risk of failure is greater and then you have to start over. Attaining success through career planning begins with self-assessment. As a career changer, you will have many life experiences to choose from when you decide which of your transferable skills you will take with you to your next career. By identifying your interests and assessing your skills, you will discover many of your "hidden talents." Let us begin by identifying your interests.

♦ Identifying Your Interests

You begin career planning by becoming aware of where your interests lie. Career specialists and counselors use several measures to identify interests and to assist the career planning process. Some of the more widely used interest inventories include the Strong Interest Inventory, Career Occupational Preference System, Self-Directed Search, and the Kuder Occupational Interest Survey. These inventories can provide a systematic method for considering interest patterns.

Although an interest inventory cannot tell you exactly what career you should follow, when used with other information, it can help you narrow your choices. All interest inventories have one basic feature in common: they compare your likes and dislikes on various subjects with those of people in certain occupational groups. One system, developed by John Holland (1985), clusters personality types and environments into six distinct groups. They are as follows:

Realistic. I'm practical and active have good physical skills. I like to work outside and to create things with my hands. I prefer to deal with things rather than ideas or people. Sometimes I have difficulty expressing things in words or communicating my feelings to others. My political and economic ideas are fairly conventional.

Investigative. I prefer to solve abstract problems and to understand the physical world rather than to act upon the world. I enjoy complicated problems and intellectual challenges. I do not like structured situations, lots of rules, or working around many people. I have unconventional values and attitudes and would like to be original and creative, especially in scientific areas.

Artistic. I prefer unstructured situations in which I can deal with problems through self-expression in artistic media. I prefer to work alone, have a great need for individualistic expression, and am sensitive and emotional. I would describe myself as independent, original, unconventional, expressive, and intense.

Social. I am sociable, responsible, humanistic, and concerned with the welfare of others. I express myself well and get along well with other people. I like to be near the center of groups and prefer to solve problems by discussing them with others. I like to see myself as cheerful, popular, achieving, and a good leader.

Enterprising. I have a great facility with words, which I can put to effective use in selling, dominating, and leading. I enjoy persuading others to my viewpoint and am impatient with work involving precision or long periods of intellectual concentration. I see myself as energetic, enthusiastic, adventurous, self-confident, and dominant.

Conventional. I prefer highly ordered activities, dislike being a leader, and enjoy working in a well-established chain of command. I like to know exactly what is expected of me and feel uncomfortable when I don't know the rules that govern a situation. I see myself as conventional, stable, well-controlled, and dependable.

You may find yourself identifying with more than one category or with a combination of these categories. Which do you feel apply to you? The following are examples of appropriate careers for each category.

REALISTIC
Electronic technician
Fire fighter
Draftsperson
Pilot
Architect
Engineer
Agricultural worker
Veterinarian
Police officer
Paramedic
Truck driver
Appliance repairer
Plumber
Surveyor
Athletic trainer
Computer repairer

INVESTIGATIVE
Biologist
Zoologist
Physician
Dentist
Optometrist
Computer programmer
Psychologist
Sociologist
Chemist
Medical lab technician
Actuary
Systems analyst
Physicist
Speech pathologist
Agronomist
Chiropractor

ARTISTIC
Writer
Journalist
Dancer
Editor
Television producer
Newscaster
Musician
Cartoonist
Graphic artist
Commercial artist
Librarian
Model
Photographer
Interpreter
Advertising director
Public relations director
Illustrator
Cinematographer

SOCIAL
Teacher
Nurse
Occupational therapist
Physical therapist
Counselor
Social worker
Clergy
Recreational worker
Dental hygienist
Community service worker

ENTERPRISING
Hospital administrator
Marketing director
Travel agent
Real estate broker
Sales representative
Lawyer
Politician
Restaurant manager
Small business owner
Academic dean
School principal

Legal assistant
Manager/supervisor
Insurance agent
Nursing home director
Purchasing agent
Financial planner

CONVENTIONAL
Accountant
Bookkeeper
Secretary
Receptionist
Computer operator
Auditor
Food service worker
Escrow officer
Airline reservations clerk
Loan officer
Claims adjuster
Banker
Bank teller
Word processing technician
Cosmetologist
Sales clerk
Dispatcher

Most interest inventories measure how closely your interests match those associated with various categories of occupations or professions and provide you with a list of careers related to these interests. At this point in your career change process you may want to take either the Strong Interest Inventory or another similar inventory or use the interest inventory developed by the U.S. Department of Labor (Exercise 4.1).

♦ Assessing Your Skills

Employers are people who are willing to pay to get a job done. Their primary interest is in the types of skills you have. Because most people cannot describe their skills "off the top of their heads," skill assessment is a major part of the career transition process.

Why should you examine your skills? You probably think most people know what they are good at. Doesn't life itself give us plenty of feedback on our strengths and weaknesses? The answer to this question is *no!*

The Johari Window (Luft & Ingram, 1963)—named for its inventors, Joseph Luft and Harry Ingram—presents four areas of self-knowledge; only one of the areas contains information that is available to both oneself and others (see Table 4.1). The upper left quadrant holds information that is known both by you and by others. For example, you may know that XYZ Company laid off 500 workers because this fact has become public knowledge. The upper right quadrant presents information that others know but you do not. For example, you may not know exactly what your supervisor thinks of your work. This quadrant is also known as the "risk area." The lower left quadrant shows your private life space. This quadrant contains information that you know but others do not;

Table 4.1 The Johari Window

	Information Known to Self	*Information Not Known to Self*
Information Known to Others	Area of free activity	Risk area
Information Not Known to Others	Private life space	Area of the unknown

Source: Adapted from "The Johari Window, A Graphic Model of Awareness in Interpersonal Relations" by J. Luft and H. Ingram in *Group Processes: An Introduction to Group Dynamics*, pp. 10–12. Copyright 1963 by National Pressbooks.

for example; you may have been offered a position at another company, but you have not told anyone. Finally, the lower right quadrant is the "area of the unknown." Information in this quadrant is not known by you or by anyone else.

Our concern here is the vast amount of unknown information about the self—specifically, those skills that exist but that are virtually unknown either to the person who has them or to others who know that person. We will attempt to uncover some of those hidden skills because they will become extremely important as you plot your new career path. But first, let us discuss what skills are.

What Is a Skill?

A skill can be defined as the ability to use one's knowledge effectively. *The Dictionary of Occupational Titles* (DOT), a publication of the U.S. Department of Labor, lists and describes over 20,000 jobs that are clustered into nine broad categories. The DOT uses the middle three digits of the nine-digit occupational code to rate the worker functions of the tasks performed in the occupation. These worker functions are related to people, data, and things. These same functions can be further categorized into these three skill groups: Functional, Adaptive, and Specific content.

According to Sidney Fine (1989), *Functional* skills are the generic behaviors related to people, data, and things that are brought into play in a work environment. *Adaptive* skills are the personality orientations an individual brings to the job. *Specific content* skills are the specific learnings and how-tos in a specific job situation. These are usually focused on specific task requirements.

Functional skills. These are competencies that enable an individual to relate to people, data, and things in some combination (orientation) according to personal preferences and to a degree of complexity appropriate to his or her potential. Included are skills like tending or operating machines; comparing, compiling, or analyzing data; and exchanging information, consulting, or negotiating with people. These skills emerge with growth, are refined and attuned in educational, training, and avocational pursuits, and then are reinforced in job-worker situations.

Adaptive skills. These are the competencies that enable an individual to manage him- or herself in relation to conformity and change and accept and adjust to the physical, interpersonal, and organizational arrangements and conditions in which a job exists. Included are punctuality, grooming, acceptance of supervision and authority, care of property, ability to get along with others, and impulse control. These skills are normally acquired in early developmental years, primarily through one's family and among one's peers and then reinforced in school, work, and adult social situations.

Specific content skills. These are the competencies that enable an individual to perform a specific job according to the specifications of an employer and according to the standards required to satisfy the market. These skills are normally acquired in a technical training school or institute, extensive on-the-job experience, or on a specific job. They are as numerous as specific products, services, and employers who establish the standards and conditions under which those products and services are produced.

Transferable Skills

The clues to your future success lie in your past. That is, the skills you take with you from one job to another (transferable skills) can be found in your previous accomplishments. Forget the thought that because you are changing careers you must start all over again and acquire an entirely new set of skills.

Transferable skills are those innate skills that make you unique. They are adaptive and functional skills. By contrast, specific content skills are primarily related to work content and may pertain only to a specific job. You acquired your technical skills through some form of training.

The range of transferability of skills in the world of work has been defined by Sidney Fine. Figure 4.2 shows the widest range to be adaptive, while the narrowest is specific content.

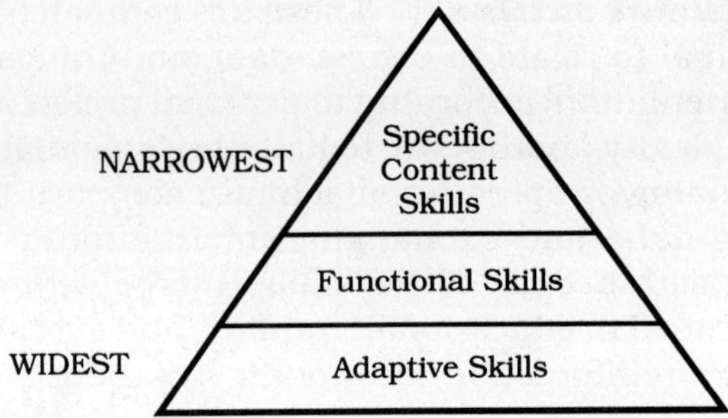

Figure 4.2 Range of transferability of skills in the world of work *Source:* © Copyright 1992 by Sidney A. Fine, Ph.D. Used by special permission. Not to be reproduced without permission.

Consider the following example:

PICKING UP BASEBALLS

One of the first jobs I ever had was working at a baseball batting cage. I used to pick up baseballs and put them back into the pitching machines, and people could try to hit me when they were hitting.

Out in back of the batting cages was a vacant lot that belonged to the owner. He had told me that if I thought of anything we could do back there that didn't cost a lot of money to build, I could be in charge of it and run it when we were done.

At the time, bicycle moto-cross was getting popular, so I thought it would be a great thing to try. The owner agreed to let me rent a bulldozer and set up a race course. From there I had to figure out a way to get about 1,000 old tires to line the track so no one would get hurt. A group of my friends and I took off from school and rented a trailer and just drove around from tire store to tire store looking for old tires. If the owner of the store didn't want to let us have the tires, I would offer him a free pass for his kids once the track opened. I didn't have any problems getting the tires.

The next problem I ran into was letting kids know about our new track. So I ended up going to all the elementary schools in the area and letting the kids know that they could ride for free for the first week but would have to pay on race day, which was Sunday.

The first day the track was open, we had over 450 kids show up to ride. My boss was so impressed that he let me have 25 percent of all the profits of the track. The first day the kids didn't have to pay to ride, but they did buy sodas and play the arcade. My boss made almost $900 extra in just one afternoon.

When the first race day came around, I couldn't believe how many people showed up. We had over 240 racers at seven dollars each, and about 800 spectators. After this, I never picked up baseballs again!

Now let's look at some of the transferable skills this person used. Consider the following:

calculating	persuasiveness	researching
problem solving	coordinating	developing
perseverance	promoting	projecting
initiative	determining	follow-through
planning	contacting	
troubleshooting	designing	

The following example is from a reentry student who was able to recall an accomplishment from her childhood.

GIRL SCOUT COOKIES

I would like to describe the time I was a Girl Scout. I had just graduated from being a Brownie and had attended a few meetings in the Girl Scouts. As most people know, Girl Scouts sell cookies. Well, our leader had given us each so many boxes of cookies to sell. I went from door to door trying to sell them, and one lady I asked said she would take 24 dozen cookies. I was so excited—I thought my troubles were over and I wouldn't have to go any further to sell the rest of my cookies. I ordered more boxes from my leader, but when I returned to the lady who wanted the 24 dozen cookies, she said she only wanted 24 cookies, not 24 dozen. I was pretty depressed about having all those cookies left, but I was determined. I worked extra hard, going from door to door until I had sold them all. At our next meeting, I turned in all the orders I had taken for cookies to my leader, and she counted them. I had sold the most of anyone. I received a really nice prize, and I was glad all my hard work had paid off.

Here are some *transferable* skills this person used:

planning	adaptability	handling detail work
evaluating	loyalty	persuasiveness
controlling	self-discipline	conscientiousness
working under stress	follow-through	goal orientation
determination	problem solving	initiative
	meeting deadlines	

Interestingly, the woman in this example used the same skills at the age of 8 that she used in her career as a real estate broker at the age of 42. So you see, these skills can be used throughout one's lifetime.

If you still find it difficult to think about your skills, use this checklist of common skills as a starting point. It will give you an idea of what your skills list might be. Have you ever done any of these?

adapted	delegated	inspected	reevaluated
administered	detected	interpreted	reorganized
allocated	directed	investigated	reviewed
approved	documented	maintained	revised
arranged	estimated	moderated	screened
assisted	expanded	operated	selected
attained	facilitated	perceived	solved
classified	founded	prepared	sorted
compared	governed	presented	stimulated
completed	identified	presided	structured
computed	implemented	processed	summarized
conceived	improved	programmed	supervised
coordinated	increased	provided	tested
dealt	indexed	recorded	
defined	initiated	recruited	

Skills Grouped According to Working Conditions and Roles

You may want to complete Exercises 4.2 and 4.3 at this time. After you have finished them, you should have several lists of skills you used—one list for each of your accomplishments. Now, what do you do with these lists? They are valuable clues to what you have done in the past that was particularly rewarding to you and what you will probably continue to do in some form.

As you study your lists, you probably will find that the same skills appear again and again throughout the ten accomplishments, like a thread woven through your life. Those skills are part of your unique make-up and are definitely *you.*

This repertoire of skills is what you will take with you to your next career. You can pick and choose from your lists and probably add a few more skills you hadn't thought of, but basically you will continue to use these "favored" skills throughout your lifetime.

Another way to view your skills is to group them according to working conditions and roles. Consider the following grouping:

MANAGEMENT SKILLS
analyzing tasks
motivating and leading people
troubleshooting
negotiating
working as a team member
planning
scheduling
organizing
assigning or delegating
directing
hiring
measuring production
setting standards
working under stress
solving problems
evaluating

COMMUNICATION SKILLS
debating
speaking in public
publicizing
reasoning
organizing
defining
writing
listening
explaining
interpreting ideas
conveying a positive image

RESEARCH AND INVESTIGATION SKILLS
experimenting
working on long-term projects
working without direction
reviewing
extrapolating
collecting data
diagnosing
writing
synthesizing
developing questions
interviewing
recognizing problems
designing
identifying problems and needs

FINANCIAL SKILLS
thinking in an orderly manner
working under stress
solving problems
calculating
handling detail work
recognizing problems
displaying finger dexterity
concentrating
budgeting
projecting
counting

MANUAL SKILLS
assembling
building
repairing
fixing
operating
monitoring
controlling
setting up
driving
cutting
doing precise machine work
working independently
operating tools or machinery

HUMAN RELATIONS SKILLS
coordinating
counseling
guiding
leading
understanding others' feelings
working under time and environmental pressures

maintaining group cooperation and support
expressing one's feelings appropriately
teaching a skill, concept, or principle

CLERICAL SKILLS
recommending
computing
examining
evaluating
filing
developing methods
improving
recording
following directions

TECHNICAL SKILLS
designing
financing
evaluating data
calculating
aligning
verifying
drafting
following specifications
adjusting
observing indicators

PUBLIC RELATIONS SKILLS
working under stress
conducting
planning
informing the public
maintaining a favorable image
consulting
writing
researching
representing

DESIGNING (ARTISTIC) SKILLS
designing
drawing
composing
painting
drafting
dealing creatively with colors, shapes, and spaces
imagining creatively
being an "idea person"
inventing
shaping
visualizing in three dimensions
executing from blueprints or patterns
innovating

SELLING SKILLS
working under stress
promoting
persuading
contacting
reviewing products
inspecting products
determining value
informing buyers
working with people

CRITICAL-THINKING SKILLS
identifying critical issues
creating innovative solutions
defining a problem
applying general principles that explain experiences
reasoning
applying appropriate criteria to strategies
analyzing data
adapting concepts to changing conditions
making decisions
comparing

Let us look at the following example, keeping in mind the preceding list.

PRIVATE PHONE LINES

As I was playing with my portable tape recorder, I discovered that it could act as an amplifier by taking my voice from a microphone and immediately sending it to a speaker plugged into the earphone jack. My best friend, who lived next door to me, had a similar recorder, and I convinced him that we could set up a private phone system between our bedrooms if only we could overcome two major obstacles: First, where could we get 300-plus feet of four-conductor wire, and second, how could we run the wire from my bedroom to his bedroom in a semi-permanent, unobtrusive manner? By sheer luck, my friend happened to mention the idea to his uncle. The next week, his uncle, a Bell Telephone employee, surprised him with a 500-foot roll of four-conductor wire. The rest was up to us.

We planned a path for the wire: out my window, up to the TV antenna, across to the nearest tree, tree-hopping toward his house for about 200 feet, across a big traverse of 100 feet from the last tree to his TV antenna, and down into his window. After all the tree climbing was done, we went to our bedrooms and hooked up our recorders. I think he was the first to speak; I heard him and replied, "I can hear you." Until then, we had thought, "Great theory, but it probably won't work." After that moment though, the world seemed a little smaller.

According to the categorized list, these are some of the skills this person used:

MANAGEMENT SKILLS
troubleshooting
planning
organizing
working under stress

COMMUNICATION SKILLS
reasoning
organizing
defining

RESEARCH AND INVESTIGATION SKILLS
experimenting
recognizing problems
designing

FINANCIAL SKILLS
calculating
projecting
counting

MANUAL SKILLS
assembling
building
cutting

HUMAN RELATIONS SKILLS
coordinating
working under time and environmental pressures

CLERICAL SKILLS
examining
evaluating
developing methods

TECHNICAL SKILLS
designing
calculating
verifying
adjusting

PUBLIC RELATIONS SKILLS
planning
consulting

DESIGNING (ARTISTIC) SKILLS
designing
dealing creatively with spaces
imagining creatively

being an "idea person"
inventing
innovating

SELLING SKILLS
contacting

CRITICAL-THINKING SKILLS
identifying critical issues
creating innovative solutions
defining a problem
applying general principles that explain experiences
reasoning
comparing

Study the preceding list of skills, and try to find a pattern. Which areas does the person tend to favor? You will note that the areas of *management, technical, designing,* and *critical thinking* were the groups where this person had the highest number of skills. Are you ready to guess what this individual does for a living? You may already have figured it out: he is an engineer. During the time I worked with him, however, he had become somewhat disenchanted with engineering. He later discovered that it was not the engineering field that he disliked but the fact that his position as an electrical engineer did not afford him an opportunity to express his creativity. He really would have been more satisfied as a design engineer, and ultimately that is the area he pursued. Do you see how skill identification works? Now make it work for you!

Skills Grouped According to People, Data, and Things

Another way to group skills is according to skills used with people, skills used with data, and skills used with things. Consider the following example:

WOODSHOP AWARD

I've always been handy with my hands, so the required projects in senior woodshop flew by, leaving me with quite a bit of extra time. Knowing what happens to good hands let idle, my instructor, who took an interest in my ability, persuaded me to tackle the construction of a cedar chest for my sister. Cedar being at a premium, I selected ash, which proved to be a mistake. Ash is what they use to make baseball bats—I'm talking *hard* here! It took me three weeks to cut and piece the chest together, but the tough part was yet to come. I had almost six more weeks of hand-sanding, two hours a day, for the desired finish.

I almost quit, until good spring weather allowed me to move outside, where I had a good view of the girls' athletic field. Without field hockey, I might not have made it. My sister's appreciation was reward enough, but I was shocked to receive the Achievement Award for woodshop for my senior class. Again, hard work prevailed.

Now let's examine this essay for the skills this person used as they relate to people, data, and things.

PEOPLE
being of service to others
consulting

DATA
following plans
organizing
writing
problem solving
creating
conducting detailed follow-through

THINGS
assembling
building
operating tools or machinery
displaying dexterity
creating
executing from models or blueprints
producing
drawing
inspecting

As you can see from the preceding list, the person in the example enjoys working mostly with things but also with some data. Of course, you would want to sample several accomplishments to see the common thread winding through them.

Describing your volunteer experiences is another excellent way of identifying your skills. How many times have you heard people say, "I wasn't paid for it, so how can I use it as work experience?" Well you can, and Table 4.2 is a good example.

♦ Summary

The first two steps in self-assessment are to identify your interests and assess your skills. You examined your interests according to the Holland typology and determined where your basic interests lie. You then categorized your skills according to whether they were adaptive, technical, or functional. Next, you analyzed your skills according to working conditions and roles, such as managerial,

Table 4.2 An example of transferable skills from a volunteer experience

Volunteer Experience	*Tasks and Responsibilities*	*General Skills, Qualities, and Traits*
Organizing and chairing an art auction as a fund-raiser for a women's organization	Contact artists to participate Decide on amount of space needed Determine equipment needed (tables, lights, and so on) Decide on location for the event Determine rental fee for booths and entrance fee Determine costs for food and materials Solicit volunteers from membership Determine committee chairpersons and tasks Contact newspapers, printers, and art associations for publicity Plan publicity strategy	Develop conceptual plan for project Communicate with the business community Set up schedule of events and working times Formulate policies, procedures, and budgets Design and coordinate physical layout Supervise and select people; delegate tasks Establish and maintain good interpersonal relationships with volunteers and businesspeople Write copy for ads; make oral presentations for publicity Motivate personnel and volunteers to support activity

TIP
It is important to communicate your experience in general terms that demonstrate transferability from volunteer experience to recognizable job skills.

communication, research and investigation, financial, manual, human relations, clerical, technical, public relations, designing (artistic), selling, and critical thinking. Finally, you determined whether you prefer to work with people, information, or things.

Be sure to complete the following exercises. They are designed to help you identify skills that are transferable from one job to another. Spend plenty of time on this chapter; it forms the crux of what we are working with—your *transferable skills.* You may want to return to this chapter when you assemble your résumé because then you will need to describe your functional skills in detail.

♦ EXERCISE 4.1 Interest Checklist

The Dictionary of Occupational Titles

The *Dictionary of Occupational Titles* (DOT) is compiled by the U.S. Department of Labor. The DOT lists and describes over 20,000 jobs, which are clustered into nine broad categories. These nine categories are divided into 82 specific divisions of occupations, which are further broken down into 979 other classifications.

The following list contains the 9 categories, 82 divisions, and 979 classifications. First, study the nine broad categories and decide which ones look most interesting to you. Next, look at the specific divisions under each of the categories you chose, and place a check mark beside those you want to learn more about. It is a good idea to research several of the occupations listed under each division because they will have certain elements in common.

ONE-DIGIT OCCUPATIONAL CATEGORIES

0/1 Professional, Technical, and Managerial Occupations
2 Clerical and Sales Occupations
3 Service Occupations
4 Agricultural, Fishery, Forestry, and Related Occupations
5 Processing Occupations
6 Machine Trades Occupations
7 Benchwork Occupations
8 Structural Work Occupations
9 Miscellaneous Occupations

TWO-DIGIT OCCUPATIONAL DIVISIONS

0/1 PROFESSIONAL, TECHNICAL, AND MANAGERIAL OCCUPATIONS
00/01 Occupations in Architecture, Engineering, and Surveying
02 Occupations in Mathematics and Physical Sciences
03 Computer-Related Occupations
04 Occupations in Life Sciences
05 Occupations in Social Sciences
07 Occupations in Medicine and Health
09 Occupations in Education
10 Occupations in Museum, Library, and Archival Sciences
11 Occupations in Law and Jurisprudence
12 Occupations in Religion and Theology
13 Occupations in Writing
14 Occupations in Art
15 Occupations in Entertainment and Recreation
16 Occupations in Administrative Specializations
18 Managers and Officials, N.E.C.*
19 Miscellaneous Professional, Technical, and Managerial Occupations

2 CLERICAL AND SALES OCCUPATIONS
20 Stenography, Typing, Filing, and Related Occupations

*Some divisions or groups end in the designation "N.E.C." (Not Elsewhere Classified). This indicates that the occupations do not logically fit into precisely defined divisions or groups, or that they could fit into two or more of them equally well.

21 Computing and Account-Recording Occupations
22 Production and Stock Clerks and Related Occupations
23 Information and Message Distribution Occupations
24 Miscellaneous Clerical Occupations
25 Sales Occupations, Services
26 Sales Occupations, Consumable Commodities
27 Sales Occupations, Commodities, N.E.C.
29 Miscellaneous Sales Occupations

3 SERVICE OCCUPATIONS
30 Domestic Service Occupations
31 Food and Beverage Preparation and Service Occupations
32 Lodging and Related Service Occupations
33 Barbering, Cosmetology, and Related Service Occupations
34 Amusement and Recreation Service Occupations
35 Miscellaneous Personal Service Occupations
36 Apparel and Furnishings Service Occupations
37 Protective Service Occupations
38 Building and Related Service Occupations

4 AGRICULTURAL, FISHERY, FORESTRY, AND RELATED OCCUPATIONS
40 Plant Farming Occupations
41 Animal Farming Occupations
42 Miscellaneous Agricultural and Related Occupations
44 Fishery and Related Occupations
45 Forestry Occupations
46 Hunting, Trapping, and Related Occupations

5 PROCESSING OCCUPATIONS
50 Occupations in Processing of Metal
51 Ore Refining and Foundry Occupations
52 Occupations in Processing of Food, Tobacco, and Related Products
53 Occupations in Processing of Paper and Related Materials
54 Occupations in Processing of Petroleum, Coal, Natural and Manufactured Gas, and Related Products
55 Occupations in Processing of Chemicals, Plastics, Synthetics, Rubber, Paint, and Related Products
56 Occupations in Processing of Wood and Wood Products
57 Occupations in Processing of Stone, Clay, Glass, and Related Products
58 Occupations in Processing of Leather, Textiles, and Related Products
59 Processing Occupations, N.E.C.

6 *MACHINE TRADES OCCUPATIONS*
60 Metal Machining Occupations
61 Metalworking Occupations, N.E.C.
62/63 Mechanics and Machinery Repairers
64 Paperworking Occupations
65 Printing Occupations
66 Wood Machining Occupations
67 Occupations in Machining Stone, Clay, Glass, and Related Materials
68 Textile Occupations
69 Machine Trades Occupations, N.E.C.

7 *BENCHWORK OCCUPATIONS*
70 Occupations in Fabrication, Assembly, and Repair of Metal Products, N.E.C.
71 Occupations in Fabrication and Repair of Scientific, Medical, Photographic, Optical, Horological, and Related Products
72 Occupations in Assembly and Repair of Electrical Equipment
73 Occupations in Fabrication and Repair of Products Made from Assorted Materials
74 Painting, Decorating, and Related Occupations
75 Occupations in Fabrication and Repair of Plastics, Synthetics, Rubber, and Related Products
76 Occupations in Fabrication and Repair of Wood Products
77 Occupations in Fabrication and Repair of Sand, Stone, Clay, and Glass Products
78 Occupations in Fabrication and Repair of Textile, Leather, and Related Products
79 Benchwork Occupations, N.E.C.

8 *STRUCTURAL WORK OCCUPATIONS*
80 Occupations in Metal Fabricating, N.E.C.
81 Welders, Cutters, and Related Occupations
82 Electrical Assembling, Installing, and Repairing Occupations
84 Painting, Plastering, Waterproofing, Cementing, and Related Occupations
85 Excavating, Grading, Paving, and Related Occupations
86 Construction Occupations, N.E.C.
89 Structural Work Occupations, N.E.C.

9 *MISCELLANEOUS OCCUPATIONS*
90 Motor Freight Occupations
91 Transportation Occupations, N.E.C.
92 Packaging and Materials Handling Occupations
93 Occupations in Extraction of Minerals
95 Occupations in Production and Distribution of Utilities

96 Amusement, Recreation, Motion Picture, Radio and Television Occupations, N.E.C.

97 Occupations in Graphic Art Work

THREE-DIGIT OCCUPATIONAL GROUPS

PROFESSIONAL, TECHNICAL, AND MANAGERIAL OCCUPATIONS

00/01 OCCUPATIONS IN ARCHITECTURE, ENGINEERING, AND SURVEYING

001 Architectural Occupations
002 Aeronautical Engineering Occupations
003 Electrical/Electronics Engineering Occupations
005 Civil Engineering Occupations
006 Ceramic Engineering Occupations
007 Mechanical Engineering Occupations
008 Chemical Engineering Occupations
010 Mining and Petroleum Engineering Occupations
011 Metallurgy and Metallurgical Engineering Occupations
012 Industrial Engineering Occupations
013 Agricultural Engineering Occupations
014 Marine Engineering Occupations
015 Nuclear Engineering Occupations
017 Drafters, N.E.C.
018 Surveying/Cartographic Occupations
019 Occupations in Architecture, Engineering, and Surveying, N.E.C.

02 OCCUPATIONS IN MATHEMATICS AND PHYSICAL SCIENCES

020 Occupations in Mathematics
021 Occupations in Astronomy
022 Occupations in Chemistry
023 Occupations in Physics
024 Occupations in Geology
025 Occupations in Meteorology
029 Occupations in Mathematics and Physical Sciences, N.E.C.

03 COMPUTER-RELATED OCCUPATIONS

030 Occupations in Systems Analysis and Programming
031 Occupations in Data Communications and Networks
032 Occupations in Computer System User Support
033 Occupations in Computer Systems Technical Support
039 Computer-Related Occupations, N.E.C.

04 OCCUPATIONS IN LIFE SCIENCES

040 Occupations in Agricultural Sciences

041 Occupations in Biological Sciences
045 Occupations in Psychology
049 Occupations in Life Sciences, N.E.C.

05 OCCUPATIONS IN SOCIAL SCIENCES
050 Occupations in Economics
051 Occupations in Political Science
052 Occupations in History
054 Occupations in Sociology
055 Occupations in Anthropology
059 Occupations in Social Sciences, N.E.C.

07 OCCUPATIONS IN MEDICINE AND HEALTH
070 Physicians and Surgeons
071 Osteopaths
072 Dentists
073 Veterinarians
074 Pharmacists
075 Registered Nurses
076 Therapists
077 Dietitians
078 Occupations in Medical and Dental Technology
079 Occupations in Medicine and Health, N.E.C.

09 OCCUPATIONS IN EDUCATION
090 Occupations in College and University Education
091 Occupations in Secondary School Education
092 Occupations in Preschool, Primary School, and Kindergarten Education
094 Occupations in Education of Persons with Disabilities
096 Home Economists and Farm Advisers
097 Occupations in Vocational Education
099 Occupations in Education, N.E.C.

10 OCCUPATIONS IN MUSEUM, LIBRARY, AND ARCHIVAL SCIENCES
100 Librarians
101 Archivists
102 Museum Curators and Related Occupations
109 Occupations in Museum, Library, and Archival Sciences, N.E.C.

11 OCCUPATIONS IN LAW AND JURISPRUDENCE
110 Lawyers
111 Judges
119 Occupations in Law and Jurisprudence, N.E.C.

12 OCCUPATIONS IN RELIGION AND THEOLOGY
120 Clergy
129 Occupations in Religion and Theology, N.E.C.

13 OCCUPATIONS IN WRITING
131 Writers
132 Editors: Publication, Broadcast, and Script

137 Interpreters and Translators
139 Occupations in Writing, N.E.C.

14 OCCUPATIONS IN ART
141 Commercial Artists: Designers and Illustrators, Graphic Arts
142 Environmental, Product, and Related Designers
143 Occupations in Photography
144 Fine Artists: Painters, Sculptors, and Related Occupations
149 Occupations in Art, N.E.C.

15 OCCUPATIONS IN ENTERTAINMENT AND RECREATION
150 Occupations in Dramatics
151 Occupations in Dancing
152 Occupations in Music
153 Occupations in Athletics and Sports
159 Occupations in Entertainment and Recreation, N.E.C.

16 OCCUPATIONS IN ADMINISTRATIVE SPECIALIZATIONS
160 Accountants, Auditors, and Related Occupations
161 Budget and Management Systems Analysis Occupations
162 Purchasing Management Occupations
163 Sales and Distribution Management Occupations
164 Advertising Management Occupations
165 Public Relations Management Occupations
166 Personnel Administration Occupations
168 Inspectors and Investigators, Managerial and Public Service
169 Occupations in Administrative Specializations, N.E.C.

18 MANAGERS AND OFFICIALS, N.E.C.
180 Agriculture, Forestry, and Fishing Industry Managers and Officials
181 Mining Industry Managers and Officials
182 Construction Industry Managers and Officials
183 Manufacturing Industry Managers and Officials
184 Transportation, Communication, and Utilities Industry Managers and Officials
185 Wholesale and Retail Trade Managers and Officials
186 Finance, Insurance, and Real Estate Managers and Officials
187 Service Industry Managers and Officials
188 Public Administration Managers and Officials
189 Miscellaneous Managers and Officials, N.E.C.

19 MISCELLANEOUS PROFESSIONAL, TECHNICAL, AND MANAGERIAL OCCUPATIONS

191 Agents and Appraisers, N.E.C.

193 Radio Operators

194 Sound, Film, and Videotape Recording, and Reproduction Occupations

195 Occupations in Social and Welfare Work

196 Airplane Pilots and Navigators

197 Ship Captains, Mates, Pilots, and Engineers

198 Railroad Conductors

199 Miscellaneous Professional, Technical, and Managerial Occupations, N.E.C.

CLERICAL AND SALES OCCUPATIONS

20 STENOGRAPHY, TYPING, FILING, AND RELATED OCCUPATIONS

201 Secretaries

202 Stenographers

203 Typists and Typewriting-Machine Operators

205 Interviewing Clerks

206 File Clerks

207 Duplicating-Machine Operators and Tenders

208 Mailing and Miscellaneous Office Machine Operators

209 Stenography, Typing, Filing, and Related Occupations, N.E.C.

21 COMPUTING AND ACCOUNT-RECORDING OCCUPATIONS

210 Bookkeepers and Related Occupations

211 Cashiers and Tellers

213 Computer and Peripheral Equipment Operators

214 Billing and Rate Clerks

215 Payroll, Timekeeping, and Duty-Roster Clerks

216 Accounting and Statistical Clerks

217 Account-Recording-Machine Operators, N.E.C.

219 Computing and Account-Recording Occupations, N.E.C.

22 PRODUCTION AND STOCK CLERKS AND RELATED OCCUPATIONS

22 Occupations in Moving and Storing Materials and Products, N.E.C.

221 Production Clerks

222 Shipping, Receiving, Stock, and Related Clerical Occupations

229 Production and Stock Clerks and Related Occupations, N.E.C.

23 INFORMATION AND MESSAGE DISTRIBUTION OCCUPATIONS

230 Hand Delivery and Distribution Occupations

235 Telephone Operators

236 Telegraph Operators

237 Information and Reception Clerks
238 Accommodation Clerks and Gate and Ticket Agents
239 Information and Message Distribution Occupations, N.E.C.

24 MISCELLANEOUS CLERICAL OCCUPATIONS
241 Investigators, Adjusters, and Related Occupations
243 Government Service Clerks, N.E.C.
245 Medical Service Clerks, N.E.C.
247 Advertising-Service Clerks, N.E.C.
248 Transportation-Service Clerks, N.E.C.
249 Miscellaneous Clerical Occupations, N.E.C.

25 SALES OCCUPATIONS, SERVICES
250 Sales Occupations, Real Estate, Insurance, Securities and Financial Services
251 Sales Occupations, Business Services, except Real Estate, Insurance, Securities, and Financial Services
252 Sales Occupations, Transportation Services
253 Sales Occupations, Utilities
254 Sales Occupations, Printing and Advertising
259 Sales Occupations, Services, N.E.C.

26 SALES OCCUPATIONS, CONSUMABLE COMMODITIES
260 Sales Occupations, Agricultural and Food Products
261 Sales Occupations, Textile Products, Apparel, and Notions
262 Sales Occupations, Chemicals, Drugs, and Sundries
269 Sales Occupations, Miscellaneous Consumable Commodities, N.E.C.

27 SALES OCCUPATIONS, COMMODITIES, N.E.C.
270 Sales Occupations, Home Furniture, Furnishings, and Appliances
271 Sales Occupations, Elecrical Goods, except Home Appliances
272 Sales Occupations, Farm and Gardening Equipment and Supplies
273 Sales Occupations, Transportation Equipment, Parts, and Supplies
274 Sales Occupations, Industrial and Related Equipment and Supplies
275 Sales Occupations, Business and Commercial Equipment and Supplies
276 Sales Occupations, Medical and Scientific Equipment and Supplies
277 Sales Occupations, Sporting, Hobby, Stationery, and Related Goods

279 Sales Occupations, Miscellaneous Commodities, N.E.C.

29 MISCELLANEOUS SALES OCCUPATIONS
290 Sales Clerks
291 Vending and Door-to-Door Selling Occupations
292 Route Sales and Delivery Occupations
293 Solicitors
294 Auctioneers
295 Rental Clerks
296 Shoppers
297 Sales Promotion Occupations
298 Merchandise Displayers
299 Miscellaneous Sales Occupations, N.E.C.

SERVICE OCCUPATIONS

30 DOMESTIC SERVICE OCCUPATIONS
301 Household and Related Work
302 Launderers, Private Family
305 Cooks, Domestic
309 Domestic Service Occupations, N.E.C.

31 FOOD AND BEVERAGE PREPARATION AND SERVICE OCCUPATIONS
310 Hosts/Hostesses and Stewards/Stewardesses, Food and Beverage Service, except Ship Stewards/Stewardesses
311 Waiters/Waitresses, and Related Food Service Occupations
312 Bartenders
313 Chefs and Cooks, Hotels and Restaurants
315 Miscellaneous Cooks, except Domestic
316 Meatcutters, except in Slaughtering and Packing Houses
317 Miscellaneous Food and Beverage Preparation Occupations
318 Kitchen Workers, N.E.C.
319 Food and Beverage Preparation and Service Occupations, N.E.C.

32 LODGING AND RELATED SERVICE OCCUPATIONS
320 Boarding-House and Lodging-House Keepers
321 Housekeepers, Hotels and Institutions
323 Housecleaners, Hotels, Restaurants, and Related Establishments
324 Bellhops and Related Occupations
329 Lodging and Related Service Occupations, N.E.C.

33 BARBERING, COSMETOLOGY, AND RELATED SERVICE OCCUPATIONS
330 Barbers

331 Manicurists
332 Hairdressers and Cosmetologists
333 Make-Up Occupations
334 Masseurs and Related Occupations
335 Bath Attendants
338 Embalmers and Related Occupations
339 Barbering, Cosmetology, and Related Service Occupations, N.E.C.

34 AMUSEMENT AND RECREATION SERVICE OCCUPATIONS

340 Attendants, Bowling Alley and Billiard Parlor
341 Attendants, Golf Course, Tennis Court, Skating Rink, and Related Facilities
342 Amusement Device and Concession Attendants
343 Gambling Hall Attendants
344 Ushers
346 Wardrobe and Dressing-Room Attendants
349 Amusement and Recreation Service Occupations, N.E.C.

35 MISCELLANEOUS PERSONAL SERVICE OCCUPATIONS

350 Ship Stewards/Stewardesses and Related Occupations
351 Train Attendants
352 Hosts/Hostesses and Stewards/Stewardesses, N.E.C.
353 Guides
354 Unlicensed Birth Attendants and Practical Nurses
355 Attendants, Hospitals, Morgues, and Related Health Services
357 Baggage Handlers
358 Checkroom, Locker Room, and Rest Room Attendants
359 Miscellaneous Personal Service Occupations, N.E.C.

36 APPAREL AND FURNISHINGS SERVICE OCCUPATIONS

361 Laundering Occupations
362 Dry Cleaning Occupations
363 Pressing Occupations
364 Dyeing and Related Occupations
365 Shoe and Luggage Repairer and Related Occupations
366 Bootblacks and Related Occupations
369 Apparel and Furnishings Service Occupations, N.E.C.

37 PROTECTIVE SERVICE OCCUPATIONS

371 Crossing Tenders and Bridge Operators
372 Security Guards and Correction Officers, except Crossing Tenders
373 Fire Fighters, Fire Department
375 Police Officers and Detectives, Public Service

376 Police Officers and Detectives, except in Public Service
377 Sheriffs and Bailiffs
378 Armed Forces Enlisted Personnel
379 Protective Service Occupations, N.E.C.

38 BUILDING AND RELATED SERVICE OCCUPATIONS
381 Porters and Cleaners
382 Janitors
383 Building Pest Control Service Occupations
388 Elevator Operators
389 Building and Related Service Occupations, N.E.C.

AGRICULTURAL, FISHERY, FORESTRY, AND RELATED OCCUPATIONS

40 PLANT FARMING OCCUPATIONS
401 Grain Farming Occupations
402 Vegetable Farming Occupations
403 Fruit and Nut Farming Occupations
404 Field Crop Farming Occupations, N.E.C.
405 Horticultural Specialty Occupations
406 Gardening and Groundskeeping Occupations
407 Diversified Crop Farming Occupations
408 Plant Life and Related Service Occupations
409 Plant Farming and Related Occupations, N.E.C.

41 ANIMAL FARMING OCCUPATIONS
410 Domestic Animal Farming Occupations
411 Domestic Fowl Farming Occupations
412 Game Farming Occupations
413 Lower Animal Farming Occupations
418 Animal Service Occupations
419 Animal Farming Occupations, N.E.C.

42 MISCELLANEOUS AGRICULTURAL AND RELATED OCCUPATIONS
421 General Farming Occupations
429 Miscellaneous Agricultural and Related Occupations, N.E.C.

44 FISHERY AND RELATED OCCUPATIONS
441 Nct, Scinc, and Trap Fishers
442 Line Fishers
443 Fishers, Miscellaneous Equipment

446 Aquatic Life Cultivation and Related Occupations
447 Sponge and Seaweed Gatherers
449 Fishery and Related Occupations, N.E.C.

454 Logging and Related Occupations
455 Log Grading, Scaling, Sorting, Rafting, and Related Occupations
459 Forestry Occupations, N.E.C.

45 FORESTRY OCCUPATIONS
451 Tree Farming and Related Occupations
452 Forest Conservation Occupations
453 Occupations in Harvesting Forest Products, except Logging

46 HUNTING, TRAPPING, AND RELATED OCCUPATIONS
461 Hunting and Trapping Occupations

PROCESSING OCCUPATIONS

50 OCCUPATIONS IN PROCESSING OF METAL
500 Electroplating Occupations
501 Dip Plating Occupations
502 Melting, Pouring, Casting, and Related Occupations
503 Pickling, Cleaning, Degreasing, and Related Occupations
504 Heat-Treating Occupations
505 Metal Spraying, Coating, and Related Occupations
509 Occupations in Processing of Metal, N.E.C.

51 ORE REFINING AND FOUNDRY OCCUPATIONS
510 Mixing and Related Occupations
511 Separating, Filtering, and Related Occupations
512 Melting Occupations
513 Roasting Occupations
514 Pouring and Casting Occupations
515 Crushing and Grinding Occupations
518 Molders, Coremakers, and Related Occupations
519 Ore Refining and Foundry Occupations, N.E.C.

52 OCCUPATIONS IN PROCESSING OF FOOD, TOBACCO, AND RELATED PRODUCTS
520 Mixing, Compounding, Blending, Kneading, Shaping, and Related Occupations
521 Separating, Crushing, Milling, Chopping, Grinding, and Related Occupations

522 Culturing, Melting, Fermenting, Distilling, Saturating, Pickling, Aging, and Related Occupations
523 Heating, Rendering, Melting, Drying, Cooling, Freezing, and Related Occupations
524 Coating, Icing, Decorating, and Related Occupations
525 Slaughtering, Breaking, Curing, and Related Occupations
526 Cooking and Baking Occupations, N.E.C.
529 Occupations in Processing of Food, Tobacco, and Related Products, N.E.C.

53 OCCUPATIONS IN PROCESSING OF PAPER AND RELATED MATERIALS
530 Grinding, Beating, and Mixing Occupations
532 Cooking and Drying Occupations
533 Cooling, Bleaching, Screening, Washing, and Related Occupations
534 Calendering, Sizing, Coating, and Related Occupations
535 Forming Occupations, N.E.C.
539 Occupations in Processing of Paper and Related Materials, N.E.C.

54 OCCUPATIONS IN PROCESSING OF PETROLEUM, COAL, NATURAL AND MANUFACTURED GAS, AND RELATED PRODUCTS
540 Mixing and Blending Occupations
541 Filtering, Straining, and Separating Occupations
542 Distilling, Subliming, and Carbonizing Occupations
543 Drying, Heating, and Melting Occupations
544 Grinding and Crushing Occupations
546 Reacting Occupations, N.E.C.
549 Occupations in Processing of Petroleum, Coal, Natural and Manufactured Gas, and Related Products, N.E.C.

55 OCCUPATIONS IN PROCESSING OF CHEMICALS, PLASTICS, SYNTHETICS, RUBBER, PAINT, AND RELATED PRODUCTS
550 Mixing and Blending Occupations
551 Filtering, Straining, and Separating Occupations
552 Distilling Occupations
553 Heating, Baking, Drying, Seasoning, Melting, and Heat-Treating Occupations
554 Coating, Calendering, Laminating, and Finishing Occupations
555 Grinding and Crushing Occupations
556 Casting and Molding Occupations, N.E.C.
557 Extruding Occupations
558 Reacting Occupations, N.E.C.

559 Occupations in Processing of Chemicals, Plastics, Synthetics, Rubber, Paint, and Related Products, N.E.C.

56 OCCUPATIONS IN PROCESSING OF WOOD AND WOOD PRODUCTS

560 Mixing and Related Occupations
561 Wood Preserving and Related Occupations
562 Saturating, Coating, and Related Occupations, N.E.C.
563 Drying, Seasoning, and Related Occupations
564 Grinding and Chopping Occupations, N.E.C.
569 Occupations in Processing of Wood and Wood Products, N.E.C.

57 OCCUPATIONS IN PROCESSING OF STONE, CLAY, GLASS, AND RELATED PRODUCTS

570 Crushing, Grinding, and Mixing Occupations
571 Separating Occupations
572 Melting Occupations
573 Baking, Drying, and Heat-Treating Occupations
574 Impregnating, Coating, and Glazing Occupations
575 Forming Occupations
579 Occupations in Processing of Stone, Clay, Glass, and Related Products, N.E.C.

58 OCCUPATIONS IN PROCESSING OF LEATHER, TEXTILES, AND RELATED PRODUCTS

580 Shaping, Blocking, Stretching, and Tentering Occupations
581 Separating, Filtering, and Drying Occupations
582 Washing, Steaming, and Saturating Occupations
583 Ironing, Pressing, Glazing, Staking, Calendering, and Embossing Occupations
584 Mercerizing, Coating, and Laminating Occupations
585 Singeing, Cutting, Shearing, Shaving, and Napping Occupations
586 Felting and Fulling Occupations
587 Brushing and Shrinking Occupations
589 Occupations in Processing of Leather, Textiles, and Related Products, N.E.C.

59 PROCESSING OCCUPATIONS, N.E.C.

590 Occupations in Processing Products from Assorted Materials
599 Miscellaneous Processing Occupations, N.E.C.

MACHINE TRADES OCCUPATIONS

60 METAL MACHINING OCCUPATIONS

600 Machinists and Related Occupations
601 Toolmakers and Related Occupations
602 Gear Machining Occupations
603 Abrading Occupations
604 Turning Occupations
605 Milling, Shaping, and Planing Occupations
606 Boring Occupations
607 Sawing Occupations
609 Metal Machining Occupations, N.E.C.

61 METALWORKING OCCUPATIONS, N.E.C.

610 Hammer Forging Occupations
611 Press Forging Occupations
612 Forging Occupations, N.E.C.
613 Sheet and Bar Rolling Occupations
614 Extruding and Drawing Occupations
615 Punching and Shearing Occupations
616 Fabricating Machine Occupations
617 Forming Occupations, N.E.C.
619 Miscellaneous Metalworking Occupations, N.E.C.

62/63 MECHANICS AND MACHINERY REPAIRERS

620 Motorized Vehicle and Engineering Equipment Mechanics and Repairers
621 Aircraft Mechanics and Repairers
622 Rail Equipment Mechanics and Repairers
623 Marine Mechanics and Repairers
624 Farm Mechanics and Repairers
625 Engine, Power Transmission, and Related Mechanics
626 Metalworking Machinery Mechanics
627 Printing and Publishing Mechanics and Repairers
628 Textile Machinery and Equipment Mechanics and Repairers
629 Special Industry Machinery Mechanics
630 General Industry Mechanics and Repairers
631 Powerplant Mechanics and Repairers
632 Ordnance and Accessories Mechanics and Repairers
633 Business and Commercial Machine Repairers
637 Utilities Service Mechanics and Repairers
638 Miscellaneous Occupations in Machine Installation and Repair
639 Mechanics and Machinery Repairers, N.E.C.

64 PAPERWORKING OCCUPATIONS

640 Paper Cutting, Winding, and Related Occupations
641 Folding, Creasing, Scoring, and Gluing Occupations

649 Paperworking Occupations, N.E.C.

65 PRINTING OCCUPATIONS

650 Typesetters and Composers
651 Printing Press Occupations
652 Printing Machine Occupations
653 Bookbinding-Machine Operators and Related Occupations
654 Typecasters and Related Occupations
659 Printing Occupations, N.E.C.

66 WOOD MACHINING OCCUPATIONS

660 Cabinetmakers
661 Patternmakers
662 Sanding Occupations
663 Shearing and Shaving Occupations
664 Turning Occupations
665 Milling and Planing Occupations
666 Boring Occupations
667 Sawing Occupations
669 Wood Machining Occupations, N.E.C.

67 OCCUPATIONS IN MACHINING STONE, CLAY, GLASS, AND RELATED MATERIALS

670 Stonecutters and Related Occupations
673 Abrading Occupations
674 Turning Occupations
675 Planing and Shaping Occupations, N.E.C.
676 Boring and Punching Occupations
677 Chipping, Cutting, Sawing, and Related Occupations
679 Occupations in Machining Stone, Clay, Glass, and Related Materials, N.E.C.

68 TEXTILE OCCUPATIONS

680 Carding, Combing, Drawing, and Related Occupations
681 Twisting, Beaming, Warping, and Related Occupations
682 Spinning Occupations
683 Weavers and Related Occupations
684 Hosiery Knitting Occupations
685 Knitting Occupations, except Hosiery
686 Punching, Cutting, Forming, and Related Occupations
687 Tufting Occupations
689 Textile Occupations, N.E.C.

69 MACHINE TRADES OCCUPATIONS, N.E.C.

690 Plastics, Synthetics, Rubber, and Leather Working Occupations
691 Occupations in Fabrication of Insulated Wire and Cable

692 Occupations in Fabrication of Products From Assorted Materials
693 Modelmakers, Patternmakers, and Related Occupations
694 Occupations in Fabrication of Ordnance, Ammunition, and Related Products, N.E.C.
699 Miscellaneous Machine Trades Occupations, N.E.C.

BENCHWORK OCCUPATIONS

70 OCCUPATIONS IN FABRICATION, ASSEMBLY, AND REPAIR OF METAL PRODUCTS, N.E.C.
700 Occupations in Fabrication, Assembly, and Repair of Jewelry, Silverware, and Related Products
701 Occupations in Fabrication, Assembly, and Repair of Tools, and Related Products
703 Occupations in Assembly and Repair of Sheetmetal Products, N.E.C.
704 Engravers, Etchers, and Related Occupations
705 Filing, Grinding, Buffing, Cleaning, and Polishing Occupations, N.E.C.
706 Metal Unit Assemblers and Adjusters, N.E.C.
709 Miscellaneous Occupations in Fabrication, Assembly, and Repair of Metal Products, N.E.C.

71 OCCUPATIONS IN FABRICATION AND REPAIR OF SCIENTIFIC, MEDICAL, PHOTOGRAPHIC, OPTICAL, HOROLOGICAL, AND RELATED PRODUCTS
710 Occupations in Fabrication and Repair of Instruments for Measuring, Controlling, and Indicating Physical Characteristics
711 Occupations in Fabrication and Repair of Optical Instruments
712 Occupations in Fabrication and Repair of Surgical, Medical, and Dental Instruments and Supplies
713 Occupations in Fabrication and Repair of Ophthalmic Goods
714 Occupations in Fabrication and Repair of Photographic Equipment and Supplies
715 Occupations in Fabrication and Repair of Watches, Clocks, and Parts
716 Occupations in Fabrication and Repair of Engineering and Scientific Instruments and Equipment, N.E.C.
719 Occupations in Fabrication and Repair of Scientific and Medical Apparatus, Photographic and Optical Goods, Horological, and Related Products, N.E.C.

72 OCCUPATIONS IN ASSEMBLY AND REPAIR OF ELECTRICAL EQUIPMENT

720 Occupations in Assembly and Repair of Radio and Television Receiving Sets and Phonographs
721 Occupations in Assembly and Repair of Motors, Generators, and Related Products
722 Occupations in Assembly and Repair of Communications Equipment
723 Occupations in Assembly and Repair of Electrical Appliances and Fixtures
724 Occupations in Winding and Assembling Coils, Magnets, Armatures, and Related Products
725 Occupations in Assembly of Light Bulbs and Electronic Tubes
726 Occupations in Assembly and Repair of Electronic Components and Accessories, N.E.C.
727 Occupations in Assembly of Storage Batteries
728 Occupations in Fabrication of Electrical Wire and Cable
729 Occupations in Assembly and Repair of Electrical Equipment, N.E.C.

73 OCCUPATIONS IN FABRICATION AND REPAIR OF PRODUCTS MADE FROM ASSORTED MATERIALS

730 Occupations in Fabrication and Repair of Musical Instruments and Parts
731 Occupations in Fabrication and Repair of Games and Toys
732 Occupations in Fabrication and Repair of Sporting Goods
733 Occupations in Fabrication and Repair of Pens, Pencils, and Office and Artists' Materials, N.E.C.
734 Occupations in Fabrication and Repair of Notions
735 Occupations in Fabrication and Repair of Jewelry, N.E.C.
736 Occupations in Fabrication and Repair of Ordnance and Accessories
737 Occupations in Fabrication of Ammunition, Fireworks, Explosives, and Related Products
739 Occupations in Fabrication and Repair of Products Made from Assorted Materials, N.E.C.

74 PAINTING, DECORATING, AND RELATED OCCUPATIONS

740 Painters, Brush
741 Painters, Spray
742 Staining, Waxing, and Related Occupations
749 Painting, Decorating, and Related Occupations, N.E.C.

75 *OCCUPATIONS IN FABRICATION AND REPAIR OF PLASTICS, SYNTHETICS, RUBBER, AND RELATED PRODUCTS*

750 Occupations in Fabrication and Repair of Tires, Tubes, Tire Treads, and Related Products

751 Laying Out and Cutting Occupations, N.E.C.

752 Fitting, Shaping, Cementing, Finishing, and Related Occupations, N.E.C.

753 Occupations in Fabrication and Repair of Rubber and Plastic Footwear

754 Occupations in Fabrication and Repair of Miscellaneous Plastics Products

759 Occupations in Fabrication and Repair of Plastics, Synthetics, Rubber, and Related Products, N.E.C.

76 *OCCUPATIONS IN FABRICATION AND REPAIR OF WOOD PRODUCTS*

760 Bench Carpenters and Related Occupations

761 Occupations in Laying Out, Cutting, Carving, Shaping, and Sanding Wood Products, N.E.C.

762 Occupations in Assembling Wood Products, N.E.C.

763 Occupations in Fabrication and Repair of Furniture, N.E.C.

764 Cooperage Occupations

769 Occupations in Fabrication and Repair of Wood Products, N.E.C.

77 *OCCUPATIONS IN FABRICATION AND REPAIR OF SAND, STONE, CLAY, AND GLASS PRODUCTS*

770 Occupations in Fabrication and Repair of Jewelry, Ornaments, and Related Products

771 Stone Cutters and Carvers

772 Glass Blowing, Pressing, Shaping, and Related Occupations, N.E.C.

773 Occupations in Coloring and Decorating Brick, Tile, and Related Products

774 Occupations in Fabrication and Repair of Pottery and Porcelain Ware

775 Grinding, Filing, Polishing, Frosting, Etching, Cleaning, and Related Occupations, N.E.C.

776 Occupations in Fabrication and Repair of Asbestos and Polishing Products, Abrasives, and Related Materials

777 Modelmakers, Patternmakers, Moldmakers, and Related Occupations

779 Occupations in Fabrication and Repair of Sand, Stone, Clay, and Glass Products, N.E.C.

78 OCCUPATIONS IN FABRICATION AND REPAIR OF TEXTILE, LEATHER, AND RELATED PRODUCTS

780 Occupations in Upholstering and in Fabrication and Repair of Stuffed Furniture, Mattresses, and Related Products
781 Laying Out, Marking, Cutting, and Punching Occupations, N.E.C.
782 Hand Sewers, Menders, Embroiderers, Knitters, and Related Occupations, N.E.C.
783 Fur and Leather Working Occupations
784 Occupations in Fabrication and Repair of Hats, Caps, Gloves, and Related Products
785 Tailors and Dressmakers
786 Sewing Machine Operators, Garment
787 Sewing Machine Operators, Non-garment
788 Occupations in Fabrication and Repair of Footwear
789 Occupations in Fabrication and Repair of Textile, Leather, and Related Products, N.E.C.

79 BENCH WORK OCCUPATIONS, N.E.C.

790 Occupations in Preparation of Food, Tobacco, and Related Products, N.E.C.
794 Occupations in Fabrication of Paper Products, N.E.C.
795 Gluing Occupations, N.E.C.

STRUCTURAL WORK OCCUPATIONS

80 OCCUPATIONS IN METAL FABRICATING, N.E.C.

800 Riveters, N.E.C.
801 Fitting, Bolting, Screwing, and Related Occupations
804 Tinsmiths, Coppersmiths, and Sheet Metal Workers
805 Boilermakers
806 Transportation Equipment Assemblers and Related Occupations
807 Structural Repairers, Transportation Equipment
809 Miscellaneous Occupations in Metal Fabricating, N.E.C.

81 WELDERS, CUTTERS, AND RELATED OCCUPATIONS

810 Arc Welders and Cutters
811 Gas Welders
812 Resistance Welders
813 Brazing, Braze-Welding, and Soldering Occupations
814 Solid State Welders

815 Electron-Beam; Electroslag; Thermit; Induction; and Laser-Beam Welders
816 Thermal Cutters and Arc Cutters
819 Welders, Cutters, and Related Occupations, N.E.C.

82 ELECTRICAL ASSEMBLING, INSTALLING, AND REPAIRING OCCUPATIONS
820 Occupations in Assembly, Installation, and Repair of Generators, Motors, Accessories, and Related Powerplant Equipment
821 Occupations in Assembly, Installation, and Repair of Transmission and Distribution Lines and Circuits
822 Occupations in Assembly, Installation, and Repair of Wire Communication, Detection and Signaling Equipment
823 Occupations in Assembly, Installation, and Repair of Electronic Communication, Detection, and Signaling Equipment
824 Occupations in Assembly, Installation, and Repair of Lighting Equipment and Building Wiring, N.E.C.
825 Occupations in Assembly, Installation, and Repair of Transportation and Material-Handling Equipment, N.E.C.
826 Occupations in Assembly, Installation, and Repair of Industrial Apparatus, N.E.C.
827 Occupations in Assembly, Installation, and Repair of Large Household Appliances and Similar Commercial and Industrial Equipment
828 Occupations in Fabrication, Installation, and Repair of Electrical and Electronics Products, N.E.C.
829 Occupations in Installation and Repair of Electrical Products, N.E.C.

84 PAINTING, PLASTERING, WATERPROOFING, CEMENTING, AND RELATED OCCUPATIONS
840 Construction and Maintenance Painters and Related Occupations
841 Paperhangers
842 Plasterers and Related Occupations
843 Waterproofing and Related Occupations
844 Cement and Concrete Finishing and Related Occupations
845 Transportation Equipment Painters and Related Occupations
849 Painting, Plastering, Waterproofing, Cementing, and Related Occupations, N.E.C.

85 EXCAVATING, GRADING, PAVING, AND RELATED OCCUPATIONS
850 Excavating, Grading, and Related Occupations
851 Drainage and Related Occupations
853 Paving Occupations, Asphalt and Concrete
859 Excavating, Grading, Paving, and Related Occupations, N.E.C.

86 CONSTRUCTION OCCUPATIONS, N.E.C.
860 Carpenters and Related Occupations
861 Brick and Stone Masons and Tile Setters
862 Plumbers, Gas Fitters, Steam Fitters, and Related Occupations
863 Asbestos and Insulation Workers
864 Floor Laying and Finishing Occupations
865 Glaziers and Related Occupations
866 Roofers and Related Occupations
869 Miscellaneous Construction Occupations, N.E.C.

89 STRUCTURAL WORK OCCUPATIONS, N.E.C.
891 Occupations in Structural Maintenance, N.E.C.
899 Miscellaneous Structural Work Occupations, N.E.C.

90 MOTOR FREIGHT OCCUPATIONS
900 Concrete-Mixing-Truck Drivers
902 Dump-Truck Drivers
903 Truck Drivers, Inflammables
904 Trailer-Truck Drivers
905 Truck Drivers, Heavy
906 Truck Drivers, Light
909 Motor Freight Occupations, N.E.C.

91 TRANSPORTATION OCCUPATIONS, N.E.C.
910 Railroad Transportation Occupations
911 Water Transportation Occupations
912 Air Transportation Occupations
913 Passenger Transportation Occupations, N.E.C.
914 Pumping and Pipeline Transportation Occupations
915 Attendants and Servicers, Parking Lots and Automotive Service Facilities
919 Miscellaneous Transportation Occupations, N.E.C.

92 PACKAGING AND MATERIALS HANDLING OCCUPATIONS
920 Packaging Occupations
921 Hoisting and Conveying Occupations

929 Packaging and Materials Handling Occupations, N.E.C.

93 OCCUPATIONS IN EXTRACTION OF MINERALS

930 Earth Boring, Drilling, Cutting, and Related Occupations

931 Blasting Occupations

932 Loading and Conveying Operations

933 Crushing Occupations

934 Screening and Related Occupations

939 Occupations in Extraction of Minerals, N.E.C.

95 OCCUPATIONS IN PRODUCTION AND DISTRIBUTION OF UTILITIES

950 Stationary Engineers

951 Firers and Related Occupations

952 Occupations in Generation, Transmission, and Distribution of Electric Light and Power

953 Occupations in Production and Distribution of Gas

954 Occupations in Filtration, Purification, and Distribution of Water

955 Occupations in Disposal of Refuse and Sewage

956 Occupations in Distribution of Steam

959 Occupations in Production and Distribution of Utilities, N.E.C.

96 AMUSEMENT, RECREATION, MOTION PICTURE, RADIO, AND TELEVISION OCCUPATIONS, N.E.C.

960 Motion Picture Projectionists

961 Models, Stand-ins, and Extras, N.E.C.

962 Occupations in Motion Picture, Television, and Theatrical Productions, N.E.C.

969 Miscellaneous Amusement and Recreation Occupations, N.E.C.

97 OCCUPATIONS IN GRAPHIC ART WORK

970 Art Work Occupations, Brush, Spray, or Pen

971 Photoengraving Occupations

972 Lithographers and Related Occupations

973 Hand Compositors, Typesetters, and Related Occupations

974 Electrotypers, Stereotypers, and Related Occupations

976 Darkroom Occupations, N.E.C.

977 Bookbinders and Related Occupations

979 Occupations in Graphic Art Work, N.E.C.

SOURCE: From *Dictionary of Occupational Titles* (1991).

Worker Trait Groups

The *Guide to Occupational Exploration* (GOE) divides occupations into 12 categories. These categories in turn group occupations according to work traits. The trait groups describe many functions and factors that are related to situations and activities required of workers, such as educational preparation. These descriptions are followed by a list of possible occupations that fall within the interest categories and worker trait groups. The list of 12 categories follows; refer to the *Guide to Occupational Exploration* for further detail.

01. ARTISTIC
01.01 Literary Arts
01.02 Visual Arts
01.03 Performing Arts: Drama
01.04 Performing Arts: Music
01.05 Performing Arts: Dance
01.06 Technical Art
01.07 Amusement
01.08 Modeling

02. SCIENTIFIC
02.01 Physical Science
02.02 Life Science
02.03 Medical Science
02.04 Laboratory Technology

03. NATURE
03.01 Managerial Work: Nature
03.02 General Supervision: Nature
03.03 Animal Training and Care
03.04 Elemental Work: Nature

04. AUTHORITY
04.01 Safety and Law Enforcement
04.02 Security Services

05. MECHANICAL
05.01 Engineering
05.02 Managerial Work: Mechanical
05.03 Engineering Technology
05.04 Air and Water Vehicle Operation
05.05 Craft Technology
05.06 Systems Operation
05.07 Quality Control
05.08 Land Vehicle Operation
05.09 Materials Control
05.10 Skilled Hand and Machine Work
05.11 Equipment Operation
05.12 Elemental Work: Mechanical

06. INDUSTRIAL
06.01 Production Technology
06.02 Production Work
06.03 Production Control
06.04 Elemental Work: Industrial

07. BUSINESS DETAIL
07.01 Administrative Detail
07.02 Mathematical Detail
07.03 Financial Detail
07.04 Information Processing: Speaking

07.05 Information Processing: Records
07.06 Clerical Machine Operation
07.07 Clerical Handling

08. PERSUASIVE
08.01 Sales Technology
08.02 General Sales
08.03 Vending

09. ACCOMMODATING
09.01 Hospitality Services
09.02 Barbering and Beauty Services
09.03 Passenger Services
09.04 Customer Services
09.05 Attendant Services

10. HUMANITARIAN
10.01 Social Services
10.02 Nursing and Therapy Services
10.03 Child and Adult Care

11. SOCIAL-BUSINESS
11.01 Mathematics and Statistics
11.02 Educational and Library Services
11.03 Social Research
11.04 Law
11.05 Business Administration
11.06 Finance
11.07 Services Administration
11.08 Communications
11.09 Promotion
11.10 Regulations Enforcement
11.11 Business Management
11.12 Contracts and Claims

12. PHYSICAL PERFORMING
12.01 Sports
12.02 Physical Feats

SOURCE: From *Guide to Occupational Exploration* (1992).

♦ EXERCISE 4.2 Making a Prioritized List of Accomplishments

List your past successes or accomplishments—things you have done that have made you feel alive, happy, and fulfilled. Start with early childhood, and treat your mind like a tape recorder: just play back the tape from as far in the past as you can. Pay attention to everything you can remember that made you feel good, that gave you a sense of accomplishment, and that made you feel proud of yourself. Free-associate; write down whatever occurs to you without analyzing it.

Maybe the first event you can remember happened when you were in grammar school; for example, when you learned to ride a bike or when you won a prize for a particular achievement. Gradually move up through your life span to the present. Remember, in all these accomplishments you need to be the doer, not the person acted upon. Perhaps the following list will give you some ideas.

- Won first prize in a spelling bee
- Learned to ride a bike
- Won a prize for selling the most cookies
- Assembled a desk
- Started a mail-order business
- Learned to fly an airplane and obtained a private pilot's license
- Drafted the blueprints for a house
- Learned a foreign language in six weeks
- Went back to school at age 50
- Staged a one-act play
- Learned to play golf
- Coached a soccer team to a winning season
- Sold my own home
- Won first place in a photography contest
- Taught myself to play the guitar

Ages 5–12

1. ______________________________
2. ______________________________
3. ______________________________
4. ______________________________
5. ______________________________

Ages 13–19

1. ______________________________
2. ______________________________
3. ______________________________
4. ______________________________
5. ______________________________

Ages 20–29

1. ______________________________
2. ______________________________
3. ______________________________
4. ______________________________
5. ______________________________

Ages 30–39

1. ______________________________
2. ______________________________
3. ______________________________
4. ______________________________
5. ______________________________

Ages 40–49

1. ______________________________
2. ______________________________
3. ______________________________
4. ______________________________
5. ______________________________

Ages 50–59

1. ______________________________
2. ______________________________
3. ______________________________
4. ______________________________
5. ______________________________

Ages 60–69

1. ____________________
2. ____________________
3. ____________________
4. ____________________
5. ____________________

Ages 70–79

1. ____________________
2. ____________________
3. ____________________
4. ____________________
5. ____________________

♦ EXERCISE 4.3 Writing about Your Accomplishments

From the list you completed in Exercise 4.2, select at least two accomplishments from each age group, for a total of no fewer than five. Then, on separate sheets of paper, write a story (at least two or three paragraphs) for each accomplishment you chose. Write each story as though you were speaking to a five-year-old child. Use as much detail as possible; try to describe how the event took place, what part you played in it, what steps you took to accomplish the task, what problems you solved, how you solved them, and how you felt about the process or event. Try to recapture the event and to reexperience the emotions you felt.

After you have finished writing about your accomplishments, your instructor may ask you to share the stories with a classmate, or you may want to ask a trusted friend or a career specialist to read them and help you identify the skills or success factors you used. You will use this list again in Chapter Eight, when you begin your résumé.

♦ EXERCISE 4.4 Volunteer Experience

Using Table 4.2 as a model, divide a sheet of paper into three columns. In the first column, list a volunteer activity or any other activity for which you did not receive any money. In the next column, list the tasks and responsibilities connected with this activity. Finally, in the third column, list all the applicable general skills, qualities, and traits you can. Make the third list as complete as possible; you will use the information in this column when you draft your résumé.

♦ Notes

FINE, S. A. (1989). *Functional job analysis scales: A desk aid* (p. 32). Milwaukee, WI: Sidney A. Fine Associates.

HOLLAND, J. (1985). *Making vocational choices: A theory of careers* (2nd ed.). Englewood Cliffs, NJ: Prentice-Hall.

LUFT, J., & INGRAM, H. (1963). The Johari Window, a graphic model of awareness in interpersonal relations. In Luft, J., *Group processes: An introduction to group dynamics* (pp. 10–12). Palo Alto, CA: National Pressbooks.

U.S. DEPARTMENT OF LABOR (1991). *Dictionary of Occupational Titles* (4th ed.) Indianapolis: JIST Works, Inc.

U.S. DEPARTMENT OF LABOR (1992). *Guide to Occupational Exploration.*

5 Making Personal Choices

"Money often costs too much."

—*Ralph Waldo Emerson*

In this chapter we will examine how people make choices. Because you are changing careers, you will be faced with many decisions. Therefore, it is necessary for you to learn what constitutes decision making, why you make the decisions you do, and what values you adhere to that affect your decision-making process at this time. First, let us examine your temperament style. (In this book, the words *temperament* and *personality* will be used interchangeably.)

After reading this chapter you should understand the following:

- The four sets of preferences that measure differences in temperament style
- That work values are those dimensions of your work that contribute to satisfaction
- That your values are directly linked to decision making

You should be able to do the following:

- Determine your temperament style
- Prioritize your career values
- Apply the eight basic steps of decision making

How many times have you actually said, "I just can't take this job another day"? Have you ever felt that you just don't seem to fit in with your work environment or that your job forces you to act phony? Do you sometimes feel like a square peg in a round hole? If so, chances are that your job does not fit your personality or your values.

♦ Temperament Styles

Personality preference theory can be traced to the Swiss-born psychiatrist Carl Gustav Jung. Jung's *Psychological Types* (1925) brilliantly outlines the classifications of personality preference. Jung's theory has become increasingly popular in the last decade, largely due to the *Myers-Briggs Type Indicator®* (MBTI®), which is based on Jung's theory.*

In the 1930s, Katharine Briggs, a devout student of Jung, became interested in observing and measuring behavioral differences. With her daughter, Isabel Briggs Myers, Briggs observed that people were often mismatched with their jobs. Many of the observations were made in the 1940s, during World War II. Later, Briggs and Myers set out to design a psychological instrument that could explain why people were not matched suitably to their jobs according to Jung's theory of personality preferences. Their efforts resulted in the *Myers-Briggs Type Indicator* (Myers, 1985), one of the most widely known and researched personality inventories. The popularity of the MBTI is at least partly due to the MBTI's excellent statistical validity and reliability.

According to Jung, eight characteristics contribute to personality:

Introversion ________________ Extraversion

Sensing ________________ Intuition

Thinking ________________ Feeling

Perceiving ________________ Judging

Jung theorized that each person has two sides to his or her personality; one side is favored, and the other is subsidiary. Every-

**Myers-Briggs Type Indicator* and MBTI are registered trademarks of Consulting Psychologists Press, Inc. For more information about personality type and the *Myers-Briggs Type Indicator* (MBTI), contact: Consulting Psychologists Press, Inc., the exclusive Publisher, at 3803 East Bayshore Road, Palo Alto, California 94303, (800) 624-1765, or Center for Applications of Psychological Type (CAPT), 2720 NW 6th Street, Gainesville, FL 32609, (800) 777-2278.

one's personality fits on a continuum; therefore, all of us have a bit of each characteristic. For example, the personality of every extraverted person contains at least a small degree of introversion. Nonetheless, even though both sides of our personality contribute to our perceptions and decisions, the favored side is always in control.

Theoretically, every person is one of 16 possible four-faceted personality types. By using the examples in this chapter, you can determine your own four-faceted personality type. Consider the following definitions, adapted from Keirsey and Bates (1984).

Introverted. You like quiet for concentration, look inward for ideas, can work contentedly alone, and like to think before acting. You may be more of a career specialist and prefer to use your skills in a narrower range than extraverts, but with more depth.

Extraverted. You love variety and action, don't mind interruptions, and like to have people around you. You are somewhat impatient with long, slow jobs and often act quickly, sometimes without thinking. You may be more of a career generalist, preferring to use your skills in a wide variety of ways.

Sensing. You like an established way of doing things, are patient with routine details, and tend to be good at precise work. You are considered very practical, and you prefer order. You would like your career to be continuous and tend to see it as a ladder, with steps based on your work experience.

Intuitive. You easily become bored if your job does not offer you variety and new challenges. You like solving new problems and are impatient with routine details. You tend to be "visionary" and to follow your inspirations whether they are good or bad. You are oriented toward career change and honestly feel you can be anything you want to be.

Thinking. You are considered rather unemotional. As a result, you can hurt people's feelings without really knowing it. You can seem rather hard-hearted at times, and your decisions are controlled by your head. You respect rules and the principles that stand behind them and like analysis and logic. You usually have a career track in mind, with a starting and an ending point.

Feeling. You enjoy pleasing people, like harmony, and are generally aware of other people's feelings. You can be influenced by other people's likes and wishes, and you dislike telling people unpleasant things. Like many feeling types, you may have personal growth as your career goal and stay in or leave a job depending on the way you feel you are growing.

Judging. You need only the essentials to get on with what you are doing and may not notice new things that need to be done. You tend to be satisfied when you have reached a decision. You have a need to settle matters and "wrap things up." Often you will make career plans but will hesitate to make moves that are not in your plan.

Perceiving. You hate schedules and routines and prefer to just let events happen. You don't mind leaving options open and may have trouble making decisions. You want to know all about a new job before you start it, and you tend to welcome new light on a subject. You prefer to take advantage of career opportunities and respond quickly to unexpected openings, good breaks, or useful connections. If you are not careful, however, you could drift in your career.

Introversion Versus Extraversion

Of the eight characteristics that contribute to personality, introversion and extraversion are the most misunderstood and subject to stereotype. Jung defined introversion as the side of the personality that prefers to look internally and to relate to ideas and concepts. Extraversion is the side of the personality that prefers to look externally and to relate to people and objects.

If someone says "he or she is an introvert," what comes immediately to your mind? Some of the adjectives I hear most frequently are *shy, retiring, low-energy, loner, bashful, dull, antisocial, quiet,* and *reserved.* If I were to ask you to describe an extravert, you might use such words as *outgoing, brash, bold, brave, aggressive, take-charge,* or *energetic.* However, these descriptions can be considered stereotypes. A person who has extraverted personality characteristics usually appears lively and outgoing to observers, whereas a person with introverted characteristics usually seems quiet and reserved. Although these notions fit the general description of these two types, there are shy extraverts as well as outgoing introverts.

Basically, introversion and extraversion have to do with *energy.* Let us examine how each of these polarities uses energy.

> Jane is a successful real estate agent. Her co-workers describe her as hard-working, dedicated, and very thorough.

> Because of her thoroughness and attention to detail, her deals almost always go through escrow without a snag. In fact, she has picked up quite a reputation in the office for having the most escrows completed. She is extremely good at detail work and frequently takes work home to complete because there is just "too much going on in the office." Financially, Jane is doing quite well, and she receives praise and encouragement from her co-workers as well as from her spouse.
>
> Jane appeared in my Changing Careers class complaining of burnout. In her native country, she had been trained to be a medical technologist, but because returning to that field here would require additional schooling, Jane chose to go into real estate instead. The more successful she was in the field, the more dissatisfied and depressed she became. In fact, Jane's physician had diagnosed her as having an ulcer. Hers is a classic case of pounding a square peg into a round hole—it just doesn't fit!

Jane is an introvert cast in the role of an extravert. As you may have guessed, a sales position requires constant external interaction with people, and sometimes you have to be "up" when you don't want to be up. In other words, working in sales requires a lot of emotional as well as physical energy. Although introverts are also capable of producing this kind of energy, they need time to "replenish the tank."

Think of yourself as having an energy tank similar to the gas tank in your automobile. You know that you have to pump gas into the tank from time to time. The same is true for you: you must replace the physical and emotional energy you expend. Extraverts and introverts differ in the way they replenish energy they have used. The extravert's energy is replenished through interaction, activity, and a fast-paced job. In fact, this actually drives them harder. Occasionally, extraverts can actually find themselves in an "overload" situation. This overload usually manifests itself by the person's seeming a little "hyper" and going in many directions at once or seeming overstimulated.

Introverts, on the other hand, replenish their energy tanks by withdrawing into themselves. You will often hear introverts say, "I have to get away for awhile," "I just need some time to think this over," "I want to sleep on this before I make a decision," or "I need a little space." This means that introverts need an absence of stimulation to bring their energy level back up. Outside stimuli actually chip away at the introvert's energy level. In addition, introverts prefer to work on tasks alone to generate new ideas and concepts.

Does this mean that introverts will not make good salespeople? Of course not! It does mean, however, that an introvert needs a balance of interaction with people and quiet concentration. When this balance becomes skewed, the person experiences discomfort. Like Jane—who eventually decided she would return to her original career in medical technology—you may find that you have been miscast in your present role.

Sensing Versus Intuition

Sensing persons are attentive to detail and facts, whereas intuitives tend to estimate or approximate factual details. Sensors are relatively tolerant of routine, specified procedures; are realistic; and prefer using skills they have already learned. Intuitives, on the other hand, like variety and challenge and work in bursts of energy. They also are more "visionary" and prefer to learn new skills.

> Nancy wanted to buy a car. As she drove to and from work, she began noticing a particular model of car that appealed to her. To save money, Nancy decided to buy the car used. When an ad appeared in the Sunday newspaper, describing the exact make and model of car she wanted, Nancy set up an appointment to see the car. After discussing a few details with the used-car salesperson, Nancy decided to buy the automobile. She drove it home the very same day.
>
> Nancy used the *intuitive* side of her personality in this transaction. Contrast this with a *sensor*, who would have inspected the vehicle thoroughly and then had it checked by a mechanic. A sensor probably would have "thought it over" before purchasing the car.

When you go to the movies or read a book, which kind of story do you prefer: one that has a definite beginning and ending and emphasizes concrete details, or one that has flashbacks and is laden with symbolism? Are you always looking for the "hidden meaning" and find enjoyment in discussing it with others? Sensors would probably prefer the former; intuitives, the latter.

Intuitive people make up approximately 25 percent of the population; sensors comprise about 75 percent. Because they are a relatively small segment of the population, intuitive people are a minority attempting to fit patterns established by and for a "sensing" majority. Intuitives are more prone to burnout than sensors because they are motivated and stimulated by variety; intuitives also change careers more frequently than sensors.

Thinking Versus Feeling

Thinking and feeling are the personality characteristics that contribute to the way we process information. In a general sense, thinking people let their heads control their hearts. Feeling people appear sensitive, empathic, appreciative, and compassionate. Thinking people are more logical and analytical. The thinking person prefers an impersonal approach as a way of making decisions whereas the feeling person makes decisions in the context of the effect it will have on oneself and others.

> Joe is a manager for a mid-sized manufacturing firm. Lately, some discord has arisen among the workers on the day shift. Of course, these problems always come to Joe's attention. Joe's method of dealing with these conflicts has been to call the workers one by one into his office and have them tell him exactly what is bothering them and what would they like Joe to do about it. Until now, this method has worked fairly well, but in the present situation one worker has been causing problems for the others by shirking his duties and consistently coming in late. In spite of this, Joe has difficulty reprimanding the worker.
>
> By contrast, the previous manager, Bill, handled such conflicts by determining who was responsible for the trouble and reprimanding the person causing the problem. In other words, Bill would get quickly to the who, what, where, when, and why of the situation. He was known for being tough but fair. Employees said they always knew where they stood with Bill. Incidentally, Bill had no qualms about reprimanding or firing someone if necessary.

Joe preferred to use the feeling side of his personality; Bill preferred to use the thinking side. Thinking persons are more objective than subjective, more impersonal than personal. They base decisions on principles rather than on values. The differences between thinking and feeling personalities account for many difficulties people have in communication. Consider the following example:

> John and Mary are about to celebrate their first anniversary. John has carefully researched a restaurant that he wants to take Mary to and asks her to be ready by seven o'clock. Excited about the upcoming event, Mary goes to her hairdresser and asks for a new hairstyle, buys a new dress, and has her

> nails manicured. Mary is somewhat late getting ready, and John is rather annoyed because they might be late for their dinner reservation.
>
> As they enter the automobile, John fails to notice Mary's new hairstyle and dress. Instead, he comments that they had better rush if they are to get to the restaurant on time. Thoroughly irritated, Mary sits in silence on the way to the restaurant. Finally, unable to control her emotions any longer, Mary "lets him have it" when they are seated for dinner.

What happened here was that Mary expected compliments and praise on her appearance, and John seemed to take her for granted. John's behavior is typical for a *thinking* person. It is not that they cannot give praise and compliments, but rather that doing so does not seem necessary at the time. Misunderstandings like the one in the example happen frequently in human communication. Thinking and feeling types see things differently—there is no single good or bad way of viewing situations. Understanding that we can look at things in different ways helps us communicate better.

Judging Versus Perceiving

Judging and perceiving contribute to the way we make decisions. Judgers prefer to have situations settled and wrapped up; perceivers prefer to be flexible and to gather as much data as possible. Perceivers tend to postpone decision making and prefer to leave situations open-ended. They can also be pulled in many directions. Judgers, on the other hand, are interested only in the essentials of getting the job done, prefer working by a schedule, and need closure on events, ideas, and relationships.

As you can see, it is easy for judgers to view perceivers as procrastinators and for perceivers to view judgers as people who leap to rash conclusions. Judgers are sticklers for time management; perceivers view time as a nebulous commodity. Judgers write the books on time management that perceivers try to comprehend and apply to their lives. The following example shows how these polarities might interact in a typical work setting.

> Joyce is holding her weekly staff meeting with the ten salespeople who work for her. She is anxious to resolve an agenda item that seems to surface at every meeting. However, every time Joyce calls for a vote, her staff never reaches a consensus. At this particular meeting, Mike reports that he needs more data before he can vote on the issue. His colleague, Sarah, says she believes the issue would be settled best by committee

> and suggests that one be set up. By this time Josh, who is sitting across from Mike and Sarah, becomes almost livid. He states, "I am getting rather tired of us having to debate this issue at every meeting. I believe we have all the data we need right now to make a decision, and I would like for us to take a vote at this time. I would like to see us settle this once and for all."

What has transpired in the example happens frequently in everyday life. Joyce is a *judging* type and is therefore decisive. Once she makes up her mind, she is set in her ways. She sees the goal for her group and feels frustrated that she is taking longer to achieve it because of this impasse. If you haven't already guessed, both Mike and Sarah are *perceivers.* They prefer to remain adaptable and leave the item open to allow for any unforeseen future events. They feel bothered by Joyce's push for closure. On the other hand, Josh is also a *judging* type who agrees with Joyce that they should resolve the item immediately. How can they extricate themselves from this dilemma? Probably through compromise. In this case, the two styles can probably form a working relationship that includes "checks and balances."

Some of you may think this theory is all very general and that it merely categorizes people into neat little boxes. However, I would ask you this: If people can understand each other a little better through studying these types, isn't that preferable to the alternative—unhappiness, depression, despair, hostility, or complacency? Remember, you cannot change who you really are, you just need to *be* who you are.

Career Choice According to Temperament

Your temperament style affects the way you choose a career. Consider the following explanations:

- *Extraverts* are career generalists who tend to use their skills in a wide variety of ways.
- *Introverts* are career specialists who tend to use their skills in a narrower range but in greater depth.
- *Sensing* types like their careers to be continuous. They see their careers as a ladder and look for the next step based on the experience they already have.
- *Intuitives* are oriented toward career change. They are likely to be inspired by the words "You can be anything you want to be." If their present job is not working out, intuitives often will decide to shift to a new field.

- *Thinking* types have a career track in mind, one with a starting point and a goal. Their goal is usually to attain a certain amount of money, prestige, or influence.
- *Feeling* types adopt personal growth as their goal. Whether they leave or stay in a job depends upon whether they feel they are growing "like a plant toward the sun."
- *Judging* types make plans for their careers. They hesitate to make moves that are not in their original plan without first establishing a new plan.
- *Perceptives* prefer to take advantage of career opportunities and respond quickly to unexpected openings, useful connections, good breaks, or brighter lights. If no opportunities arise for a while, perceptives can appear to drift in their careers. *Source:* Adapted from "A Taxonomy of Career Orientation," *The Type Reporter,* 1984.

What type are you? Can you pick yourself out from the preceding descriptions? Everyone has a four-faceted personality type. Determine your own personality type according to the MBTI by choosing one preference from each of the polarities that were discussed in this chapter. If you cannot decide which personality type you are, remember that everyone can identify with all eight characteristics to some extent. You will, however, have a *preference* (however slight) for one trait more than the other.

If you are using the MBTI, your scores will indicate the consistency with which you choose one attitude or function over the other. The four preferences in your MBTI code indicate 1 of 16 possible types. Figure 5.1 lists words that describe each type.

Temperament and Transition

When you are going through a crisis or a major life transition—such as changing careers—you may find yourself preferring to use the auxiliary side (that is, the other side of the polarity) of your personality. That is why it is important to let some time elapse before you move into another position. Here is an example of one midlife career changer:

> Robert, age 45, felt completely burned out in his job as a social worker. In fact, his situation had become so severe that he sought psychiatric help and was given a medical leave of absence. Robert's four temperament preferences were introverted, intuitive, feeling, and judging. Robert decided to investigate the financial career clusters because he wanted a complete change from his previous career. After a relatively

ISTJ	ISFJ	INFJ	INTJ
factual thorough systematic dependable steadfast practical organized realistic duty bound sensible painstaking reliable	detailed conscientious traditional loyal patient practical organized service-minded devoted protective meticulous responsible	committed loyal compassionate creative intense deep determined conceptual sensitive reserved holistic idealistic	independent logical critical original systems-minded firm visionary theoretical demanding private global autonomous
ISTP	**ISFP**	**INFP**	**INTP**
logical expedient practical realistic factual analytical applied independent adventurous spontaneous adaptable self-determined	caring gentle modest adaptable sensitive observant cooperative loyal trusting spontaneous understanding harmonious	compassionate gentle virtuous adaptable committed curious creative loyal devoted deep reticent empathetic	logical skeptical cognitive detached theoretical reserved precise independent speculative original autonomous self-determined
ESTP	**ESFP**	**ENFP**	**ENTP**
activity-oriented adaptable fun-loving versatile energetic alert spontaneous pragmatic easygoing persuasive outgoing quick	enthusiastic adaptable playful friendly vivacious sociable talkative cooperative easygoing tolerant outgoing pleasant	creative curious enthusiastic versatile spontaneous expressive independent friendly perceptive energetic imaginative restless	enterprising independent outspoken strategic creative adaptive challenging analytical clever resourceful questioning theoretical
ESTJ	**ESFJ**	**ENFJ**	**ENTJ**
logical decisive systematic objective efficient direct practical organized impersonal responsible structured conscientious	conscientious loyal sociable personable responsible harmonious cooperative tactful thorough responsive sympathetic traditional	loyal idealistic personable verbal responsible expressive enthusiastic energetic diplomatic concerned supportive congenial	logical decisive planful tough strategic critical controlled challenging straightforward objective fair theoretical

Figure 5.1 Brief descriptors of the 16 MBTI types. *Source: Reproduced by special permission of the Publisher, Consulting Psychologists Press, Inc., Palo Alto, CA 94303. From* Introduction to Type in Organizations *by S. K. Hirsh & J. M. Kummerow. Copyright 1990 by Consulting Psychologists Press, Inc. All rights reserved. MBTI and* Myers-Briggs Type Indicator *are registered trademarks of Consulting Psychologists Press, Inc. Further reproduction is prohibited without the Publisher's written consent.*

brief period as a claims adjuster, he decided that the field did not fit his work style, so he began to look again at the human services field. Robert finally found a position in the state system that allowed him more autonomy and client contact.

What happened in this case is quite common: when people find themselves in a very stressful situation, they naturally tend to want to try a new tactic. The auxiliary can seem like a welcome relief. In Robert's case, the claims adjuster position suited his sensing side well but left his intuitive side wanting more. In retrospect, Robert realized that he preferred his intuitive side to the sensing side, and he returned to his original field, but to a different job.

Remember, you cannot change who you really are. Personality characteristics are not good or bad; they just *are*. Use this insight to determine your behavioral style so that you can choose a work environment conducive to your success and happiness.

♦ Your Values Are Showing

Just what are values? Values are the things or ideas that are important to you in your daily life. As used in this chapter, the term *work value* means the way you feel about the task itself and the contribution it makes to others. Everything we do, every decision we make, and every action we take are based on our beliefs, attitudes, and values—whether we hold them consciously or unconsciously.

Many people have contributed greatly to our understanding of the valuing process. In particular, credit is due to Raths, Harmon, and Simon (1966), who define values as those elements that show how a person decides to use his or her life. Work values are those dimensions of our work that contribute to our satisfaction. To value something involves the following:

PRIZING

Do you feel strongly about and cherish a conviction very much?

Do you speak up in public about a prized conviction, strongly affirming it when appropriate?

CHOOSING

Do you consider the alternatives available to you before taking a stance?

Do you examine the consequences of a stance before taking it?

Do you make a decision independent of external pressures to feel, think, or act a certain way?

ACTING
Do you back up your feelings and beliefs with action?
Do you consistently act on your feelings and beliefs?

When you can answer yes to each of these questions in reference to a personal conviction, you truly value that conviction. If you answer no to any of these questions, you need to reexamine your convictions with reference to the value in question. Try using these three elements with the following list of work values. These work values play an integral part in the amount of satisfaction you get from your job.

Work Values

The following is a list of work values.

Help society. Do something to contribute to the betterment of the world.
Help others. Be involved in helping other people in a direct way, either individually or in small groups.
Public contact. Have a lot of day-to-day contact with people.
Work with others. Have close working relations with a group; work toward common goals as part of a team.
Affiliation. Be recognized as a member of a particular organization.
Friendships. Develop close personal relationships with people as a result of work activities.
Competition. Engage in activities in which I pit my abilities against those of others in situations where there are clear win-and-loss outcomes.
Make decisions. Have the power to decide on policies and courses of action.
Work under pressure. Work in situations where time pressure is prevalent; where the quality of my work is judged critically by supervisors, customers, or others; or both.
Power and authority. Control the work activities or (at least partially) the destinies of others.
Influence people. Be in a position to change other people's attitudes or opinions.
Work alone. Do projects alone, without any significant amount of contact with others.
Knowledge. Engage in the pursuit of knowledge, truth, and understanding.
Intellectual status. Be regarded as a person of high intellectual prowess or as an acknowledged expert in a given field.

Artistic creativity. Engage in creative work in any of several art forms.

Creativity (general). Create new ideas, programs, organizational structures, or anything else not following a format previously developed by others.

Aesthetics. Be involved in studying or appreciating the beauty of ideas and events.

Supervision. Be directly responsible for the work done by others.

Change and variety. Have work responsibilities that frequently change in their content and setting.

Precision work. Work in situations where there is very little tolerance for error.

Stability. Have a work routine and job duties that are largely predictable and not likely to change over a long period.

Security. Be assured of keeping a job and receiving a reasonable financial reward.

Fast pace. Work must be done rapidly.

Recognition. Be recognized for the quality of my work in some visible or public way.

Excitement. Experience a high degree of (or frequent) excitement in my work.

Adventure. Have work duties that involve frequent risk-taking.

Profit/gain. Have a strong likelihood of accumulating large amounts of money or other material gain.

Independence. Be able to determine the nature of work without significant direction from others; not to have to do what others tell me.

Moral fulfillment. Feel that my work contributes significantly to a set of moral standards that I feel are very important.

Location. Find a place to live (town, geographical area) that is conducive to my life-style and affords me the opportunity to do what I enjoy most.

Community. Live in a town or city where I can become involved in community affairs.

Physical challenge. Have a job that makes physical demands that are rewarding to me.

Time freedom. Have work responsibilities with no time schedule; no specific working hours required.

Values and Career Change

Unlike our basic temperament, our values can change. That is why assessing values is so important for career changers. Values clarification works on the same principle as a barometer—you must constantly check it for variances. The following demonstrates how we can view our work differently depending on our present circumstances.

> Katharine, a reentry student, has just gone through a major crisis in her life—a divorce. Before her divorce, Katharine prioritized her values as follows (from most important to least important): help society, aesthetics, adventure, fast pace, profit/gain, excitement, moral fulfillment, security, change and variety, stability. After the divorce, Katharine revised her list to the following: security, stability, profit/gain, knowledge, affiliation, friendships, influence people, make decisions, power and authority, change and variety.

Now let us examine how values affect decision making in midlife. Consider the following case:

> Carrie, age 47, has been in education all her life. Now, however, she is beginning to think she should "move up" to the rank of administrator. Carrie had started her career path as a high school English teacher and then had worked as a high school guidance counselor. Many of her fellow teachers have remarked that Carrie would be a good human resources administrator, and they have encouraged her to pursue that route. However, after Carrie clarified her values, she felt her values were being met in her current job. Her values, in rank order, are as follows: (1) independence, (2) time freedom, (3) change and variety, (4) creativity, and (5) helping others. Given those values, it is understandable that Carrie chooses to remain in a teaching and counseling position. As Carrie says, "Why would I want to give up a position with all that flexibility and time freedom for one that would definitely be more confining and not give me an opportunity to work on a one-on-one basis with students?"

Carrie had become accustomed to having several weeks off in the summer to pursue other activities. Further, she didn't think she was motivated toward power and authority or other values commonly associated with a supervisory position.

At this point, take a good look at your present values. What is important to you *now*? How have your values changed from five years ago? Ten years ago? What values emerge as you contemplate your career change? Before we leave the topic of values clarification, let us discuss the internal forces that affect your behavior or

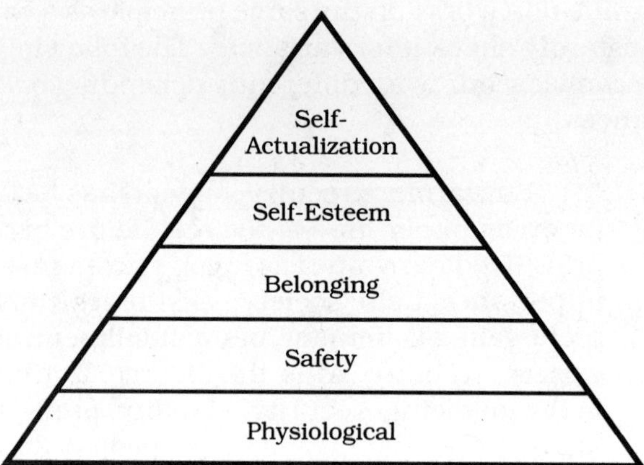

Figure 5.2 Maslow's hierarchy of needs. *Source: Adapted from Abraham H. Maslow,* The Farther Reaches of Human Nature *(1971).*

cause you to act in a particular way. These internal forces are referred to as needs, and motives develop from needs.

Motivated Needs

So far we have discussed your belief system and your attitude toward change. We also have examined your values to determine what is most important to you in a new career. Still another element comes into play at this time: what *motivates* you. Refer to Figure 5.2, Abraham Maslow's hierarchy of needs (1971). According to Maslow, five basic needs are common to all human beings. These needs progress from basic to complex, socially oriented needs as follows:

1. Physiological needs: basic survival needs, such as food, water, oxygen, sleep, and warmth.
2. Safety needs: an environment where you feel protected (shelter, law and order, and security) and free from fear and anxiety.
3. Love and belongingness needs: relationships, affiliation, friends, affection, and love.
4. Self-esteem needs: self-respect, appreciation, recognition, status, and a sense of self-worth.
5. Self-actualization needs: realizing your talents, developing your highest potential, being creative, and fulfilling your mission in life.

As you study Maslow's hierarchy of needs, ask yourself, "At what level am I operating now?" Clearly, when people are out of work and are preoccupied with finding ways to put food on the table and a roof over their heads, they have little time or desire to work on relationships and self-actualization needs. In a period of unemployment, this can mean that a person will take a job, any job, just to pay the bills.

Maslow's hierarchy of needs may also explain why relationships are often tested when a person is unemployed. It is difficult to cultivate relationships to gain recognition, appreciation, or status when all one's efforts are used to meet basic physiological needs. In a time of personal crisis (such as being unemployed), it becomes crucial to satisfy each level of needs to bring about a balance in life. As needs at one level are fulfilled, the next need level begins to emerge, and you are motivated to satisfy those needs. You may want to reflect on your own hierarchy of needs as you proceed to more significant decision making.

♦ Decision Making

We are constantly in a position of having to make decisions: what to wear to work, what to order from the menu, what car to buy, whether to leave a salaried position and start a business, how to invest money. The list can go on and on. Some decisions are insignificant; others can have a very real and lasting effect on our lives.

Throughout your life you have been bombarded with decisions to make, some large and some small. Some decisions were relatively easy to make, and others were extremely difficult. In fact, in some cases you may still wonder if you made the right decision. One of those cases could be your choice of career. You are on that threshold once again. By now, you have probably concluded that you really want to change careers. You may even have come to the conclusion that you need a change in your life-style.

Now we have completed the self-assessment portion of the career change model (see Figure 4.1 on page 58). The last component in the model is decision making. Decision making is a logical process that involves eight basic steps, which lead from one phase to another.

Eight Basic Steps to Decision Making

1. *Identify* the decision to be made. Are you really ready for a career change? Are you in the wrong field, or do you just feel burned out in your particular job?
2. *Gather* information on your interests, skills, abilities, and temperaments. Ask, "Who am I?" This step is the self-assessment portion of the career planning model.

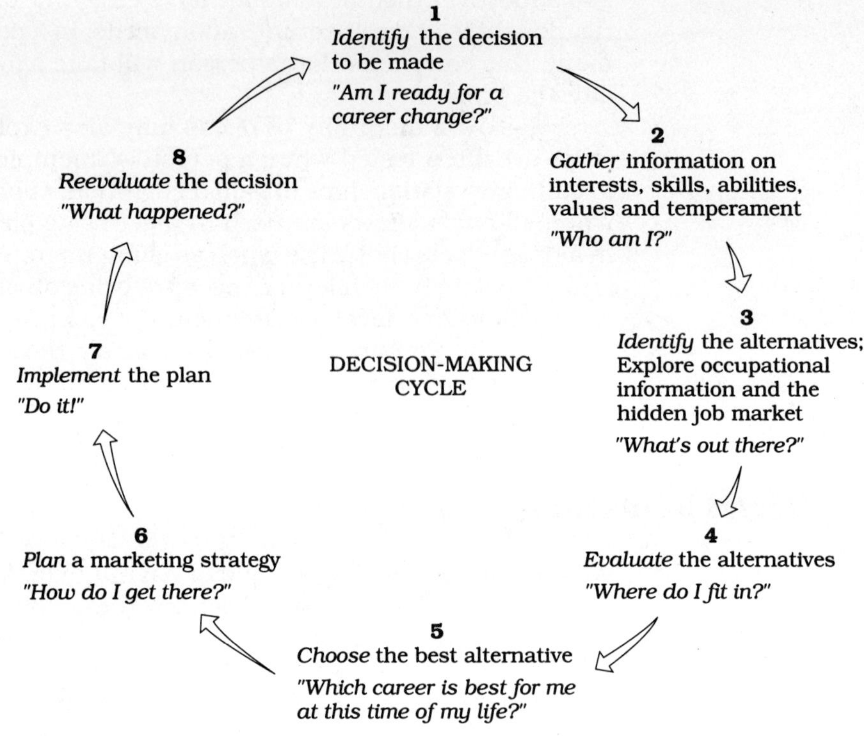

Figure 5.3 Decision-making cycle for changing careers

3. *Identify* the alternatives; explore occupational information and the "hidden" job market. Ask, "What is out there ?" After you have a clear picture of who you are, you can research what is out there and compare the various career alternatives to your own attributes.
4. *Evaluate* the alternatives. Ask, "Where do I fit in?" This involves finding a career match for your talents.
5. *Choose* the best alternative. Ask, "Which career is best for me at this time of my life? Have I weighed the pros and cons of my options and found what fits my particular needs?"
6. *Plan* a marketing strategy. Ask, "How do I get there?" This involves taking inventory of your present skills and packaging them to attract the attention of an employer who needs those skills. This step culminates in a résumé, which in turn leads to the interview and subsequent follow-up.
7. *Implement* the plan. Say, "Do it." You may want to identify your support systems and use them as you put your plan into action.

8. *Reevaluate* the decision. Ask, "What happened?" Not all plans work out the way we would like them to. Maybe you will need to go back to step 1 and reevaluate your initial decision.

Figure 5.3 depicts the decision-making cycle for changing careers.

In the next chapter you will have an opportunity to explore your options. This will involve doing occupational research, locating contacts, and interviewing for information. So let's move right along!

♦ Summary

As you have seen in this chapter, personal choices involve taking a careful look at your temperament style and your values. You have examined your temperament style according to a model, based on the *Myers-Briggs Type Indicator*, that focused on the eight characteristics that contribute to personality. You have measured your values according to what you prize, choose, and act upon. Finally, you have learned to apply the eight basic steps to decision making: (1) identifying the decision to be made, (2) gathering information, (3) identifying the alternatives, (4) evaluating the alternatives, (5) choosing the best alternative, (6) planning a marketing strategy, (7) implementing the plan, and (8) reevaluating the decision.

The following exercises are designed to help you determine what you valued most in a career choice five years ago and ten years ago, as well as what you value most now. You will also identify the values represented in your past accomplishments. Finally, you will prioritize your present career values. Remember, unlike the other elements in the self-assessment process, your values can and do change. You may want to revisit this chapter before you embark on your career-changing campaign.

♦ EXERCISE 5.1 What Do You Value Most?

Review the list on pages 115–116. Select ten of the values to which you personally subscribe and write them below. After you have done so, rank those values in order of their importance to you. For example, even if you value time freedom and independence equally, you must list only one value in the number-one slot.

1. ______________________________

2. ______________________________

3. ______________________
4. ______________________
5. ______________________
6. ______________________
7. ______________________
8. ______________________
9. ______________________
10. ______________________

RANKED LIST OF VALUES

1. ______________________
2. ______________________
3. ______________________
4. ______________________
5. ______________________
6. ______________________
7. ______________________
8. ______________________
9. ______________________
10. ______________________

Now that you have ranked your values in order of importance, rank them according to your present priorities and your priorities five and ten years ago.

	I VALUE	*NOW*	*FIVE YEARS AGO*	*TEN YEARS AGO*
1.				
2.				
3.				
4.				
5.				
6.				

	I VALUE	*NOW*	*FIVE YEARS AGO*	*TEN YEARS AGO*
7.				
8.				
9.				
10.				

♦ EXERCISE 5.2 Values Represented in Accomplishments

Go back to Exercise 4.3. Review each of the five accomplishments you wrote about. What values are represented there?

What themes do you find running through the stories?

What issues do these values in the stories represent? (For example, did you often find yourself taking charge of a situation or event? This could mean that you value supervision.)

Do these issues suggest that you need to make major decisions or commitments in the near future? Why or why not?

♦ EXERCISE 5.3 Prioritizing Matrix for Ranking Work Values

List 10 or 12 major work values you identified in the previous exercises that you would want to express in your occupation. Place each in one of the blank lines in Column A of the following matrix. Each work value is designated by a letter. For each letter pair in Column B

Prioritizing matrix for ranking work values

Column A (List in random order)	Column B (Compare and circle each choice)	Column C (Count for each letter)	Column D (Rank in order)
a	a a a a a a a a a b c d e f g h i j	a	1.
b	b b b b b b b b c d e f g h i j	b	2.
c	c c c c c c c d e f g h i j	c	3.
d	d d d d d d e f g h i j	d	4.
e	e e e e e f g h i j	e	5.
f	f f f f g h i j	f	6.
g	g g g h i j	g	7.
h	h h i j	h	8.
i	i j	i	9.
j		j	10.

Source: Taken from *The 1993 What Color Is Your Parachute? A Practical Manual for Job-Hunters and Career Changers*, by Richard N. Bolles, p. 223. Copyright © 1992 by Richard N. Bolles. Adapted with permission.

of the matrix, ask yourself, "Which of these two work values is most important to me?" Circle the letter that corresponds to the value you have chosen. When you have finished circling all your choices, record in Column C the total number of times you chose each value. If two values were chosen the same number of times, go back to the place in Column B where the two tying values were paired, and note which letter you have circled. Indicate the final rank of each value in Column D. (See Table 5.1 for an example of this exercise.)

Table 5.1 Prioritizing matrix for ranking work values (example)

Column A (List in random order)	Column B (Compare and circle each choice)	Column C (Count for each letter)	Column D (Rank in order)
a Public contact	(a) a (a) a a a a a (a) b (c) d (e) (f) (g) (h) (i) j	a 3	1. i
b Help others	b b b b b b b (b) (c) (d) (e) (f) (g) (h) (i) j	b 1	2. h
c Affiliation	(c) c c c c c (c) d (e) (f) (g) (h) (i) j	c 2	3. f
d Influence people	d d d d d d (e) (f) (g) (h) (i) (j)	d 1	4. g
e Creativity (general)	e e e e (e) (f) (g) (h) (i) j	e 4	5. e
f Change and variety	(f) f f (f) g (h) (i) j	f 6	6. a
g Recognition	g g (g) (h) (i) j	g 6	7. c
h Independence	h (h) (i) j	h 8	8. b
i Time freedom	(i) j	i 9	9. d
j Excitement		j 1	10. j

♦ Notes

HIRSH, S. K., & KUMMEROW, J. M. (1990). *Introduction to type in organizations* (2nd ed.). Palo Alto, CA: Consulting Psychologists Press.

JUNG, C. G. (1925). *Psychological types.* London: Routledge and Kegan Paul.

KIERSEY, D., & BATES, M. (1984). *Please understand me.* Del Mar, CA: Prometheus Nemesis.

MASLOW, A. H. (1970). *Motivation and personality* (2nd ed.). New York: Harper & Row.

MASLOW, A. H. (1971). *The farther reaches of human nature.* New York: Viking Press.

MYERS, I. B., & McCAULLEY, M. H. (1985). *Manual: A guide to the development and use of the Myers-Briggs Type Indicator.* Palo Alto, CA: Consulting Psychologists Press.

RATHS, L., SIMON, S., & HARMIN, M. (1966). *Values and teaching.* Columbus, OH: Merrill.

A taxonomy of career orientation. *The Type Reporter* (1984). Vol 1, no. 2, p. 4.

6 Exploring Your Options

"The greatest thing in the world is not so much where we stand, as in what direction we are moving."

—Oliver Wendell Holmes

Now that you have examined your goals and objectives; taken inventory of your interests, skills, and accomplishments; and examined your personal choices, you have completed the internal information gathering, or self-assessment, stage of the Steps to Success Model. You are now ready to explore your options by moving to the next stage, external information gathering.

After reading this chapter you should understand the following:

- Where to locate written career information
- That several computerized career guidance programs are available through colleges and universities
- The importance of conducting an informational interview and the value of networking in the career-change process
- The geographic considerations involved in making a career change

You should be able to do the following:

- Locate career information in your college, university, or local public library
- Conduct an informational interview
- Determine whether to focus your career change horizontally or vertically or to make a complete change

In this stage you will explore your options both through research using written information and through interviewing for information, which involves talking to people in career areas in which you are interested. Both methods are necessary to your success in changing careers. Networking cannot be used as a substitute for library research, and vice versa.

♦ Sources of Occupational Information

Occupational information falls into two basic categories: the information you gather from written sources and the information you gather from other people. First, we will examine written sources of information.

Written Information

The staff at your local library or the career planning and placement center at your local college or university should be able to help locate the following sources.

U.S. Government Publications

The *Dictionary of Occupational Titles* (DOT): Published by the U.S. Department of Labor, the DOT lists over 35,000 job titles and over 20,000 different occupations. It is especially useful for writing résumés because it lists the specific tasks for each occupation. For example:

PARALEGAL ASSISTANT
Researches law, investigates facts, and prepares documents to assist lawyers. Researches and analyzes law sources such as statutes, recorded judicial decisions, legal articles, treaties, constitutions, and legal codes to prepare legal documents such as briefs, pleadings, appeals, wills, contracts, deeds, and trust instruments for review, approval, and use by an attorney. Appraises and inventories real and personal property for estate planning. Investigates facts and law of case to determine causes for action and to prepare case accordingly. Files pleadings with court clerk. Prepares affidavits of documents and maintains document file. Delivers or directs delivery of subpoenas to witnesses and parties to action. May direct and coordinate activities of law office employees. May prepare office accounts and tax returns. May specialize in litigation, probate, real estate, or corporation law. May search patent files to ascertain originality of patent application and be designated patent clerk.

The *Occupational Outlook Handbook* (OOH): Also published by the U.S. Department of Labor, the OOH is updated every other year. It includes information on job descriptions, places of employment, training, educational requirements, and salary ranges.

The *Guide to Occupational Exploration* (GOE): The data in this publication are organized into 12 interest areas, 66 worker trait groups, and 348 subgroupings. The GOE is also published by the U.S. Department of Labor.

The *Occupational Outlook Quarterly:* This publication may be of interest to you because it provides quarterly updates of occupational projections and other useful information, such as cost-of-living comparisons, on a nationwide basis.

Directories

There are numerous directories that contain information on corporations, associations, and foundations. In these directories you will find entries that include names and addresses of employers, the number of employees who work for them, and the names of top-level executives. Some of these directories contain information for a particular geographical area; these are particularly helpful when you begin marketing yourself for a job. Many times these directories are published through the local chambers of commerce.

Business and Industrial Directory: Look for directories that are specific to geographic regions and subjects.

California Manufacturers Directory: Lists companies by location and product. There is also an additional section on import/export businesses. Look for other directories that cover your particular geographic location.

College Placement Annual: Contains information on firms and governmental agencies that relates to occupational opportunities.

Consultants and Consulting Organizations Directory: A Reference Guide to Concerns and Individuals Engaged in Consultation for Business, Industry, and Government: Contains contact information about thousands of individuals and organizations both in the United States and abroad.

Contacts Influential: A complete catalog of firms and personnel of a particular geographical location; listings by firm name, type of business, ZIP code area, name of key executives, and numerically by telephone number; contains a market planning section; includes monthly updates.

Directory of American Firms Operating in Foreign Countries: Published in three volumes.

Directory of Corporate Affiliation: The family tree of every major corporation in America, or the "Who Owns Whom."

Directory of Executive Recruiters: Contains information on 1,479 executive search firms in the United States, Canada, and Mexico. Offers tips on how to work with recruiters and what to look for in a search firm.

Dun and Bradstreet Billion Dollar Directory: Complements the *Million Dollar Directory* series by specifically identifying U.S. ultimate parent companies that have large corporate families. Shows corporate linkage and ownership of subsidiaries and divisions.

Dun and Bradstreet Middle Market Directory: Lists companies with assets between $500,000 and $1 million.

Dun and Bradstreet Million Dollar Directory: Encyclopedia of business facts in three volumes. Information on over 120,000 of America's top businesses, listed alphabetically, geographically, and by product classification.

Encyclopedia of Associations: A guide to national and international nonprofit organizations. Includes information on location, size, and objectives of more than 14,500 trade associations, professional societies, labor unions, and fraternal and patriotic organizations.

Guide to American Directories: Describes 3,300 directories, subdivided into over 400 areas.

Literary Market Place with Names and Numbers: Includes lists of book publishers, types of books published, agents and agencies, wholesalers, exporters and importers, and magazine and newspaper publishers. Includes listings of services and suppliers to the book publishing industry.

Martindale-Hubbell Law Directory: Complete legal directory in seven volumes. Includes listings of law firms in the United States, their staffs, and biographical sketches of personnel.

Moody's Industrial Manual; Bank and Finance Manual; OTC Industrial Manual; and Transportation Manual: Lists publicly owned companies in their respective subject areas. Each volume has two unique features: (1) the history of the company, name changes, mergers, and other corporate information; and (2) the "additional companies formerly included" section, which helps you trace name changes.

National Trade and Professional Associations and Labor Unions of the United States and Canada: Lists over 6,300 trade associations; labor unions; professional, scientific, or technical societies; and other national organizations composed of groups united for a common purpose. Includes membership, annual budget, and publications.

Peterson's Engineering, Science, and Computer Jobs (Peterson's Guides): Describes entry-level opportunities for technical bachelor's, master's, and doctoral degree holders, including salary ranges, starting assignments, training programs, summer and co-op programs, and international placements. Also contains information for mid-career professionals. Covers nearly 1,000 companies hiring technical graduates.

Places Rated Almanac: Published by Rand McNally. Identifies communities with a population over 500,000 in terms of low crime rates, good transportation facilities, cultural activities, and economic opportunities.

Research Centers Directory: A guide to thousands of university-related and other nonprofit research organizations, based in the United States and Canada, doing research in agriculture, business, conservation, education, engineering and technology, government, law, life sciences, math area studies, physical and earth sciences, social sciences, and humanities.

Sheldon's Retail and Phelon's Resident Buyers: Lists department stores, women's specialty stores, and chain stores.

Southern California Business Directory and Buyers Guide: A complete listing of companies according to products and services in the Southern California area. Includes a list of the top 100 corporations and the top 50 privately held companies. Look for similar directories for your geographical location.

Standard & Poor's Register of Corporations, Directors and Executives: Contains an alphabetical list showing business affiliations, business addresses, and residence addresses of people serving as officers, directors, trustees, and partners in business and professional organizations.

Standard Directory of Advertising Agencies and *Standard Directory of Advertisers:* A guide to 17,000 corporations; includes alphabetical and trade name indexes.

Standard Rate & Data Service: Directories of national and local media, including business publications, consumer magazines, professional journals, newspapers, and radio and television stations. Gives names and titles of personnel, circulation statistics, advertising rates, and other information.

The Foundation Directory: The standard reference work for information about private grant-making foundations in the United States.

Thomas Grocery Register, Volumes I, II, and III: Lists grocery store suppliers and products.

Thomas Register of American Manufacturers: Provides in-depth information on products and services, company location, divisions, subsidiaries, and sales offices. Includes products and services volumes, company volumes, and catalog volumes.

Walker's Manual of Western Corporations, Volumes I and II: Describes financial institutions and corporations that are publicly owned and headquartered in the 13 Western states. In Volume II, "Over-the-Counter Margin Stocks" and "Companies No Longer Described" are featured.

Who's Who in Electronics: Lists manufacturers and suppliers of electronic components and equipment.

Who's Who in Finance and Industry: Lists persons who have accomplished conspicuous achievements that distinguish them from the majority of their business contemporaries. Also contains names of incumbents in specified positions, including principals of financial and industrial concerns capitalized at or above a certain amount.

TIP
If you fail to locate information on a company, and you know the name of the company and the state in which it is located, you can send for or telephone the State Corporation Office for information. The articles of incorporation document that companies must file to become a corporation usually contains: the company name; place of business; date of incorporation; nature of the business; names and addresses of directors, officers, and incorporators; the name and address of the agent; and capitalization.

Do not forget to use your local telephone directory. The White Pages list government agencies and departments; the Yellow Pages list other places of employment. Let your fingers do the walking!

Magazines and Periodicals

The Readers' Guide to Periodical Literature, available at any library, is your guide to magazines that contain articles on any career you wish to research. Keeping up with the latest research in your field of interest is an excellent way to keep abreast of what is happening in the ever-changing labor market. You are likely to obtain the latest information or to uncover job titles that are not mentioned in government publications. There is a vast variety of magazines on all business-related topics. The following are some that you might find useful:

Advertising Age
Business Week
Entrepreneur
Entrepreneurial Woman
Forbes
Fortune
The Futurist
Inc.
Kiplinger's Changing Times
Modern Maturity
Professional Careers Magazine (Engineering and Computer Science)
Success
Working Woman

Other written sources include annual reports, newspapers, trade journals, and in-house bulletins.

Computer-Based Occupational Information Systems

Computer technology has become an integral part of many professions, including career counseling. Using computer guidance programs will not eliminate all your library research, but it can enhance it and save you some time.

There are two basic types of computerized guidance systems. One type is *interactive.* The program will ask you questions, give you a list of possible responses, and respond according to the answers you give. The information you receive is shown on the computer's screen. You also will be able to press a key to obtain a printout of the information.

The other type of system is *information retrieval.* Information retrieved from a computer data bank is often quite general. For example, occupations may be listed in their broadest terms, such as "managers," or "teachers," without any subgroups. For that reason, you should supplement these programs with the other types of written information discussed in this chapter.

Some computer-based career guidance programs that may be available to you are Discover, Choices, Guidance Information System (GIS), Career Information System (CIS), and System of Interactive Guidance and Information (SIGI Plus). There are also programs that contain a library of occupational and educational information that is up to date and localized to the area where you live. One such program is the National Career Information System (NCIS).

As of this writing, 15 states belong to NCIS. They have computer-aided labor market and occupational information localized for their state and even for regions of the state. The CIS is used in high schools, colleges, universities, public libraries, job training facilities, and other locations. The 15 NCIS members are Alaska, California (which calls its system EUREKA), Colorado, Georgia, Hawaii, Idaho, Illinois, Minnesota, Montana, Nebraska, Nevada, Metro Guide (New York City), Ohio, Oregon (which developed the system), and Wyoming. Other states are developing their own systems.

All of these systems contain units or sections that develop lists of occupations for you to explore. And, as with localized systems, you can obtain some idea of the salary range in the geographical area in which you are interested. Most college and university career centers have one or more of these systems available for student use at a nominal fee. Be sure to take advantage of it.

♦ Information Interviewing and Networking

What Is an Information Interview?

Interviewing for information is a process of gathering facts about people, activities, and occupations related to a particular career field. The interview will introduce you to the people and work environments that interest you. You can use information interviewing to get a better idea of jobs in which you might use your skills, what those jobs are called, and the environments that suit you best.

Information interviewing will enable you to screen out occupations you would dislike or organizations for which you would not want to work. The interview will also help you develop the necessary rapport with someone who can hire you and will expose you to the vocabulary that pertains to the particular company or field.

When conducting the information interview, you are not trying to hide the fact that ultimately you are looking for a position. You are on an active job search campaign, with the specific purpose of finding the right position. It is very important that every potential employer is aware of this. Also, it is realistic to assume that the persons you interview will not have or know of an opening at the exact time you are talking with them.

When you ask people for a job, you put them under pressure. When you make it clear that you do not expect them to have a job opening or to know of one, you take the pressure off them; they become more willing to listen to you and to remember you favorably. Interviewing for information also allows you to learn more about the job you eventually want.

Locating contacts. The following is a list of possible sources of information concerning career opportunities. Use this list to identify people who can help you. Do not leave anyone out—you never know who they might know!

- Relatives and neighbors
- Friends, colleagues, and other work acquaintances
- Professors and teachers
- Past employers and co-workers
- Owners of small businesses (especially those with whom you do business)
- Professionals, including doctors, dentists, lawyers, accountants, pharmacists, bankers, financial planners, brokers, and other consultants
- People you know through the activities of your children or other family members
- Members of professional associations or other organizations

- People with whom you have worked on community, school, or religious activities
- Members of the religious community, such as priests, rabbis, and ministers

List everyone you know who works in the field you want to enter. Broaden the list to include employees of firms you have worked for in the past few years, alumni of your college who are already in that profession, and any other people you know.

You can also get names from other sources, including the Yellow Pages, business directories, chambers of commerce, and newspaper articles. Another way to establish contacts is to look for people who are doing what you think you might enjoy. Watch for interesting newspaper and magazine articles, as well as television and radio programs, that mention people doing what you want to do. Contact these people for more information.

Making an appointment. A telephone call is usually the best way to contact the person you want to interview. Most secretaries are trained to screen their employer's calls; therefore, you may need to use special techniques to get to speak to the appropriate person. Consider the following example:

Secretary: May I tell him who is calling?
John: Yes, it's John Jones.
Secretary: What is the nature of the call?
John: I am doing some research on your company and feel the answers should come from Mr. Smith personally.
or
I am writing a paper on advertising, and I would like to have permission to use ABC Company as an example.
or
I have a technical question concerning your company that I feel only Mr. Smith can answer. May I speak to him for just a minute, please?

Obtaining information from contacts. The following list contains some of the questions that you may want to ask in an information interview.

1. How did you get into this field?
2. What academic preparation did you have?
3. What do you like most about your job?
4. What do you like least?
5. What are the responsibilities of your job?
6. What personal qualities do you feel are important in your work?
7. Please describe the tasks you do in a typical day.

8. What are the prospects for someone entering your field today?
9. If you were to advise someone about entering this field, what would you say to them?
10. Can you suggest any other sources of information?
11. What advice would you give me for locating and obtaining a job in this field?
12. Can you supply me with the names of three other people who might be able to tell me more about this field?

Evaluating the information. Ask yourself the following questions after each interview:

1. Does this person use the skills I want to use?
2. Would I be qualified for this job?
3. Do I understand what the job entails?
4. Would I enjoy working in this capacity?
5. Did I get additional ideas for alternatives?
6. What positive impression do I now have about this area of work?
7. Would I enjoy working for this company?
8. What are the goals (needs, concerns) of this area of work or company?
9. Which of my personal assets could I offer this field or company?

What Is Networking?

Networking involves using personal contacts to advance your own cause. It is one of the most powerful ways to develop contacts and leads. There are many avenues and opportunities for networking, some of which are part of your normal daily activities.

Many people have been asked for résumés after they have conducted the information interview. Also, do not be alarmed if you actually get a job offer after the information interview. As you know, this was not the purpose of the interview, but keep in mind that it does happen!

You will also develop several contacts through interviewing for information. Even though the intent of the interview was only to gather information, undoubtedly you will find that several of the people you interview are very willing to help you advance your career or to give you the names of individuals who know people in organizations in which you may be interested. Remember to ask each person you interview for the names of three *more* people who might be able to assist you . . . and so the list grows. Figure 6.1 is a graphic example of how you can develop contacts. Note how quickly you can expand your network if you ask each contact for three leads.

Another point to remember is not to be shy or to keep your job search to yourself. Tell everyone you know that you are looking for a job; that means your friends, neighbors, teachers, and any service professionals that you have occasion to contact. Tell as many people as you can, because this process really works!

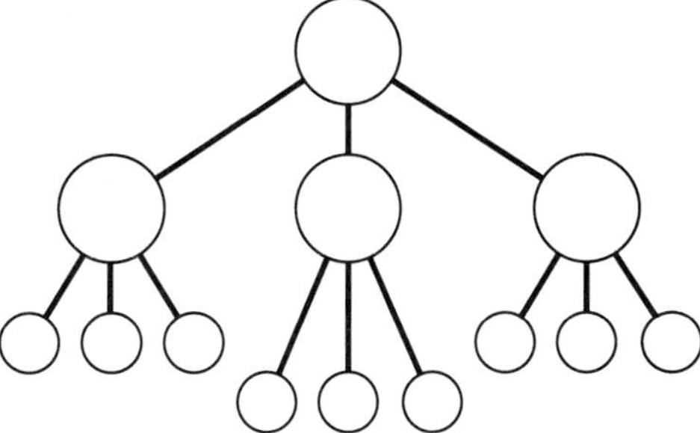

Figure 6.1 Developing Contacts

It is also a good idea to have a résumé with you *just in case* someone asks for one. If you do not yet have a résumé you wish to share, say, "I am in the process of revising my résumé, but I will send you one within a few days." Of course, then you must do it.

♦ Labor Market Considerations

Now that you have gathered both written and verbal information, you will want to sort it out and decide what it means. In Chapter One, we discussed labor market trends in general. Now concentrate on trends in your geographic location. Not only will you want to look at geographic considerations, but you will also want to consider whether you wish to move up or down from your present level of employment.

Once you have assessed where you currently fit, you can prepare to move up the ladder. Figure 6.2 illustrates how jobs are related in a large manufacturing company. Whether you are interested in manufacturing or some other field, ask your immediate supervisor and the personnel department for information on routes for advancement. If you are not employed, go out to various companies and interview for information.

After considering the economic conditions in your area, you may also want to consider moving from one industry to another. Some ideas on that subject are also presented in this chapter.

Geographic Considerations

If you are the primary or secondary breadwinner in your household, your ability to move will be somewhat restricted. Therefore, your research may be limited to a particular location. However, in an economic down cycle, it may be more important to be opportunity-driven. Once the number of companies in your industry and within your geographic limits is exhausted, you may wish either to think

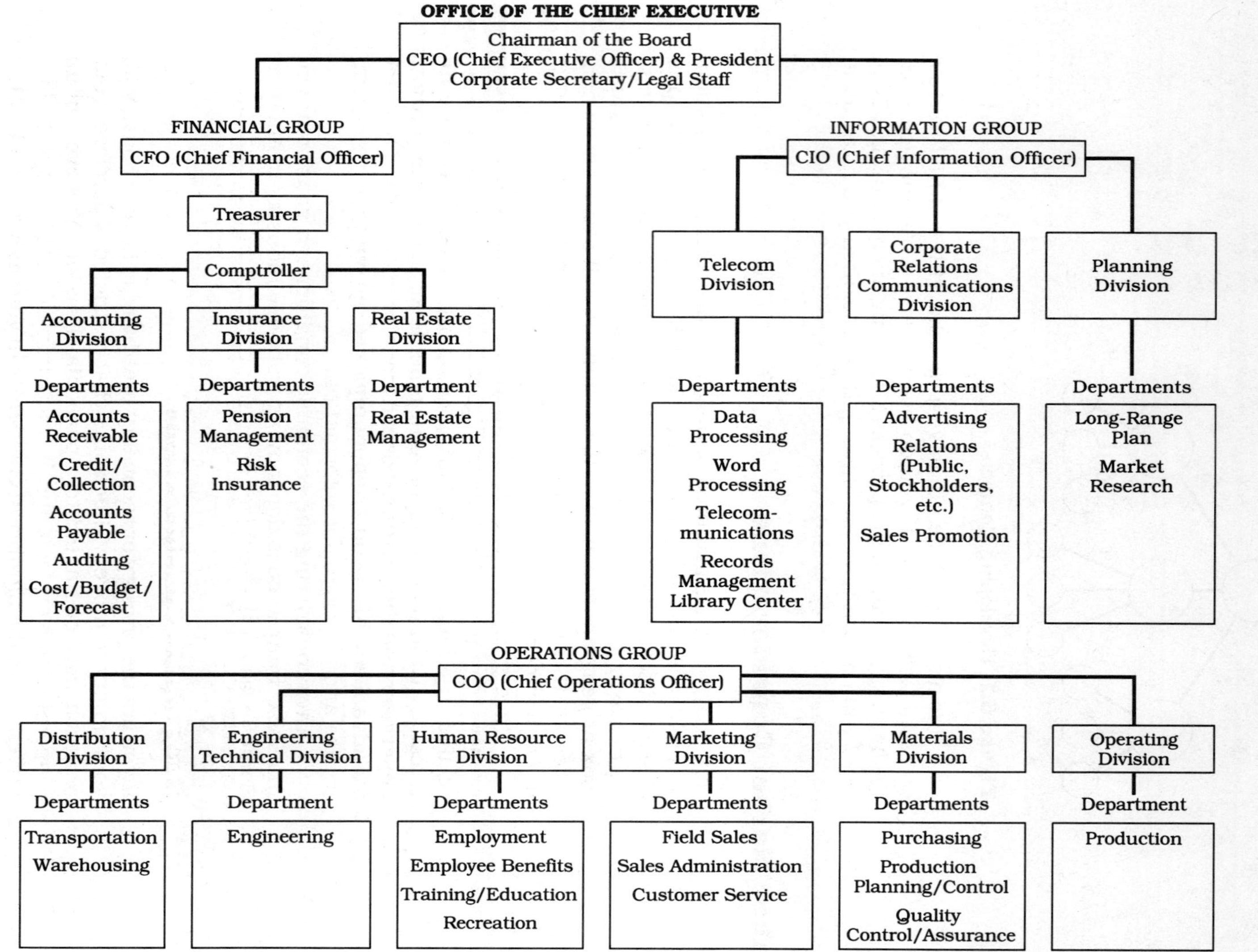

Figure 6.2 A typical organization chart for a large manufacturing company. *Source: From the* Careerism Newsletter, *vol. XXI, no. 11, November, 1991, p. 128. Copyright © 1991 by WWW/Services, Inc. (The Information Company) Box 10046, Rochester, NY 14610. Reprinted by permission.*

about other types of work in which you could use your training and experience or to relocate.

We now return to your values and personal preferences. You may want to review Chapter Five, because this is the point at which your values will have a definite effect on your decision making. Consider this decision: whether to move to a new geographical location for a position in a similar industry or to stay and look for work in a different industry. Refer to your prioritized list of values. What is most important to you? Use this as a guide to resolving the conflict, and move on to decision making.

Making a Vertical Move

A vertical move involves moving up or down from your present career level. In the following examples, you will see that a college instructor working in a small college or university could consider a position as dean at a small college or university a vertical move. A salesperson in a large company with a good track record might consider moving up to sales manager in a medium-sized company. A vertical move for a computer programmer in a medium-sized company would be a data processing manager in a medium-sized or small company. A personnel recruiter responsible for recruiting nationwide for a large company could make a vertical move by becoming a human resources manager at a small or medium-sized company. These examples can also be presented as follows:

Present Position	*Small, Medium, or Large Company, Organization, or Institution*	*Your Goal*	*Small, Medium, or Large Company, Organization, or Institution*
College instructor	Medium	Dean	Small
Salesperson	Large	Sales manager	Medium
Computer programmer	Medium	Data processing manager	Medium or small
Personnel recruiter	Large	Human resources manager	Medium or small

Source: Adapted from *Super Job Search: The Complete Manual for Job-Seekers and Career-Changers* (p. 41, 42, 43) by P. K. Studner, 1990.

The organizational chart in Figure 6.2 shows a typical line of responsibility for a large company.

Making a Horizontal Move

A horizontal move is one that involves moving from one industry to another while moving up or down the hierarchy. Consider the following example:

At age 47, Ivan was dismissed from his management position in a food service company specializing in airline catering. It had taken Ivan 18 years to rise to the top in his industry. By looking at horizontal moves that he could make, Ivan found many parallel industries that could use his expertise and years of experience. Here are some of his options:

RELATED CAREERS	*NEW MARKETS*
Procurement manager	Convalescent hospitals
Management consultant	Food brokerage businesses
Market research	Government
Product development	Hospitals (public and private)
Self-employment	Hotels
	Schools (public and private)

Of course, this list could be expanded. The idea here is to see how you can branch out into new markets, using your skills in related careers. Once you see the possibilities, you will not feel so confined to your present position.

Making a Complete Change

After considering the vertical and horizontal markets, you might still want to consider a complete career change. Here are a few examples:

Past Position	*New Career*
Administrator of a large metropolitan hospital	Stockbroker
Advertising coordinator	Technical editor
High school physical education teacher	Real estate salesperson
Registered nurse	Marketing representative for a line of hospital beds
Beauty salon owner	Sales representative for a beauty supply company
Homemaker, volunteer, and church fund-raising chairperson	Owner of a catering business

Pros and Cons of Small and Large Companies

A career changer who has worked for the government or for a large corporation has worked in a completely different environment from someone who has spent his or her working life in a small business. There are definite advantages and disadvantages of each environment.

Large companies. Large companies offer a greater degree of security than small ones, and there are more opportunities for movement. Large companies may also offer greater opportunities to travel and to relate to other parts of the company because larger corporations have multiple divisions and branch offices that make such moves possible. Further, on-the-job training is more readily available in large companies, such as General Electric or Xerox. In addition, benefit packages may be more extensive in larger companies because size gives them more power to negotiate with insurance companies for better rates.

On the negative side, large companies move very slowly. They can be very structured, with several layers of management. You might also be expected to do everything "by the book."

Small companies. Working for a smaller company can offer more flexibility. You may have greater opportunities to solve problems and to see how all parts of the business are run. Often a small company has less bureaucracy and fewer managers; therefore, each person is given more responsibility. Also, some small companies offer investment opportunities in the form of stock options.

On the negative side, small companies can impede your career growth because they usually have little room at the top of the ladder. Small companies may also lack such resources as capital and personnel. In addition, you might have a very loose job description in which you actually do the work of several people; for example, instead of having a personnel department, you may *be* the personnel department.

As you can see, working either for large or for small companies has both advantages and disadvantages. When making your decision on the type of working environment you would enjoy most, you may want to review the material about temperament styles and values found in Chapter Five.

Pros and Cons of the Public and Private Sectors

Some issues to consider when comparing the differences between the public and private sectors are employment opportunities, growth and promotion, salary, and benefits. You will find that large public employers and large private companies have many similarities.

Employment opportunities. Although several career opportunities may exist in government, a mid-career changer is more likely to have to start at an entry-level position. This is because most federal and state agencies try to promote from within, thus leaving more openings at the bottom or entry level.

Growth and promotion. The broad diversity offered by large public employers may mean more opportunities for advancement. On the other hand, some people find working for a large bureaucracy stifling, even though there usually is more job security. Large private companies are becoming more aware of the important role they play in helping women and minorities move ahead. Similarly, public employers and companies working under a government contract must adhere to affirmative hiring practices, thereby offering more opportunities to minorities and women. There still are relatively few women in upper management in smaller companies, but recent labor market statistics show that this is changing slightly.

Salaries. Salaries for federal, state, and local government workers have traditionally been lower than salaries in the private sector. Private employers have more flexibility to pay for qualified workers. Again, this varies with location. Consult your local resources for the most recent information.

Benefits. Most retirement programs for public employees are excellent, and insurance benefits are usually quite good. You will find that insurance benefits vary from company to company in the private sector. Generally speaking, the larger the employer, the better the coverage.

In considering these issues, you come back to your values, such as creativity, security, or any others discussed in Chapter Five.

♦ Summary

Chapter Six focused on the external information-gathering stage of the career change process. One source of information on careers is written information available through your local college or university career planning and placement center or your local public library. A list was provided in this chapter to guide you in researching careers. The second source of occupational information is other people. By now you should understand the concepts of *networking* and *informational interviewing*. You need to practice the techniques discussed in this chapter until they become second nature to you. This will be a continuous process until you find the job you really want.

You also had an opportunity to evaluate labor market considerations, such as geographical location, moving up or down from your present level, moving from one industry to another, or making a complete change. You studied the advantages and disadvantages of working for a small or a large company, and you compared the pros and cons of working in the public or the private sector.

♦ EXERCISE 6.1 Locating Contacts

Refer to the list of sources on pages 134 and 135 that could provide you with career information. Fill in the following blanks with names of people who you believe could help you.

1. Relatives and neighbors: ______________________________

____

____

____

2. Friends, colleagues, and other work acquaintances: ________

____

____

____

3. Professors and teachers: ______________________________

____

____

____

4. Past employers and co-workers: _________________________

____

____

____

5. Owners of small businesses: ___________________________

____

____

____

6. Professionals (doctors, dentists, lawyers): _______________

____

____

____

7. People you know through the activities of your children or other family members: ______________________________

____

____

____

8. Members of professional organizations or other associations:

____

____

____

9. People with whom you have worked in community, school, or religious activities: ______________________________

____

____

____

10. Members of the religious community: ______________________________

____

____

____

♦ EXERCISE 6.2 Conducting an Information Interview

Select one person from the list you completed in Exercise 6.1. Using the questions supplied on pages 135 through 136, as well as the information contained in this chapter, conduct an information interview. Write a brief report of your findings.

♦ EXERCISE 6.3 Evaluating the Information

After you have completed the interview, evaluate the information according to the following points. Write your response to each in the blanks provided.

1. Does this person use the skills I want to use? If so, what are those skills? ______________________________

____

____

2. Would I be qualified for this job? Why or why not? ________

3. Do I understand what the job entails? ________

4. Would I enjoy working in this capacity? Why or why not?

5. Did I get additional ideas for alternatives? What were they?

6. What positive impression do I now have about this area of work? ________

7. Would I enjoy working for this company (institution, person)? Why or why not? ________

8. What are the goals (needs, concerns) of this area of work or company? ________

9. Which of my personal assets could I offer this company?

____

____

____

____

10. Did I obtain the names of three other people who might be able to tell me more about this field? Who are they? ____________

____

____

____

As you correspond with prospective employers, record each contact on a 4 × 6 inch card. A written record of the transaction might look like this:

Sample Contact File

Company: ____________________________________

Address: ____________________________________

Contact person: ______________________________

Telephone number: ____________________________

Résumé left as calling card: ____________________

Résumé and cover letter sent: ___________________

Interview: ___________________________________

Follow-up and comments: _______________________

____

____

My Personal Job Search Contract

1. I will begin my job search on ______________________.
(Date)

2. By ______________ , I will have completed _________ hours
(Date)
of library research.

3. I will enlist the support of _________ friends and relatives in
(Number)
my job search campaign.

4. By ______________, I will have set up ________ appoint-
   (Date) (Number)
   ments for informational interviews.
5. By ______________, I will have conducted ________ infor-
   (Date) (Number)
   mational interviews.
6. By ______________, I will have conducted another ________
   (Date) (Number)
   informational interviews.
7. By ______________, I will have conducted another ________
   (Date) (Number)
   informational interviews.
8. Each week, I will follow up on ______________ referrals.
9. I expect to have my first job interview on ______________.
   (Date)
10. I will begin my new job or career on ______________.
    (Date)

♦ Notes

Careerism Newsletter (1991). Rochester, NY: WWW/Services, Inc.

NAVE, J. R., & NELSON, L. M. (1991). *Mid-career crisis.* New York: Putnam.

STUDNER, P. K. (1990). *Super job search: The complete manual for job-seekers and career-changers.* Los Angeles: Jamenair.

7 Developing a Plan of Action

"Don't believe what your eyes are telling you. All they show is limitation. Look with your understanding, find out what you already know, and you will see the way to fly."

—*Richard Bach,* Jonathan Livingston Seagull

In this chapter you will learn to set your goals and list the objectives needed to reach them. By integrating what you have learned in the self-assessment stage, you will determine what work activities you would most enjoy and what work situations you would prefer. You will also decide whether or not self-employment is for you.

After reading this chapter you should understand the following:

- The difference between goals and objectives
- What work activities and situations are important to you
- The pros and cons of running your own business

You should be able to do the following:

- Set your goals and list your objectives
- Write your own job description
- Determine whether or not self-employment is for you

Planning takes time and energy. It is like a road map—you must use it to begin your journey. Yes, you can venture out on a trip without a map, and you might eventually end up at your destination. But think how much easier it would have been if all the roads you took and the intermediate stops had been predetermined!

The same is true with your life; now is the time to review your life goals.

♦ Life Goals and Objectives

If you were to interview several successful people and ask them what the key to their success is, chances are they will tell you they set goals and objectives for themselves. Goal setting provides direction. Remember that classic saying: "If you don't know where you are going you will probably end up somewhere else." This is often the case with most people—they fail to plan.

Goals

First, you must distinguish a goal from an objective. A goal is the end result of what one is trying to reach. For example, a goal for you could be to find a new career that is satisfying to you in this stage of your life. Goals are general and long-range.

Objectives

Objectives, on the other hand, are more specific and describe the steps you must take to reach your goal. The chapters in this book are written so that you can use them as tools for reaching objectives; meeting your objectives will lead you to attaining your ultimate goal—a career change.

Steps to Goal Setting

As you begin to set goals and list objectives, follow these five basic steps: (1) define your goal, (2) identify obstacles, (3) develop strategies, (4) set up a time line, and (5) determine rewards.

1. *Define Your Goal.* What exactly do you want? You need to be able to define your goal in terms of measurable objectives. For example, let us say your goal is to change careers. A better way of defining this goal could be that you want to be established in your new career one year from now. Set up intermediate checkpoints for progress between now and the desired completion date.

2. *Identify Obstacles.* Obstacles can be real or imagined and can involve mental and physical limitations. You must disclose all the barriers or inhibitors that could keep you from reaching your goal. For example, obstacles could include lack of motivation, lack

of a support system, or not having enough time to spend on the process. Another obstacle might be the difficulty of locating job openings in your chosen field. Locating these openings may take longer than you anticipated. Therefore, you may have to take an intermediate step, such as finding temporary employment to tide you over until you land the job of your choice. Always have a second plan to fall back on when the original plan does not work.

3. *Develop Strategies.* In this step, you will set up a specific plan to achieve your goal. You need to be flexible and innovative and to develop alternative strategies. For example, one strategy might involve spending a minimum of ten hours per week attending networking meetings and doing library research. You might also plan ways to enlist the assistance of your family and friends as part of your support network.

4. *Set a Time Line.* If you fail to set a time line, you probably will procrastinate or let the process drag on too long. Set up a time chart with very specific milestones. A typical milestone would be, "By March 15 I will have completed six informational interviews." The Personal Job Search Contract you completed in Exercise 6.3 will be useful for this step.

5. *Determine Rewards.* To stay on target and to not become discouraged, you will need to set up your own motivation system. This motivation should be in the form of rewards—whatever is important for you. For example, after you have completed three informational interviews, you could treat yourself to a movie, a special meal, or anything else that pleases you.

Making a major life transition, such as a career change, can take a while, so it is important to feel that you are making progress. By following a plan, you have checkpoints to indicate your progress and to give you incentive to continue. Try it; you'll like it! (See Exercise 7.2.)

Another point to remember is that age need not be an inhibitor to a successful career change. Consider the following:

> Jane entered the world of work at age 56 with no formal education and a wealth of volunteer experiences. Her first job was as a receptionist, but within two years she had worked her way to a sales position in the fur salon of an exclusive department store. After nine years in this job, she is seeking new challenges and opportunities. At age 67, Jane is thinking of either becoming a sales representative for a cosmetics firm or going into business for herself as a consultant or fashion show coordinator.

♦ Write Your Own Job Description

How many of you have had an opportunity to structure your own job or to write your own job description? This would indeed be ideal, but it happens infrequently in modern-day business. However, if you cannot focus on your needs and motivation, you will have difficulty setting goals and objectives. It is now time to write down your thoughts about what an ideal job or work situation would be for you. Exercise 7.3 gives you an opportunity to write your ideal job description using the categories presented in the following section.

What Is Important to You?

1. *Work Activities.* What types of activities are involved in your ideal job? Do you like to work with data, whether compiling, organizing, computing, or summarizing them? Do you like to work with people by teaching, training, supervising, or counseling them? Do you like to work with things—repairing, assembling, operating, or building them? What do you find yourself doing when no one is *telling* you what to do? What would you like to do even if you were not paid for it? When you think of your ideal career this way, it is more like play or something you would become involved with if left to your own resources.

2. *Work Situations.* What situations appeal to you? Are you happiest performing duties that change frequently, or do you enjoy routine tasks? Do you prefer using your personal judgment to make decisions, or using standards that can be measured or checked?

3. *Skills.* Focus on skills you enjoy using. You have a wealth of skills—some innate, and some acquired through formal education or on-the-job training. Think of physical skills, such as motor coordination, strength, or endurance. Consider skills associated with working with people, such as teaching, advising, training, or counseling. You might also contemplate designing, drawing, writing, or other artistic skills.

4. *Working Conditions.* Do you see yourself in an office setting? Outdoors? Do you like to work by yourself or with a partner? Would you rather be a team leader or a team member? Do you prefer to be managed or to practice self-management? Do you like a lot of hustle and bustle, or do you prefer a quiet environment?

5. *Education and Training.* How much training or education do you currently possess? How much time are you willing to spend retraining? What are your educational goals? Do you want to work

toward an associate's degree, a bachelor's degree, a master's degree, or a doctorate? State an educational major if you can.

6. *Geographical Location.* In what size of community would you prefer to work and live? Would you rather live and work in a rural, suburban, or large urban area? What size population do you consider ideal? Do you want to be near recreational areas, cultural centers, colleges, and universities? Consider all the desirable features in your ideal location. At this point, do not try to focus on any one city or location; just fantasize.

7. *Type of Organization.* Do you like working for a large or a small company? What type of institution—public or private? Would you rather work for yourself? Be as specific as possible.

8. *Personal Characteristics.* What type of work environment is most conducive to your temperament? What kinds of people do you want to work with on a daily basis? What are the interests of the people with whom you would like to work? If you could choose the people you work with, what would their characteristics be (for example, diplomatic, flexible, friendly, trustworthy, high achievers)?

9. *Salary.* What would your ideal salary be (monthly or yearly)? Do you know what you are worth in the job market? What is the smallest salary you could accept to continue in your accustomed life-style? In considering this, keep in mind the cost-of-living differences among geographical locations.

10. *Personal Values.* What kind of personal satisfaction do you need in your work? What is important to you on the job: security, independence, variety, creativity, high income potential, status, or creativity?

Dare to Dream

Do you remember how exciting it was to play "make believe" when you were a child? As adults we have learned to put away such thoughts in lieu of more practical, sound ideas. In doing so, we lose that richness of imagination. Now we must work at tuning in to our imagination and creativity. One form of tapping our creativity and hidden resources is called "brainstorming." Brainstorming can be defined as that burst of inspiration that comes from listening to the ideas of other people. Many corporate meetings are turned into brainstorming sessions for the purpose of generating new ideas and creativity.

Another way to bring out your creativity is to indulge in a guided fantasy exercise. Have someone read you the following fantasy. It should be read slowly and softly. Close your eyes, take a few deep breaths, and relax.

Imagine you are starting a typical day about five years from now. It's a workday, and you're trying to decide what to wear. Look over your collection of clothes. What do you finally decide to wear? (Pause) Imagine you are checking yourself out in a mirror. How do you look? How do you feel as you think ahead to your day at work? Nervous? Calm? Excited? Afraid? (Pause)

You are eating breakfast now. Is there anyone with you, or are you eating alone? (Pause) You're ready to head for work. Do you stay home? If not, how do you get to work? How far is it? (Pause)

You're entering your workplace now. Stop for a moment and try to get a mental picture of your workplace. Where is it? What does it look like? (Pause) What people are there? How many? What are they doing? (Pause) Complete your morning's work right up to lunchtime. Form an image of the things you do on your job. Think about what you are actually doing. Are you working with ideas or adding figures? Are you working with people, talking with them, helping them in some way?

Are you using tools or running a machine? Do you work mostly by yourself or with lots of people? Are you mostly inside or outdoors? (Pause) Now it's lunchtime. Where do you go? Who are the people you are with? What are they like? What are you talking about? (Pause)

Return to work now and finish the workday. Is anything different from the morning's work? What is the last thing you do before you quit for the day? (Pause) Your workday is coming to an end. Has it been mostly a satisfying day or a frustrating day? What has made it so? (Pause) Open your eyes when you are ready, and just sit quietly for a moment. (Adapted from Morgan & Skovholt, 1977)

Keep these thoughts in mind; you will be referring back to them from time to time.

♦ Is Self-Employment for You?

If independence, time freedom, variety, and creativity were work values to which you assigned a high priority in Chapter Five, then self-employment may be for you. Who knows? You may want to join the ranks of such well-known entrepreneurs as Mary Kay Ash of Mary Kay Cosmetics, Inc., of Dallas, Texas. Mary Kay Cosmetics rewards its salespeople with pink Buicks and Cadillacs for success in selling the product line. Countless women are now driving pink Buicks and Cadillacs due to their success with this company. Did you know that Calvin Klein, famous for the jeans of the same name, began his career in 1962 as a $75-a-week apprentice designer? In 1968, he used his savings of $12,000 to launch his own company, Calvin Klein Ltd. Within a decade, he and his partner had built the business into a $100 million fashion empire.

We could go on and on naming famous entrepreneurs. But what about *you?* What are your secret ambitions? Let us examine some ways you can be your own boss.

Facts to Consider

To be your own boss you generally need to purchase a franchise, establish your own business, or buy a company from its current owner. However, before you decide to "walk on the wild side," you should consider some important facts.

1. The opportunities for entrepreneurship should be quite good in the 1990s. According to the U.S. Department of Labor, the largest number of occupations will be in the service sector, and many of these will be in small start-up businesses.
2. Nearly 90 percent of all new jobs will be created by small businesses. As large Fortune 500 companies continue to reduce their ranks and to downsize their middle management, many of these displaced people will become entrepreneurs by starting their own small businesses. Over 600,000 new businesses are started each year.
3. According to Naisbitt and Aburdene (1990), the welfare state will be increasingly privatized. This will result in a nationwide movement toward getting people off welfare and into private-sector jobs. This trend will affect both large and small businesses as more people are placed in job programs.
4. The days of women as a minority in the work force are over (Naisbitt & Aburdene, 1990). Women are starting new businesses twice as fast as men are. In Canada, one-third of small businesses are owned by women. In France, women own one-fifth of the small businesses. In Britain, since 1980 the number of self-employed women has increased three times as fast as the number of self-employed men.
5. Starting your own business entails an inherent amount of risk. According to the latest figures from the U.S. Department of Commerce, only 16 percent of self-owned businesses are successful. The chance of a new business closing within seven years is about 50 percent. However, franchise operations are given better odds; 90 percent of franchised businesses are successful (Naisbitt & Aburdene, 1990).

Franchised Businesses

Although franchising is frequently and inaccurately described as an industry or business, it actually is neither of these. Rather, it is a method of doing business—a way of marketing a product, a service, or both. Franchising has been adopted and used in a wide variety of industries and businesses. For instance, the fast-food business contains numerous examples of franchising—McDonald's, KFC, Domino's Pizza, Burger King, Baskin-Robbins, and so forth. Other types of franchised businesses include auto parts dealers, convenience stores, automotive dealers, and personal and business services.

Franchising has several advantages. You generally receive a proven business format; that is, a way of selling goods or providing services that is likely to succeed in most areas. Most franchisors also offer training programs that teach their franchisees how to train, hire, and fire personnel. The risk of failure is greatly reduced because franchisees can take advantage of the managerial and financial expertise available through the home office. In larger cities, most newspaper classified ads for franchises generally appear in the "Business Opportunities" section.

If you were to talk to people who have started their own businesses, you would find that they all have something in common: they prefer to be their own boss, they like the potential for financial reward, and they love the challenge. As an example, consider this midlife career changer:

> At age 30, facing divorce and with five young children to raise, Patricia knew she had no other choice but to somehow enter the work force. Her options were rather limited because she had dropped out of school in the tenth grade. She returned to school through adult education, completed a nurse's aide course, earned a degree at a community college, and became a registered nurse. Over the next five years, Patricia developed management and leaderhip skills and attained the position of Director of Nurses at a large metropolitan hospital. But the story does not end here. Patricia decided she needed even more of a challenge—she changed careers in order to fulfill her strong desire for independence and creativity. She obtained the requisite training and started operating a small financial planning business from her home. To market her business, Patricia decided to finance a radio program by taking a second mortgage on her home. Now, six years later, she is the successful owner of a business that grosses nearly a million dollars annually.

Who Is the Entrepreneur?

Now that you have seen that others just like you have successfully started their own businesses, consider some of the preliminary planning you should do before starting your own business. At this point, it would be a good idea to take the entrepreneur's quiz in Exercise 7.4.

The following are preliminary points to consider in planning a business of your own:

1. Have experience in the line of business you plan to enter. If you have not worked in that particular industry, then consider getting a job with a successful owner of that business for three months, six months, or more, and learn as much as you can about the business from that person. Knowledge is very expensive when paid for in the currency of your own mistakes.
2. Have management experience. Having had a job in which you supervised people and were responsible for important expenditures will be helpful.
3. Consult an attorney if necessary. If you are unsure about what to do or if you are about to risk a lot of money, then you might want to speak with an attorney.
4. Obtain accounting advice. As a business owner, you will have to prepare many reports on your business for federal, state, city, and county governments. Your accounting and bookkeeping system should be a useful, valuable management tool. To operate a business successfully, you will always need current financial information, and you will need it promptly.
5. Make a capital needs study. Forecast your sales, expenses, and profit, and prepare a cash flow chart. An accountant can assist you in preparing these documents. It is important that you know where you are going financially.
6. Know your local banker, and be sure he or she knows you. Local bankers know the area, the average income, and the competitive situation, as well as real estate and rental values. Make good use of their expertise.
7. Contact an insurance broker. Have the broker submit suggested coverage for fire and personal liability insurance. Know the importance of and types of coverage. Discuss the broker's suggestions with your lawyer and accountant.
8. If you belong to a trade association, contact its office and the association manager. Trade organizations have a wealth of material, much of which you should study.
9. Know the executive officers of your chamber of commerce; they have much knowledge about the area and can give you informative printed material.

10. Visit your local library. The librarian will place in your hands most of the reading material you need. Time spent at the library can provide adequate information upon which to make sound decisions.
11. If you feel the need, avail yourself of counseling by a professional consultant in marketing, production, accounting, and so on. Contact your banker, attorney, or accountant to secure the names of consultants who specialize in the particular area of business operation in which you feel you need advice and assistance.
12. Attend management courses offered for the benefit of small-business owners. Call colleges and adult schools near you for lists of courses. Lack of management competence causes about 90 percent of small-business failures.
13. Visit the Small Business Administration office nearest you. The SBA is a federal agency created to encourage and assist small business. It provides financial assistance in the form of loans, advance payments, and business development expenses. One word of caution, however: do not go to the SBA with the thought that you are going to be *taught* how to run your business. Go with your business plan in hand. (Adapted from "Checklist for Going into Business" by the Service Corps of Retired Executives, U.S. Small Business Administration.)

Sources for Further Information

The federal government offers several publications through the Small Business Administration, 1441 L Street, NW, Washington, DC 20401; telephone: (800) 368-5855. Some of these publications are free; others are for sale. In addition, the Consumer Information Center publishes a free booklet entitled *More than a Dream: Running Your Own Business.* To obtain this booklet, write to the Consumer Information Center, Department 616J, Pueblo, CO 82009. You can also order the following publications through the Consumer Information Center: "Starting and Managing a Business from Your Home," and "Financial Management: How to Make a Go of Your Business." Finally, the bibliography at the end of this book includes a list of works that may provide you with useful information.

♦ Summary

This chapter should prompt you to develop a plan of action. First, you must decide on a goal and then identify the steps you must take to reach your goal. These steps take the form of objectives. Here is where you incorporate what you learned about yourself in the self-assessment stage. You should be able to integrate your interests, skills, temperament, and values and to determine the best working environment for you.

Dare to dream—write your own job description. Review what is important to you. You may want to investigate the possibility of self-employment. Supplement the information on self-employment presented in this chapter by consulting some of the sources listed in this chapter as well as those listed in the bibliography. Now proceed to the written exercises, where you can start to put your plans on paper.

♦ EXERCISE 7.1 Lifetime Goals

Answer each of the following questions. Write quickly. Aim for quantity rather than quality at first; you can always go back and revise your answers.

1. What are your lifetime goals?

2. What are your goals for the next three years?

3. If you were given six months to live, what would your final goals be?

4. Review your answers to questions 1 through 3, and make any changes or additions you wish.

5. Select one or two goals from each list (for a maximum of six), and rank them in order, with the most important goals first.

Now that you have your goals arranged by priority, choose one to work on today. It need not be the one to which you have assigned first priority. Remember, this is just a practice to prepare you for implementing your decision to change careers.

♦ EXERCISE 7.2 Setting Your Career Goal

Complete steps 1 through 5.

1. Write your goal statement; include measurable outcomes.

2. List all the obstacles you can think of that could prevent you from reaching your goal.

3. Design a strategy for overcoming each obstacle you listed in step 2.

4. Set up a time line with checkpoints. What will you have accomplished at each point?

5. Set up a reward system for yourself. How will you reward yourself when you have accomplished an objective?

♦ EXERCISE 7.3 Describing Your Ideal Job

Using the following categories as a guide, describe the ideal job for you. Write your responses for each category. Be creative and intuitive; let your imagination run wild. Remember, it is important that you do not have a preconceived idea of what your job title would be or what company you would work for. Simply let your thoughts flow. Erase from your mind old thoughts, negative statements, or "shoulds" left over from previous job searches or unsuccessful career attempts. If necessary, review the section entitled "What Is Important to You?" for a detailed description of the categories given in this exercise.

Work Activities:

Work Situations:

Skills:

Working Conditions:

Education and Training:

Geographical Location:

Type of Organization:

Personal Characteristics:

Salary:

Personal Values:

♦ EXERCISE 7.4 Entrepreneur's Quiz

If becoming your own boss appeals to you, take this entrepreneur's quiz to see if you have what it takes to become an entrepreneur; this quiz may offer you some insight.

The Entrepreneur's Quiz

1. An entrepreneur is most commonly the __________ child in the family. (a) eldest (b) middle (c) youngest (d) doesn't matter
2. An entrepreneur is most commonly (a) married (b) single (c) widowed (d) divorced
3. An entrepreneur is most typically a (a) man (b) woman (c) either

4. An individual usually begins his or her *first* entrepreneurial company at which age? (a) teens (b) twenties (c) thirties (d) forties (e) fifties
5. Usually an individual's entrepreneurial tendency first emerges at which of these ages? (a) teens (b) twenties (c) thirties (d) forties (e) fifties
6. Typically, entrepreneurs have reached the following educational level by the time they begin their first serious business venture: (a) grammar school (b) high school diploma (c) bachelor's degree (d) master's degree (e) doctoral degree
7. An entrepreneur's primary motivation for starting a business is (a) to make money (b) to not work for anyone else (c) to be famous (d) as an outlet for unused energy
8. The primary motivation for entrepreneurs' high ego and need for achievement is based upon their relationship with their (a) spouse (b) mother (c) father (d) children
9. An entrepreneur brings which of these items from business to business? (a) desk (b) chair (c) all office furniture (d) none of these items
10. To be successful in an entrepreneurial venture, you need an overabundance of (a) money (b) luck (c) hard work (d) good ideas
11. Entrepreneurs and venture capitalists (a) get along well (b) are best of friends (c) are cordial friends (d) are in secret conflict
12. A successful entrepreneur relies on which of these groups for critical management advice? (a) internal management team (b) external management professionals (c) financial sources (d) no one
13. Entrepreneurs are best as (a) managers (b) venture capitalists (c) planners (d) doers
14. Entrepreneurs are (a) high risk takers (b) gamblers (c) moderate risk takers (take a few chances) (d) doesn't matter
15. The only necessary and sufficient ingredient for starting a business is (a) money (b) a customer (c) a product (d) an idea

ANSWERS

1. (a) eldest
2. (a) married
3. (a) man
4. (c) thirties
5. (a) teens
6. (d) master's degree
7. (b) to not work for anyone else
8. (c) father
9. (b) chair
10. (b) luck
11. (d) are in secret conflict
12. (b) external management professionals
13. (d) doers
14. (c) moderate risk takers
15. (b) a customer

NUMBER OF QUESTIONS ANSWERED CORRECTLY	*SCORE*
11 or more	Successful entrepreneur
10–11	Entrepreneur
9–10	Latent entrepreneur
8–9	Potential entrepreneur
7–8	Borderline entrepreneur
7 or less	Hired hand

SOURCE: Adapted from the book: *How to Start, Finance, and Manage Your Own Small Business.* By Joseph R. Mancuso. © 1978. Used by permission of the publisher, Prentice-Hall/ A division of Simon & Schuster, Englewood Cliffs, NJ.

♦ Notes

MANCUSO, J. R. (1978). *How to start, finance, and manage your own small business.* Englewood Cliffs, NJ: Prentice-Hall.

MORGAN, J. I., & SKOVHOLT, T. M. (1977). Using inner experience: Fantasy and daydreams in career counseling. *Journal of Counseling Psychology, 24,* 391–397.

NAISBITT, J., & ABURDENE, P. (1990). *Megatrends 2000.* New York: Morrow.

SERVICE CORPS OF RETIRED EXECUTIVES (SCORE). *Checklist for going into business.* Management Aid, Number MP 12. Los Angeles: U.S. Small Business Administration.

8 Marketing Yourself: Résumés and Cover Letters

"He is not only idle who does nothing, but he is idle who might be better employed."

—*Socrates*

A résumé is the most important factor in determining whether or not you obtain that all-important interview with the employer. In this chapter you will enter the final phase of the Steps to Success Model: marketing yourself. Your résumé is a marketing tool that advertises your assets to prospective employers; the cover letter introduces you to these employers. Résumés and cover letters have only one purpose: to get you an interview.

After reading this chapter you should understand the following:

- That an effective résumé is a highly personal and individual summary of your background, experience, training, and skills
- The similarities between marketing a product and marketing your skills
- How to emphasize your strongest skills for redirecting your career

You should be able to do the following:

- Recognize the three basic résumé styles and know the advantages and disadvantages of each

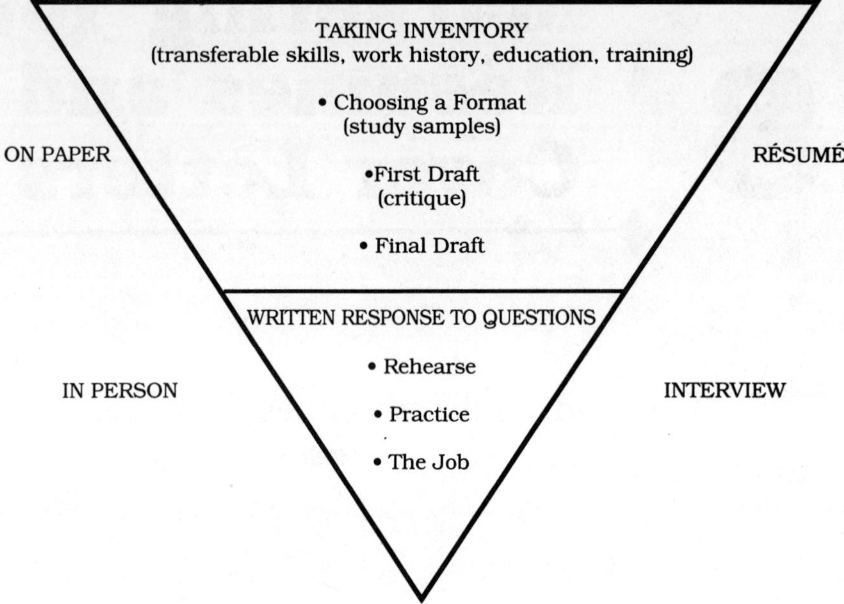

Figure 8.1 Marketing model: Selling yourself

- Write a résumé that effectively markets your experience, training, and skills
- Write a cover letter that gets the attention of a prospective employer

An effective résumé is a highly personal, individual summary of your background, experience, training, and skills. Therefore, you should write your own résumé rather than have someone write it for you. To change jobs successfully, you must remember that you are marketing a product—and that product is *you*.

This chapter and Chapter Nine contain the marketing strategies for changing careers. Figure 8.1 is a model for marketing yourself on paper and in person.

♦ The Résumé as a Marketing Tool

Whether you are marketing yourself or a product, you must be able to answer five basic questions:

1. Who is the current market competition?
2. To whom is the product marketed?
3. Is the advertising and promotion budget sufficient?

4. Have you promoted enough enthusiasm in the sales force?
5. How does the product stack up with competition? Is it competitively priced?

These five points can also apply to your job search.

1. *Identify competition.* Unless you are competing for an in-house position where you could possibly identify your competition, there is no accurate way to determine who is vying with you for a particular job. Therefore, you must "out-market" your competitors regardless of how well-qualified they may be. In the final analysis, what counts is who did the best job of selling to the employer.

2. *Identify your market.* This step should be relatively easy for you because this material was covered extensively in Chapter Six. In addition, in Chapter Seven you developed a plan of action. Now you are ready to put it to work.

3. *Evaluate your advertising budget.* Successful job hunting depends more on your personal effort than on the amount of money you spend. In fact, you do not need to spend much money at all.

4. *Promote enthusiasm in the sales force.* The people you must convince are the contacts and leads you have uncovered in your market research. They can prove invaluable to you. If you are applying directly to human resources staff, you must convince them that you have made their jobs easy by making it unnecessary for them to advertise the position again. Thus, you have saved the employer time and money because you are *the right person* for the job.

5. *Make the product competitive.* To identify your competition in the labor market you must test-market your résumé. Have someone whose judgment you respect critique your résumé. Have the reviewer pretend to be the employer to whom you have sent your résumé. Most people make the mistake of sending out hundreds of résumés, either to respond to ads or to "cold-canvass" employers. Obviously, this does not work. Even worse, it makes job-seekers feel rejected and gives them an inaccurate impression of the labor market. Résumés sent in this manner are "shotgun-blasted" rather than targeted to the appropriate person.

Résumé Styles

Functional

This style is especially effective for career redirection because it allows you to emphasize your strongest skills, talents, achievements, and capabilities. In a functional résumé, you can display these attributes prominently and link them to your experience. This style is excellent for people who have gaps in their work history or whose work experience is unrelated to the job they are seeking.

The functional résumé style is different from others because it calls attention to your transferable skills. Your qualities are organized by the functions that relate to the job objective and summary of qualifications.

ADVANTAGES
- Provides flexibility in emphasizing strengths and areas of accomplishment
- Enables a prospective employer to place you in a job where your greatest assets can be used
- Makes it easier for you to select the capabilities you want to use in your new career
- Reduces the possibility of being placed in a field or position in which you no longer want to work
- Conceals gaps in your work history
- Allows you to examine your accomplishments in a positive manner and to uncover "hidden" assets

DISADVANTAGES
- Takes time and effort and is more difficult to write
- Employers may view your résumé negatively if you omit work history

Chronological

(Also known as *historical.)* In a chronological résumé, you present your work experience and education in chronological order, beginning with the most recent first. This style tends to combine your talents and therefore does not allow those special talents to stand out. Although this résumé style is useful for depicting your promotions within a company through a historical account, it may not be appropriate for older workers who are sensitive about their age. Because of these drawbacks, the strictly chronological style is not recommended.

ADVANTAGES:
- Easy to write
- Emphasizes career longevity
- Stresses growth and continuity in specific job categories

DISADVANTAGES
- Boring
- Makes it difficult to redirect your career
- Deemphasizes your transferable skils

- Makes it easy to detect gaps in employment
- Emphasizes your most recent employment regardless of whether it is the most important
- Can place older workers at a disadvantage because it emphasizes dates

Combination

This style includes some qualities of the functional style, but employers and job titles are listed in reverse chronological order.

The combination style seems to be a healthy compromise between the functional and chronological styles because it appeals to employers while allowing you to market your transferable skills. Several examples of the combination style are presented in this chapter.

Writing Your Résumé

Before you begin your first draft, let us consider what goes into the résumé. By this time you have decided on the direction you want your career to take, so you now have an objective (although it could be a temporary one).

Think of the objective as the topic sentence. Everything else in your résumé should support it. Leave out anything that does not relate to your objective.

Your writing style should reflect activity, or the "can-do" attitude that employers desire. Therefore, begin each entry in your résumé with an active verb rather than a passive one. (Consult the list on page 170 for ideas.) An example follows:

VERB	*NOUN*
conducted	sales seminar
WHY	*RESULT*
to increase productivity;	increased profits by 20 percent

According to Robert Half, CPA (president of Robert Half, Inc., an organization specializing in placement of financial and data processing personnel), the most effective résumés incorporate three basic positive elements:

1. *Your positive image.* You should accentuate the positive and eliminate (or deemphasize) the negative. You can highlight the positive by positioning the most important elements of your background first and by allotting a larger amount of space to these elements.
2. *Your positive contribution.* You should indicate how you contributed in your previous employment (for example, you helped

ACTION VERBS THAT DEMONSTRATE FUNCTIONAL SKILLS

accomplished
acted
adapted
administered
advanced
advised
allocated
analyzed
applied
approved
arbitrated
arranged
assisted
attained
blended
brought
built
carried out
cataloged
changed
classified
collaborated
compared
completed
computed
conceived
conducted
constructed
consulted
contracted
controlled
coordinated
corrected
counseled
created
dealt
decided
decreased
defined
delegated
derived
designated
detected
developed
devised
directed
disapproved
discovered
distributed
documented
doubled
edited
encouraged
engineered
enlarged
escalated
established
estimated
evaluated
examined
expanded
experienced
explored
facilitated
finalized
formulated
founded
functioned
governed
grouped
guided
handled
harmonized
harnessed
headed
identified
implemented
improved
increased
indexed
initiated
inspected
installed
instituted
interpreted
introduced
invented
investigated
justified
led
localized
located
made
maintained
managed
mastered
mechanized
merged
moderated
monitored
motivated
negotiated
opened
operated
ordered
organized
originated
overcame
performed
pioneered
planned
prepared
presented
presided
processed
produced
programmed
promoted
provided
purchased
quadrupled
raised
recommended
recorded
recruited
rectified
reduced
reevaluated
reorganized
repaired
replaced
reshaped
restored
reversed
reviewed
revised
saved
scheduled
screened
selected
serviced
set up
solved
sorted
sparked
specified
standardized
started
stimulated
straightened
strengthened
succeeded
summarized
supervised
supported
surpassed
systematized
tested
trained
transacted
transcribed
transferred
transformed
translated
tripled
underwrote
unified
upgraded
validated
varied
verified
vitalized
won
worked
wrote
yielded

increase profits, improved customer or client relations, or handled a department better than expected).

3. *Your positive appeal.* At the end of the résumé, you should lightly "toot your own horn." Without appearing pompous, you should point out that you are a hard worker, have a flair for accomplishing work, can interrelate well, and are an energetic, ambitious self-starter.

For five years, Half researched and analyzed thousands of résumés from all over the country. He discovered that the most effective résumés incorporated these three basic *positive* elements. He also found that regardless of the style of presentation (chronological, functional, or combination), employment candidates who used all three positive elements achieved optimum results. As the number of elements used decreased, so did the results; those who used none of the positive elements did very poorly in their job search. (Adapted from "How to Write (or Read) a Resume," by Robert Half, May 1981, *The Practical Accountant*, pp. 63–67.)

Salary is not discussed in the résumé, even if you are responding to an advertisement that asks you to list your salary expectations. You cannot win on this one—you will either sell yourself short or price yourself out of the job. If you are asked about your salary expectations, simply say that you would like to discuss them in an interview or that salary is negotiable. Salary expectations have no place on a résumé. Also, be sure you do not include a lot of "filler" in your résumé. Nothing is more distracting and counterproductive than listing entry after entry—or page after page—of irrelevant, inconsequential, or unimportant information.

Study the sample résumés in this chapter. Do not feel discouraged if you do not find your actual job objective among these samples. What is important is the way the material is presented and how it "speaks" for the applicant. Read the comments for each résumé, and decide which sample best fits your needs. Then complete Exercises 8.1 through 8.4 *before* you begin your first draft.

Sample Résumés

The following pages contain nine sample résumés (Figures 8.2 through 8.10). Figures 8.9 and 8.10 are "before" and "after" versions of the same résumé. The remaining seven résumés are in their completed form. Four of the sample résumés follow the combination style, two are chronological, and three are functional. Five of the résumés are two pages long; the others are only one page. Every sample résumé in this chapter has special components for you to examine. Study them carefully, and refer to them as you complete your first draft. Feel free to "mix and match" elements as well.

Format:
Block—two page
Style:
Combination

Anil Patel
2705 East Ocean Blvd.
Long Beach, CA 90803
(310) 439-9566

OBJECTIVE:
Managerial position for hardware and software technical support in a computer environment.

A summary of qualifications section provides an overall recap of Anil's experience. This sets the tone for the rest of the résumé.

SUMMARY OF QUALIFICATIONS
Over 20 years of experience with computers—both hardware and software—in a field environment, interfacing with customers and management at all levels. Major troubleshooter for a Fortune 500 company on computer mainframes, using both hardware and software diagnostic skills. Managerial responsibility for service personnel on large-scale computer sites.

A summary of skills section—an element of the functional résumê—was added to support the objective. This section amplifies the components necessary for the position.

SUMMARY OF SKILLS
Managerial. Project manager for installation of ten Xerox 530 systems in the Los Angeles County Community College District. Managed personnel for service of computer hardware at large-scale computer sites, including the University of California, Irvine; the Orange County Department of Education; and Hughes Ground Systems, Fullerton.

Hardware. Diagnostician and senior field engineer involved with troubleshooting large mainframes nationwide. Scheduled installations, upgrades, and service in a timely manner. Organized customer meetings and resolved complaints. Trained customer engineers in specialized hardware courses and made hardware presentations to software engineers and marketing personnel.

Software. Used operating system software CONTROL PROGRAM 5 (CP5). Responsible for seven large time-sharing sites in Los Angeles and Orange County. Responsible for system generation, new-release upgrades, patching, and benchmarking for potential new customers. Also responsible tor improvements in operating procedures for many customers. Languages used include Assembler, BASIC, FORTRAN, and COBOL.

Because Anil has had longevity and growth with the same company, his work history is presented chronologically.

WORK HISTORY
Field Supervisor — Honeywell Federal Systems
Anaheim, CA
Managed and supervised all maintenance functions. Initiated preventive maintenance programs. Interfaced with customers concerning all installation, upgrades, and service. Responsible for nine technicians and a variable number of sites during this period. Acquired knowledge of MS-DOS, WordPerfect, and Lotus 1-2-3. (1981–present)

Figure 8.2 Sample résumé: block format, two pages, combination style

Senior Site Specialist — Honeywell Information Systems, Los Angeles, CA
Employed as a site specialist during development of a major operating system, troubleshooting, defining, and redefining problems in both hardware and software (CP5). (1979-1981)

Senior Software Specialist — Honeywell Information Systems, Los Angeles, CA
Responsible for seven large time-sharing sites in Los Angeles and Orange County area. (1976-1979)

Senior Field Engineer — Xerox Corporation, Los Angeles, CA
Worked as a local site engineer maintaining large systems in the Los Angeles area. As a diagnostician and senior field engineer, provided technical support for large systems throughout the United States. (1969–1976)

EDUCATION

Higher National Certificate in Electrical Engineering, Durham, England. (This is a five-year course administered jointly by the Institute of Electrical Engineers and the Council for National Academic Awards CNAA].)

OTHER TRAINING

"The Essentials of Management." Five-day AMA-sponsored course. (1989)

Software Specialist training. (1975 and a further course in 1977)

"The Principles of Management." Nine-day course sponsored by Xerox Corp. (1975)

Diagnostic training, including Assembler language, error logs, system software, and problem-solving methods. (1970)

Anil does not have a college degree in management, therefore, his industry-sponsored training is listed.

Figure 8.2 *(continued)*

Format:
Block–two page
Style:
Functional

Margarita G. Rodriguez
246 Carnation Drive
Costa Mesa, CA 92626
(714) 746-6016

OBJECTIVE: Entry-level marketing position in an advertising agency or graphic design firm

Margarita wants to change her work environment as well as her job title. She wants to transfer her public relations, supervisory, and administrative skills to a position in which she can better use them. For this reason, a functional résumé will best support her objective.

PUBLIC RELATIONS/COMMUNICATIONS

- Represented several lines of cosmetics; advised customers about skin treatment, choice of colors, and make-up techniques
- Represented musician/composer marketing musical services to advertising agencies and companies
- Currently a liaison between Associate Director and other hospital administrators, outside agencies, Fire Marshal, OSHA, and the Health Department

SUPERVISORY/TRAINING

- Eighteen years' experience giving private piano and flute lessons to adults and children; organized recitals; planned programs; developed lesson plans geared to individual students' interests, needs, and abilities
- Trained and supervised office workers in general office duties
- Counseled junior and senior high school students in residence at summer music clinics; organized free-time activities; supervised junior counselors

ADMINISTRATIVE

- Researched, compiled, and prepared data for director to use in proposals and reports; gathered information through telephone communication and reference materials
- Coordinated studio recording sessions, including contracting players; arranged meetings from start to finish; followed up on action items, acting as liaison between members and chair
- Experience as office manager; responsible for all office functions, including budget and projections, proofreading, editing, and composing; developed filing system for complex flow of information

Figure 8.3 Sample résumé: block format, two pages, functional style

The work history is placed on page 2, where it does not attract as much attention. Margarita cannot show direct experience in marketing; therefore, she must play up her transferable skills. Remember, your résumé should portray *your positive image.*

EDUCATION

Bachelor of Music, University of Wisconsin at Madison, 1975

WORK HISTORY

1979–present	South Coast Medical Center Environmental Health & Safety Office Administrative Assistant
1978–1979	ABC Musical Instruments Costa Mesa, CA Marketing Clerk
1977–1978	I. Magnin Department Store Santa Ana, CA Sales Clerk
1975–1976	Studio 9 Music Services Madison, Wisconsin Office Manager

ADDITIONAL WORK EXPERIENCE

1970–present	Professional flutist providing music for parties, weddings, business functions, and church services. Co-founder and member of Musette, a guitar and flute duo.
1967–1986	Private piano and flute instructor for children and adults.
1976–1977	Product advertising model.

References furnished upon request.

Figure 8.3 *(continued)*

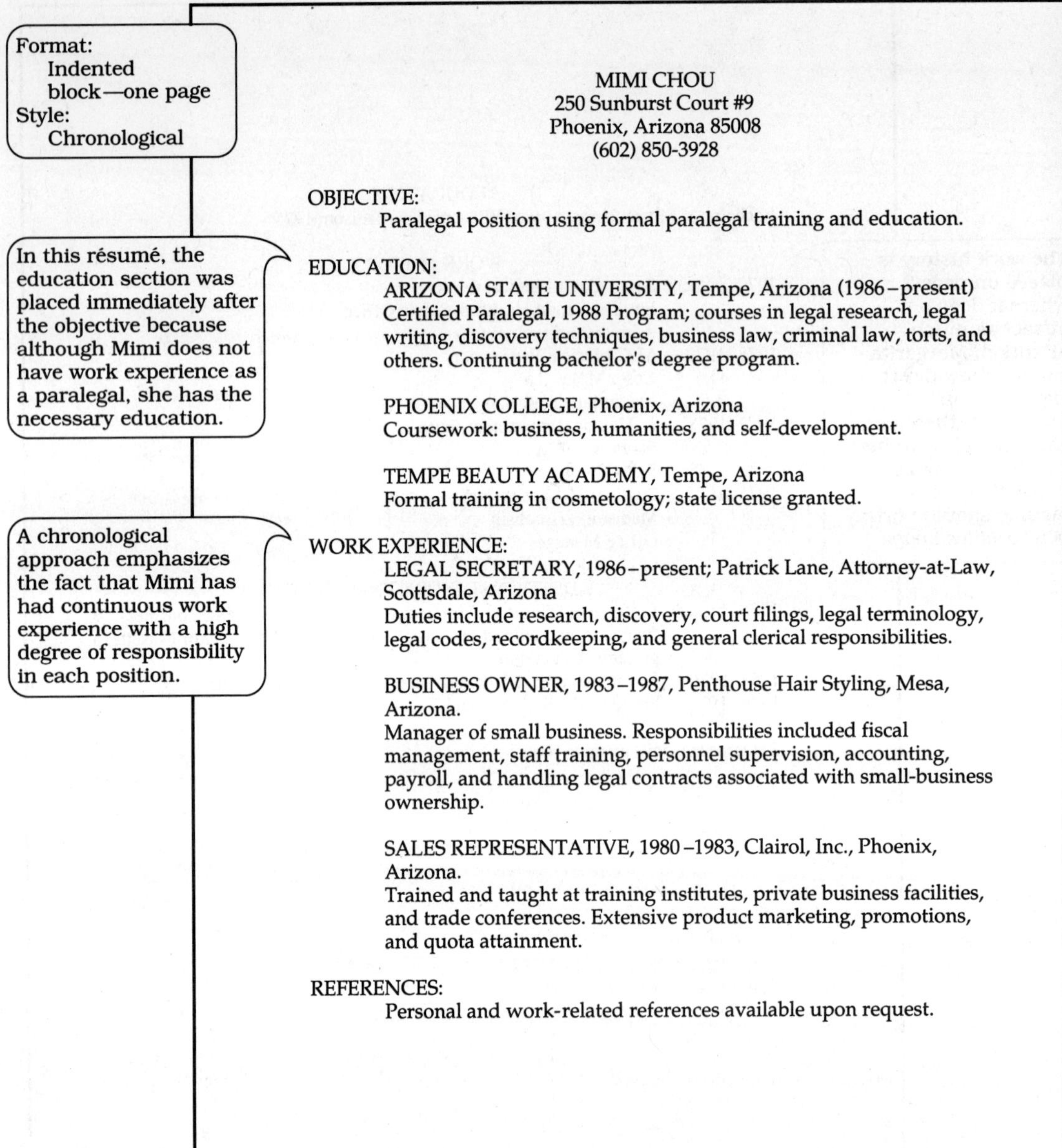

Figure 8.4 Sample résumé: indented block format, one page, chronological style

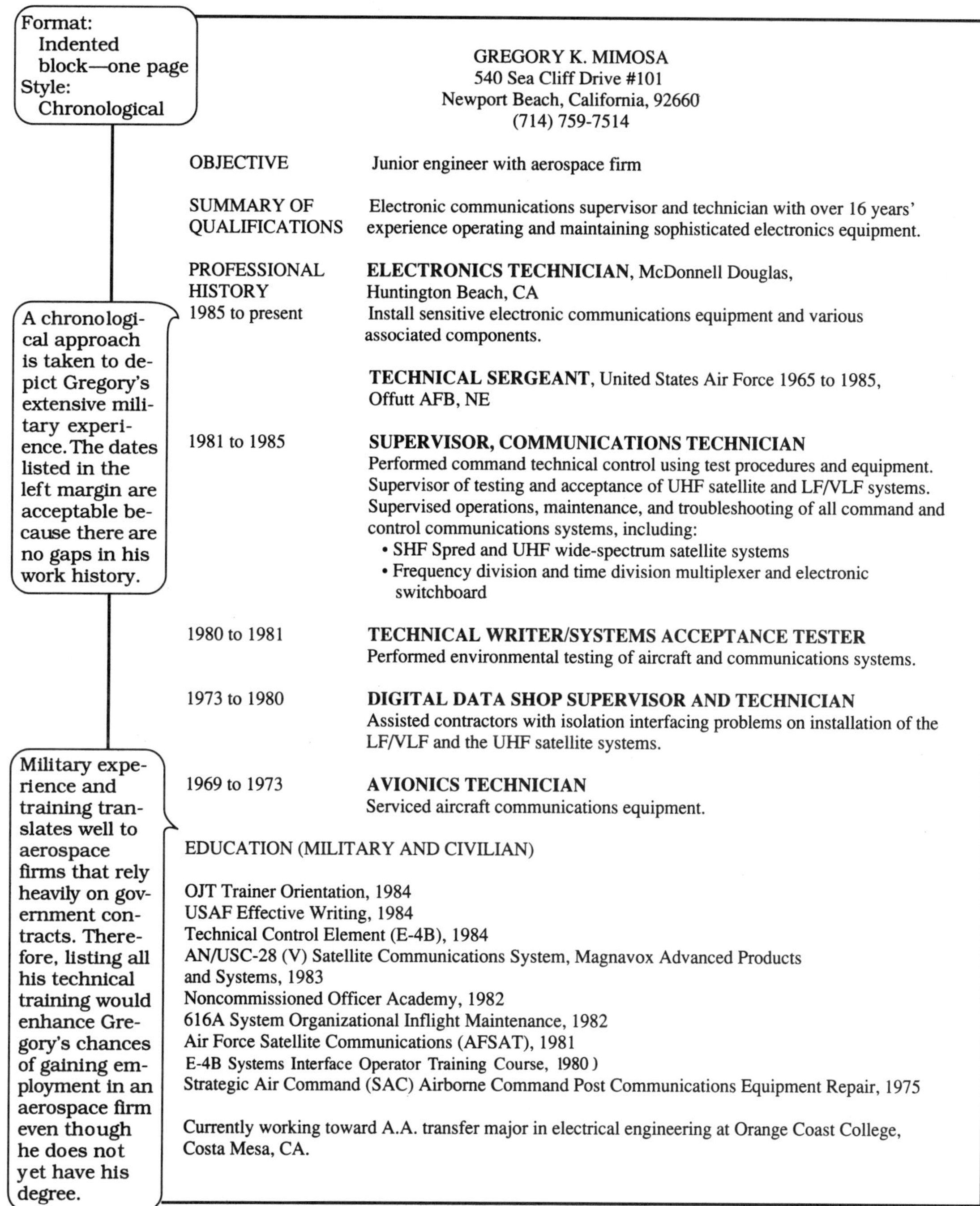

GREGORY K. MIMOSA
540 Sea Cliff Drive #101
Newport Beach, California, 92660
(714) 759-7514

OBJECTIVE — Junior engineer with aerospace firm

SUMMARY OF QUALIFICATIONS — Electronic communications supervisor and technician with over 16 years' experience operating and maintaining sophisticated electronics equipment.

PROFESSIONAL HISTORY

1985 to present — **ELECTRONICS TECHNICIAN**, McDonnell Douglas, Huntington Beach, CA
Install sensitive electronic communications equipment and various associated components.

TECHNICAL SERGEANT, United States Air Force 1965 to 1985, Offutt AFB, NE

1981 to 1985 — **SUPERVISOR, COMMUNICATIONS TECHNICIAN**
Performed command technical control using test procedures and equipment.
Supervisor of testing and acceptance of UHF satellite and LF/VLF systems.
Supervised operations, maintenance, and troubleshooting of all command and control communications systems, including:
- SHF Spred and UHF wide-spectrum satellite systems
- Frequency division and time division multiplexer and electronic switchboard

1980 to 1981 — **TECHNICAL WRITER/SYSTEMS ACCEPTANCE TESTER**
Performed environmental testing of aircraft and communications systems.

1973 to 1980 — **DIGITAL DATA SHOP SUPERVISOR AND TECHNICIAN**
Assisted contractors with isolation interfacing problems on installation of the LF/VLF and the UHF satellite systems.

1969 to 1973 — **AVIONICS TECHNICIAN**
Serviced aircraft communications equipment.

EDUCATION (MILITARY AND CIVILIAN)

OJT Trainer Orientation, 1984
USAF Effective Writing, 1984
Technical Control Element (E-4B), 1984
AN/USC-28 (V) Satellite Communications System, Magnavox Advanced Products and Systems, 1983
Noncommissioned Officer Academy, 1982
616A System Organizational Inflight Maintenance, 1982
Air Force Satellite Communications (AFSAT), 1981
E-4B Systems Interface Operator Training Course, 1980)
Strategic Air Command (SAC) Airborne Command Post Communications Equipment Repair, 1975

Currently working toward A.A. transfer major in electrical engineering at Orange Coast College, Costa Mesa, CA.

Figure 8.5 Sample résumé: indented block format, one page, chronological style

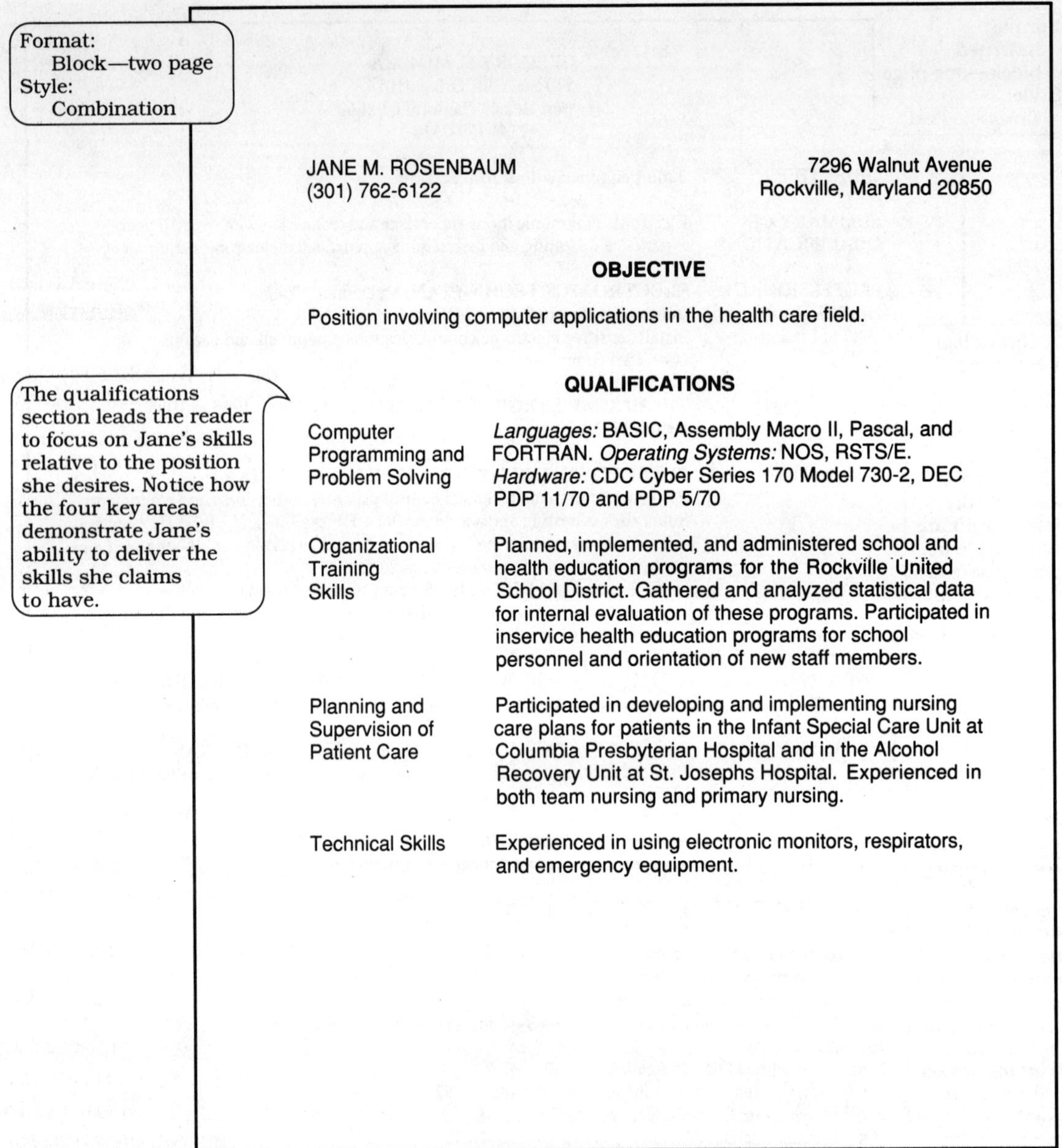

Format:
Block—two page
Style:
Combination

The qualifications section leads the reader to focus on Jane's skills relative to the position she desires. Notice how the four key areas demonstrate Jane's ability to deliver the skills she claims to have.

JANE M. ROSENBAUM
(301) 762-6122

7296 Walnut Avenue
Rockville, Maryland 20850

OBJECTIVE

Position involving computer applications in the health care field.

QUALIFICATIONS

Computer Programming and Problem Solving	*Languages:* BASIC, Assembly Macro II, Pascal, and FORTRAN. *Operating Systems:* NOS, RSTS/E. *Hardware:* CDC Cyber Series 170 Model 730-2, DEC PDP 11/70 and PDP 5/70
Organizational Training Skills	Planned, implemented, and administered school and health education programs for the Rockville United School District. Gathered and analyzed statistical data for internal evaluation of these programs. Participated in inservice health education programs for school personnel and orientation of new staff members.
Planning and Supervision of Patient Care	Participated in developing and implementing nursing care plans for patients in the Infant Special Care Unit at Columbia Presbyterian Hospital and in the Alcohol Recovery Unit at St. Josephs Hospital. Experienced in both team nursing and primary nursing.
Technical Skills	Experienced in using electronic monitors, respirators, and emergency equipment.

Figure 8.6 Sample résumé: block format, two pages, combination style

Jane's work history is somewhat abbreviated but still conveys longevity and stability on the job. This was done to deemphasize the fact that Jane is indeed changing careers.

WORK HISTORY

Registered Nurse 1981–present
St. Josephs Hospital, Rockville, MD
Plan, implement, and evaluate nursing care for patients in the Alcohol Recovery Unit.

School Nurse 1980–1981
Gaithersburg Public School District, Gaithersburg, MD
Served as health resource person for school administrator and staff. Performed state-mandated screening. Developed and implemented school health education programs.

Public Health Nurse 1978–1980
Montgomery County Health Department, Rockville, MD
Provided health education, counseling, and follow-up services for patients with communicable and childhood diseases.

Registered Nurse 1977–1978
Columbia Presbyterian Hospital, New York, NY
Performed nursing duties in the 24-bed Infant Special Care Unit. Shared responsibility of evening charge nurse.

Public Health Nurse 1974–1977
Maternity Infant Care, Family Planning Project, New York, NY
Coordinated services to high-risk prenatal patients and infants. Conducted prenatal, family planning, and infant care classes.

EDUCATION

University of Maryland, College Park, MD 1984–present
Completed nine units in computer science; working toward M.S. in computer science

Montgomery College, Rockville Campus, Rockville, MD 1983–present
A.A., computer science, 1987

Columbia University, New York, NY 1972–1974
B.S., nursing, 1974

Seminar, "Applications in Health Care," Montgomery College, April 1984

References available upon request.

Figure 8.6 *(continued)*

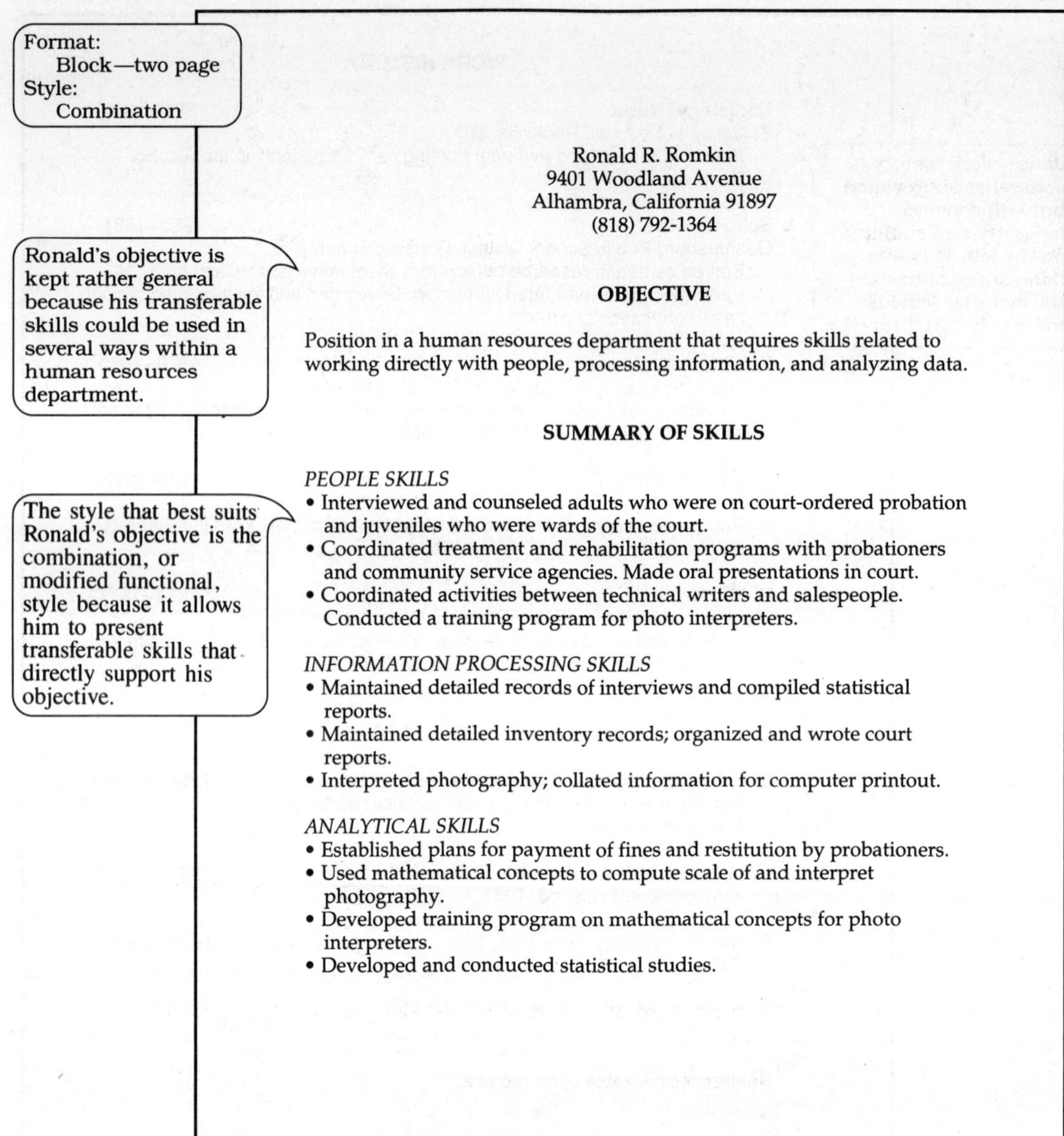

Format:
Block—two page
Style:
Combination

Ronald R. Romkin
9401 Woodland Avenue
Alhambra, California 91897
(818) 792-1364

Ronald's objective is kept rather general because his transferable skills could be used in several ways within a human resources department.

OBJECTIVE

Position in a human resources department that requires skills related to working directly with people, processing information, and analyzing data.

SUMMARY OF SKILLS

The style that best suits Ronald's objective is the combination, or modified functional, style because it allows him to present transferable skills that directly support his objective.

PEOPLE SKILLS

- Interviewed and counseled adults who were on court-ordered probation and juveniles who were wards of the court.
- Coordinated treatment and rehabilitation programs with probationers and community service agencies. Made oral presentations in court.
- Coordinated activities between technical writers and salespeople. Conducted a training program for photo interpreters.

INFORMATION PROCESSING SKILLS

- Maintained detailed records of interviews and compiled statistical reports.
- Maintained detailed inventory records; organized and wrote court reports.
- Interpreted photography; collated information for computer printout.

ANALYTICAL SKILLS

- Established plans for payment of fines and restitution by probationers.
- Used mathematical concepts to compute scale of and interpret photography.
- Developed training program on mathematical concepts for photo interpreters.
- Developed and conducted statistical studies.

Figure 8.7 Sample résumé: block format, two pages, combination style

The work history is placed on page 2, where it attracts less attention. The jobs Ronald held before his present one are not listed because they go back further than ten years and do not support his objective.

EMPLOYMENT HISTORY

Adult Probation Officer Los Angeles County Probation Department
Whittier, California

Supervised 200 to 500 probationers. Interviewed and counseled probationers and maintained detailed records of interviews. Made referrals to community service agencies and worked with other criminal justice agencies. Collected fines and restitution. Enforced court orders, organized and wrote court reports, and testified in court. (September 1978–present)

Juvenile Probation Officer Los Angeles County Probation Department
Downey, California

Supervised 30 to 60 juveniles in Juvenile Hall. (1973–1978)

EDUCATION

Pepperdine University, Los Angeles, California. Completed 12 graduate units in psychology.

Ohio State University, Columbus, Ohio. B.A. degree, sociology.

MILITARY EXPERIENCE

Photo-Radar Intelligence Officer United States Air Force
Beale AFB, California

Interpreted photography taken by reconnaissance aircraft. Read out photography and collated information for computer printout. Trained others concerning mathematical concepts and procedure for determining scale of photography.

Figure 8.7 *(continued)*

Format:
Block—one page
Style:
Functional

Notice how Carmen states her objective: she attracts the attention of potential employers by stating what she can do for them.

From her previous jobs, Carmen has extracted several accomplishments that demonstrate that she is qualified to work as an events planner. She cannot show direct experience in this field, so she must allude to skills that can be generalized from one context to another.

In this résumé, the work experience section is abbreviated and includes only job titles. The dates are listed first to show job stability.

CARMEN VALDEZ
2021 LARKSPUR LANE
HUNTINGTON BEACH, CALIFORNIA 92647
(714) 524-9907

OBJECTIVE

A position as an events planner in which my communication, people, and organizational skills would be an asset to an organization valuing its public relations and service.

SUMMARY OF SKILLS

- Created a plan according to a theme for a wide variety of special events (for example, holiday gatherings, retirement banquets, reunions, weddings, and special-occasion parties), with successful results.
- Planned and coordinated all details for luncheon conferences for 350 to 500 professionals in the community. Actively participated at the conference site.
- Organized in-house meetings and conferences with attention to detail, keeping needs and purpose in perspective.
- Facilitated a marketing and public relations campaign. Acted as a liaison for the department, marketing, and the advertising agency.
- Developed brochures and advertisements; researched, wrote, and initiated policies and methods of tracking responses and dealing with the public.
- Managed and monitored efficient administration and operation of facility and its events within set budgetary allowances.

EXPERIENCE

October 1986–present: Assistant Administrative Analyst
July 1984–October 1986: Administrative Assistant II
Department of Psychiatry, University of California, Irvine Medical Center, Orange, California.
October 1978–July 1984: Managing Cosmetologist, The Clip Joint, Huntington Beach, California

EDUCATION

Currently enrolled at Coastline Community College; working toward a transfer degree in public relations. Completed courses in sociology, gourmet catering, and college writing.

Figure 8.8 Sample résumé: block format, one page, functional style

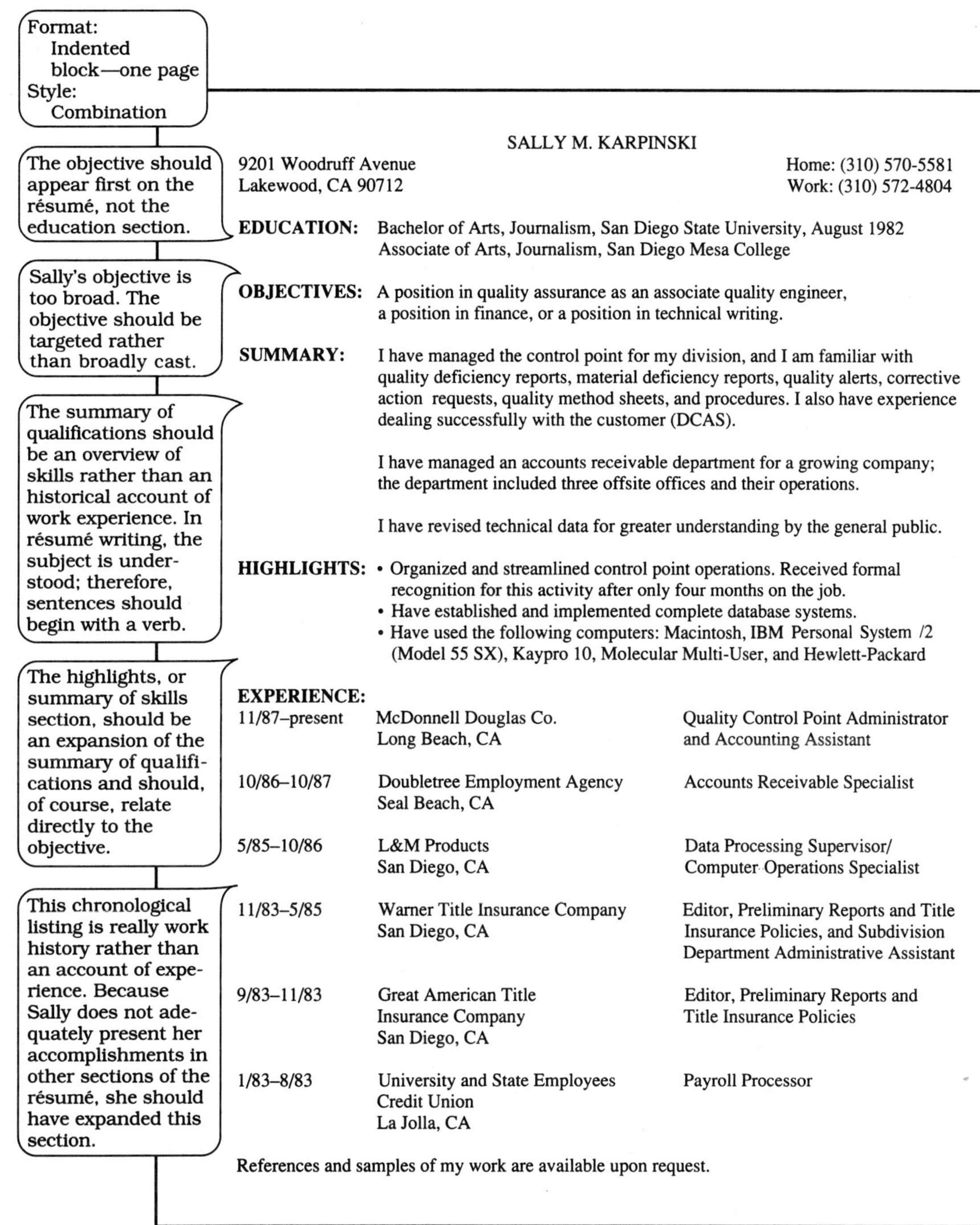

Figure 8.9 Sample résumé: indented block format, one page, combination style ("before" version)

Format:
Indented
block—two pages
Style:
Combination

The objective clearly states the position Sally is seeking.

The education section appears early in the résumé because Sally's work experience does not necessarily support her objective. In addition, the major courses are listed to give her further credibility.

The summary section is broad enough to encompass all of Sally's transferable skills. This is extremely important because she is moving from one career to another.

The highlights section includes excerpts drawn from Sally's work and college experiences that further enhance the objective.

SALLY M. KARPINSKI

9201 Woodruff Avenue
Lakewood, CA 90712

Home: (310) 570-5581
Work: (310) 572-4804

OBJECTIVES: Seeking the position of Public Relations Specialist/Practitioner

EDUCATION: Bachelor of Arts, Journalism, San Diego State University; Associate of Arts, Journalism, San Diego Mesa College

Major courses included: Public relations, advertising, broadcasting, psychology, news writing, layout and pasteup, magazine writing, and editing.

SUMMARY: Over five years of experience in the accounting field in positions requiring data management skills, people skills, and attention to detail. Streamlined operations in several positions by recommending and implementing improvements. Used creative ability to solve problems. Used writing skills in correspondence, public service, and persuasion.

HIGHLIGHTS:

- Held position of Assistant Feature Editor on Mesa College newspaper staff for one year. Also served on advertising staff for the same period.
- Researched and wrote three front-page stories for San Diego newspaper during college internship.
- Managed an accounts receivable department for a growing company; the department included three offsite offices and their operations.
- Organized quality department data and streamlined control point operations. Received formal recognition for improvements after only four months on the job.
- Managed the control point for the Quality Department of Division 1K at McDonnell Douglas Co. Controlled documentation regarding the quality of hardware and software produced by Division 1K.
- Operational knowledge of Macintosh, IBM Personal System /2 (Model 55 SX), Kaypro 10, Molecular Multi-User, and Hewlett-Packard computers.

Figure 8.10 Sample résumé: indented block format, two pages, combination style (revised version)

The work history has been expanded to include Sally's duties and accomplishments on the job. Moreover, it has been placed on the second page, where it will receive less attention. Remember, Sally is selling her transferable skills!

WORK HISTORY:

Quality Control Point Administrator and Accounting Assistant
McDonnell Douglas Company, Long Beach, CA
As quality control point: Track eight different types of documentation on Macintosh computer. Reorganize computer databases. Streamline control point operations and originate new ways to eliminate delinquencies. Interface with customer (government representatives). Generate customized reports upon request from management.
As accounting assistant: Resolve problems preventing invoices from being payable. Provide customer service to vendors. Work with buyers to correct errors. Process invoices for payment and audit checks for accuracy. (1987–present)

Accounts Receivable Specialist
Doubletree Employment Agency, Seal Beach and Huntington Beach, CA
Filled vacancies in the accounting departments of various companies while seeking permanent employment following relocation from San Diego. Used IBM PCs at most companies. (1986–1987)

Data Processing Supervisor/Computer Operations Specialist
L&M Products, San Diego, CA
Controlled and supervised all aspects of accounts receivable for the company and all its satellite operations. Created and maintained databases for offices in Texas and Arizona. Conducted troubleshooting and research of problems. Maintained information for five customer databases to provide company's status. Generated reports and assisted in analyzing information obtained. (1985–1986)

Editor, Preliminary Reports and Title Insurance Policies, and Subdivision Department Administrative Assistant
Warner Title Insurance Company, San Diego, CA
Prepared documents for recording with the County Recorder. Priced title charges for escrow. Arranged for transmittal of funds from bank in Texas. Composed supplementary reports to inform customers of changes in their title policies. Handled all aspects of time-shares. Conducted research regarding property and backgrounds of customers. (1985–1986)

Editor, Preliminary Reports and Title Insurance Policies
Great American Title Insurance Company, San Diego, CA
Checked preliminary title reports and title insurance policies for accuracy. Put together presentation packages for customers. (1983)

Payroll Processor
University and State Employees Credit Union, La Jolla, CA
Maintained computerized payroll accounts. Performed daily closing and balancing of administrative office bank account audit. (1983)

Figure 8.10 *(continued)*

The main concern in writing your résumé is to portray skills and talents adequately, not to compress or condense material for the sake of keeping the résumé to one page. However, research indicates that your résumé should not be more than two pages long because the reader's attention span rarely exceeds this limit.

When you have completed your first draft, have someone critique it. (See Exercise 8.5.) You may need to tailor your résumé to each position for which you apply. This task has been made easier with word processing. Simply store all the information on a disk, and make changes as necessary. Several quick-print stores, located throughout the country, can give you assistance in both formatting and printing your résumé. Many of these businesses also have computers available for customer use. Have your résumé printed on quality bond paper, and use matching stationery for your cover letter.

♦ Cover Letters

The cover letter, or letter of application, introduces you and asks for an interview. With very few exceptions, it should accompany a résumé. The cover letter creates attention and leads the reader to the résumé. Sometimes an employer will offer an interview on the basis of an outstanding cover letter. *Do not underestimate the importance of a good cover letter.*

Cover Letter Outline

Think of the cover letter as a sales letter. The opening paragraph should be designed to create *attention.* There are several such openings: summary, name, request, and question. All four of these openings appear in the sample cover letters in this chapter.

The middle paragraph (or paragraphs) should create *desire.* There are several ways of generating an employer's desire for an interview. You can mention education, work experience, ability to work with others, interest in your field, interest in the employer's company, and your responsibilities on previous work assignments. Choose your strongest traits, and expand on them in the middle paragraph. You may want to reemphasize certain points listed on the résumé or bring out additional facts not given there. It is easier to state your interest in the company or to give examples of your ability to work with others in this section of the letter than it is in the résumé.

The closing paragraph calls for *action.* It should "close the sale." After you have built up a desire, you must make it easy for the

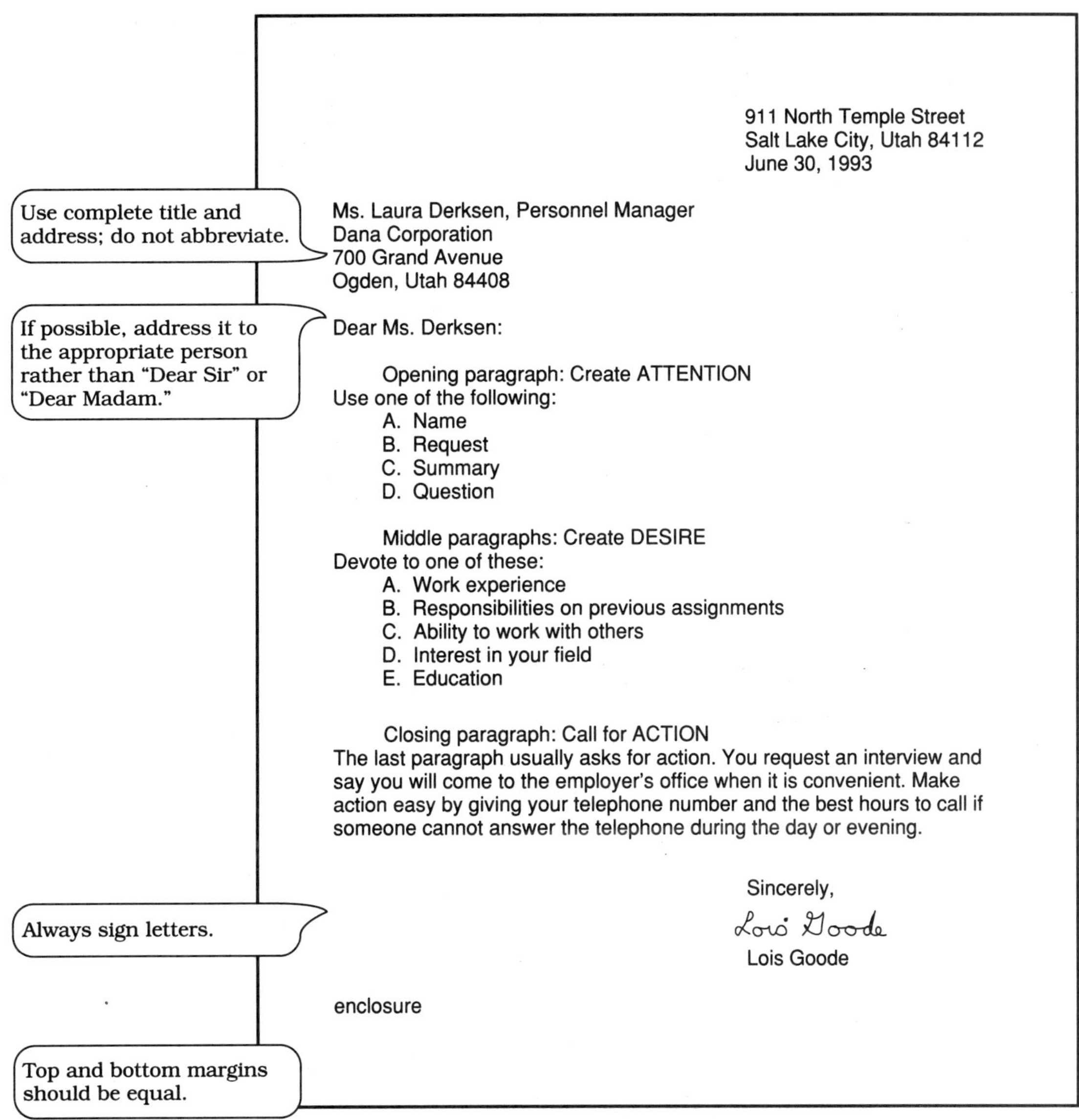

911 North Temple Street
Salt Lake City, Utah 84112
June 30, 1993

Ms. Laura Derksen, Personnel Manager
Dana Corporation
700 Grand Avenue
Ogden, Utah 84408

Dear Ms. Derksen:

Opening paragraph: Create ATTENTION
Use one of the following:
A. Name
B. Request
C. Summary
D. Question

Middle paragraphs: Create DESIRE
Devote to one of these:
A. Work experience
B. Responsibilities on previous assignments
C. Ability to work with others
D. Interest in your field
E. Education

Closing paragraph: Call for ACTION
The last paragraph usually asks for action. You request an interview and say you will come to the employer's office when it is convenient. Make action easy by giving your telephone number and the best hours to call if someone cannot answer the telephone during the day or evening.

Sincerely,

Lois Goode

Lois Goode

enclosure

Figure 8.11 Outline of cover letter. *Source: Adapted from* Resume Writing Made Easy (4th Ed.), *by L. Coxford. Copyright 1991. Reprinted by permission from Gorsuch Scarisbrick.*

employer to buy. You also need to clearly state when you will be available to talk to the employer. Be specific; give telephone numbers where you can be reached both at work and off work. You may have a tremendous background and sell yourself very well, but if the employer cannot reach you, everything could be lost! (See the cover letter outline in Figure 8.11.)

525 Sturgeon Drive
St. Helena, CA 95392
December 1, 1993

Stuart Head
Employment Manager
Embassy Suites Hotel
200 North State Street
Napa, CA 95390

Dear Mr. Head:

I am interested in the position of banquet coordinator and salesperson for the Embassy Suites Hotel. I am currently employed in a similar position at the Ritz Hotel in St. Helena, California, and am interested in furthering my career in marketing and business administration. In support of my goal, I am currently enrolled at Napa Valley College.

I have a great deal of experience in organizing and planning social events, banquets, receptions, and wedding parties. I possess strong leadership qualities and the ability to motivate and supervise people. Additionally, I have had several years of successful sales experience and enjoy interacting with the public.

I have enclosed my résumé for your information. I would be very pleased to be associated with the hotel and would like to meet with you personally. Please do not hesitate to contact me at (209) 537-1008. Thank you for your consideration.

Sincerely yours,

Megan Laramore

Megan Laramore

enclosure: résumé

Figure 8.12 Sample cover letter with a summary opening

Sample Cover Letters

Figures 8.12 through 8.15 are sample cover letters, each with a different type of opening. Determine which of these letters might work best for you in your own particular situation. Figure 8.16 is a sample letter written in response to a newspaper ad. If you cannot resist the temptation to respond to want ads, use this letter as your guide.

8777 Newell Place
Thousand Oaks, CA 90081
March 31, 1993

Dr. Anne R. Schmidt
District Superintendent
Thousand Oaks School District
2008 San Jose Avenue
Thousand Oaks, CA 90081

Dear Dr. Schmidt:

I am interested in the position of instructional aide to the Speech and Language Handicapped classroom of Dickerson Elementary School. Jack Carson, currently on your staff as a speech and language pathologist, suggested I write you. I feel my education, skills, and desire to work in this area make me a strong candidate for this position.

As you can see by the enclosed résumé, my previous education has given me a considerable understanding of the difficulties of SLH children, their specific needs, and the detailed remediation processes used to help them. I feel my knowledge, management training, and experience with both the public and SLH children can be an asset to the pathologist and the pupils.

I will telephone your secretary next week to see when we might set up an appointment to further discuss the instructional aide position and any other ways I could serve the school district.

Sincerely,

Marilyn M. Wilson

Marilyn M. Wilson

enclosure: résumé

Figure 8.13 Sample cover letter with a name opening

8207 Colima Road, #5
Whittier, CA 90605
April 13, 1993

Mr. Robert Weidner
Human Resources Manager
AT&T Corporation
3469 Browning Avenue
City of Commerce, CA 90040

Dear Mr. Weidner:

I have been following the development of the Human Resource Center at Browning Avenue in the City of Commerce and feel it is a perfect way to assist AT&T in becoming a leader in the communication field of today. I view your center as producing better ways to motivate employees to produce inner satisfaction within their selected fields while providing increased profitability for AT&T.

I would like to be considered for the position of trainer within your Human Resource Division. My customer interfacing skills and administrative experience at AT&T will be an asset to you in increasing your productivity through human resource training.

I have enclosed my résumé and would enjoy meeting with you to discuss how I can help your organization.

Sincerely,

Shana Donahue

Shana Donahue

enclosure: résumé

Figure 8.14 Sample cover letter with a request opening

1715 North Rosemead Blvd., #208
Rosemead, CA 91207
May 11, 1993

Mr. Arthur M. Moore
Volunteer Coordinator
Altadena Recreation and Community Services
200 South Rosemead Boulevard, Suite 344
Altadena, CA 91208

Dear Mr. Moore:

Can you use someone with a strong background in the life sciences and an absolute passion for the outdoors, and who enjoys sharing them with others?

These are the qualifications you are seeking in a naturalist, as published in your internship listing. I believe my experience and education make me the person you are looking for to fulfill your needs.

My lifelong career goal is to work in a park that is nature-oriented.

As you can see from the enclosed resume, my varied experience, along with my interest and education in ecology and the natural sciences, make me confident that I can meet the demands of a naturalist internship.

If my qualifications meet your needs, Mr. Moore, may I discuss with you the possibility of working at the Walnut Creek Nature Center?

Sincerely,

Lewis T. Janowsky

Lewis T. Janowsky

enclosure

Figure 8.15 Sample cover letter with a question opening

PURCHASING MANAGER

Leading wholesale grocery distributor has immediate employment opportunity for general merchandise purchasing manager with minimum six years related work experience including minimum three years supervisory experience. Applicants must have demonstrated knowledge of health and beauty care and general merchandise items, vendors, and demonstrated knowledge of pricing and merchandising techniques. Demonstrated ability to plan, initiate and control activities and knowledge of industry facilities/personnel is required. Good salary, outstanding company benefits. Apply in person 8am to 3pm M-F or send detailed resume including salary history in confidence to:

700 Pacific Coast Highway, #102
Huntington Beach, CA 92648
September 14, 1993

Post Office Box 808
Los Angeles Times
Los Angeles, CA 90041

Ladies/Gentlemen:

This is in response to your advertisement for a purchasing manager, which appeared in the *Los Angeles Times* on Sunday, September 13. As the following comparison shows, my experience and background match the requirements for this position.

Your Requirements	My Qualifications
Six years' purchasing experience	Eight years' experience as a buyer
Supervisory experience	Supervised a staff of 20 people
Knowledge of health and beauty care products	Owner of a beauty salon for ten years
Knowledge of merchandising techniques	Demonstrated ability to price and merchandise beauty care products

I am very interested in this position because it fits my qualifications perfectly! As additional information, I have enclosed a copy of my résumé, which further details my experience and training.

I would like to discuss the position with you at your earliest possible convenience. I can be reached at (714) 594-2800.

Sincerely,

Danielle Keller

Danielle Keller

enclosure

Figure 8.16 Sample letter responding to an advertisement

♦ Summary

This is the first of the two chapters on marketing. You must first use a résumé to attract a prospective employer's attention. This chapter included several sample résumés and cover letters. Use these samples and the following written exercises to help you present yourself in the best possible light.

♦ EXERCISE 8.1 Résumé Worksheet: Work History

Complete the following worksheet before you begin the first draft of your résumé. There is room to describe three work positions and three educational programs. Use separate sheets of paper if necessary to describe additional experiences.

Work Experience (full- and part-time)

Job title: ______________________________

Company, agency, or institution: ______________________________

Type of business (if not clear from company name): ______________________________

____

Division or department: ______________________________

Location: ______________________________

Dates of employment: ______________________________
From To

Major responsibilities: ______________________________

____

____

____

____

____

____

____

Major accomplishments: ______________________________

____

____

____

____

____

____

____

Number of persons supervised: ______________________________

Work Experience (full- and part-time)

Job title: ______________________________

Company, agency, or institution: ______________________

Type of business (if not clear from company name): __________

____

Division or department: ________________________

Location: ______________________________

Dates of employment: ________________________
From To

Major responsibilities: ________________________

____

____

____

____

____

____

____

Major accomplishments: ________________________

____

____

____

____

____

____

____

Number of persons supervised: ____________________

Work Experience (full- and part-time)

Job title: ______________________________

Company, agency, or institution: ______________________

Type of business (if not clear from company name): __________

____

Division or department: ______________________________

Location: ______________________________

Dates of employment: ______________________________
From To

Major responsibilities: ______________________________

____

____

____

____

____

____

____

Major accomplishments: ______________________________

____

____

____

____

____

____

____

Number of persons supervised: ______________________________

Other Work Experience (volunteer work, community service)

____

____

____

____

____

____

____

____

____

Education (List all degree and certificate programs, company-sponsored seminars, and other special training or licenses.)

Degree or certificate: ______________________________

Major or special emphasis: ______________________________

____

Name of college, university, or training institution: ____________

____

Dates of education or training: ______________________________
From To

Courses relevant to career objective: ______________________________

____

____

____

____

Special licenses or certificates: ______________________________

____

____

Education (List all degree and certificate programs, company-sponsored seminars, and other special training or licenses.)

Degree or certificate: ______________________________

Major or special emphasis: ______________________________

____

Name of college, university, or training institution: ____________

____

Dates of education or training: ______________________________
From To

Courses relevant to career objective: ______________________________

____

____

____

____

Special licenses or certificates: ______________________________

____

____

Education (List all degree and certificate programs, company-sponsored seminars, and other special training or licenses.)

Degree or certificate: ______________________________________

Major or special emphasis: __________________________________

____

Name of college, university, or training institution: __________

____

Dates of education or training: ______________________________
From To

Courses relevant to career objective: _________________________

____

____

____

____

Special licenses or certificates: ______________________________

____

____

Special Recognition (List any special awards or professional recognition you may have received.)

____

____

____

____

Special Skills (For example, list your ability to speak a foreign language or your knowledge of computer software.)

____

____

____

♦ EXERCISE 8.2 Résumé Worksheet: Taking Inventory of Your Past

The following worksheet will help you take stock of your past achievements. Complete one for each job you have held.

Name of Company: ______________________________

Title of Position: ______________________________

Length of Employment: ______________________________

1. Describe in detail what you did on this job during an average day, week, and month. Include specific responsibilities, number of persons supervised, budgets controlled, programs managed, and sales generated.

____

____

____

____

____

____

____

____

____

____

2. Describe the skills, abilities, and talents you demonstrated in carrying out your duties. For example, list your ability to solve problems, achieve goals, introduce innovative techniques, or reduce costs; leadership qualities, such as planning, staffing, organizing, and controlling; and human relations skills.

____

____

____

____

____

____

____

♦ EXERCISE 8.3 Résumé Worksheet: Transferring Your Skills to the Job Objective

Analyze your entries in Exercises 8.1 and 8.2. Then transfer your skills to your job objective.

1. Describe your job objective. (Keep it general, and refine it as you progress).

   ____

   ____

   ____

   ____

   Write your job objective by filling in the blanks:

   A ______________ position in which skills in ______________ ,

   ______________ , and ______________ would be an asset in an

   organization valuing ____________________________ .

2. Write your summary of qualifications. (This is perhaps the most important *and* the most difficult portion of the résumé to write. Write as much as you can, then edit it later.)

   ____

   ____

   ____

   ____

   ____

   ____

3. Identify the skills you used in previous jobs that you can apply to your current job objective. Relate this as closely as you can to a particular job description or to what you think an employer would look for.

   ____

   ____

   ____

   ____

   ____

   ____

4. Select at least four skills that you used extensively. Expand on each skill, and describe how you used it. Think in terms of what you accomplished. (It is easier if you begin with an active verb. See the list of action verbs on page 170.)

   a. ______________________________

   ____

   ____

   b. ______________________________

   ____

   ____

   c. ______________________________

   ____

   ____

   d. ______________________________

   ____

   ____

♦ EXERCISE 8.4 Résumé Critique Form

Use the following résumé critique form to evaluate your résumé.

	Excellent	*Good*	*Average*	*Poor*
1. Appearance. Does the résumé *invite* someone to read it?				
2. Format. Are the key points attractively placed on the page?				
3. Actuals. Does the résumé state what you have actually done?				
4. Trends. Does it imply you are keeping up with trends (for example, recent education, computer knowledge)?				
5. Plan. Does it show initiative? 6. Grasp. Does it demonstrate that you have a grasp of your field?				
7. Positive Image. Does it accentuate the positive and eliminate the negative?				
8. Positive Contribution. Does it show how you made positive contributions in previous jobs?				

(continued)

	Excellent	*Good*	*Average*	*Poor*
9. Positive Appeal. Do you "toot your own horn"?				
10. Competitive. Will the résumé make you stand out from other job-seekers?				

♦ EXERCISE 8.5 Résumé Critique

Have someone critique your résumé. The reviewer can be a career counselor, a teacher, a friend, or someone who has seemed receptive during informational interviews.

♦ Notes

COXFORD, L. M. (1991). *Résumé writing made easy.* (4th ed.). Scottsdale, AZ: Gorsuch Scarisbrick.

HALF, R. (1981, May). How to write (or read) a resume. *The Practical Accountant,* pp. 63–67.

9 Marketing Yourself: Interviewing

"We are still responding to the old challenges—not the new ones."

—Toynbee

You are now beginning the final phase of the Steps to Success Model. So far, you have made decisions about why you want to change careers and how much of a change you actually want to make. You have taken inventory of your skills and determined what is most important to you in your next career. You then explored your options and developed an action plan. You have also written a résumé that effectively markets your experience, training, and skills. Now it is time to prepare for that face-to-face encounter known as the interview.

After reading this chapter you should understand the following:

- That a typical interview format has four phases
- How to respond to difficult questions
- How to prepare for your interview in advance

You should be able to do the following:

- Provide your own answers to at least 20 of the most commonly asked interview questions
- Sell your skills, experience, and special accomplishments
- Follow up after the interview with an appropriate letter

♦ Interviewing with Confidence

An employment interview is a meeting between two interested parties—a buyer and a seller—to explore what each has to offer the other. You are asked to an interview because someone in the company feels you are qualified for a specific job and wants to know more about you. It is up to you to convince the interviewer that you are the best candidate for the job. You may have to go through several interviews at one company, just as a salesperson may have to make several calls to one prospective buyer.

It is important that you keep your self-esteem high. Each interview will bring you closer to the employment situation that is right for you. As with many skills, interviewing techniques are improved with practice. What you can do is to make sure you arrive at an interview adequately prepared.

Typical Interview Format

Phase 1: The Opening. The first thing to remember is the portance of a *warm, personal greeting.* The interviewer usually extends his or her hand first. The next few minutes are usually devoted to establishing rapport and opening lines of communication. This opening time sometimes takes the form of "chitchat." Even though you may wish to get down to basics right away, view this time as a relaxation period for both of you. The opening phase usually sets the tone of the interview and is directed by the company representative—that is, the interviewer. The interviewer will inform you of the purpose and scope of the interview. As you begin the interview, remember to smile, be genuine, and act friendly. There is no substitute for a good first impression.

Phase 2: The Information Exchange. The interviewer will move from the casual opening exchange to a more specific level of conversation. The interviewer will ask you some direct questions about your background and qualifications. Sometimes you will have to respond to an open-ended question or request, such as "Tell me about yourself." This part of the interview gives you a chance to answer "where," "why," and "when" questions about your background. Now is the time to describe volunteer activities or work experience that may not appear on your résumé. For example, you can state that as a volunteer you organized dinner and entertainment arrangements for 500 people.

View this phase as a chance to elaborate upon your strong points and to maximize what you have to offer. However, be careful not to monopolize the conversation. During this time, the interviewer will usually present some information about the organization. Here is your chance to ask questions, such as "What type of orientation and training may be part of the job?" and "What are some of the career paths within the company?" Be sure to listen attentively and not interrupt the interviewer.

Phase 3: Discussion of Company Openings. Phase 3 begins when the interviewer believes that your skills and interests have been identified and that he or she can see how you might fit into the organization. At this time, you might want to clarify your job objective and ask specific questions about the job and the organization. This is the phase in which the interviewee can become more involved in the process and become more assertive. You must gain more information by asking direct questions about the specific position, thus determining whether it meets your desires. You should ask questions regarding the responsibilities connected with the position, why the job is open, where the person is who had the job before, how many people you would supervise, and the size of the budget you would manage.

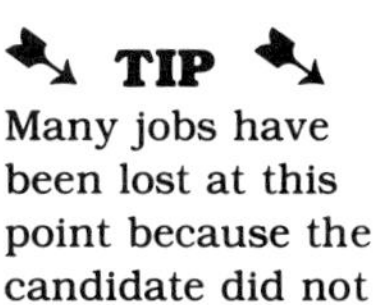

TIP

Many jobs have been lost at this point because the candidate did not appear enthusiastic enough.

The interviewer's description of company operations and activities may help you recall some questions you had in mind. Do not ask questions about salary at this point. Instead, let the interviewer bring up the subject of money and fringe benefits—perhaps they are to be covered in a later interview. Never ask about salary in an initial interview!

Phase 4: Summing Up. This phase allows both of you to clarify any information if necessary and to make some final comments. If the interviewer is interested in you, he or she will probably become more specific about the job. However, if the interviewer does not start to become more specific, it is time for summing up. Ask about the next step: Will there be another interview? When? How soon can you expect to hear from the interviewer? If your first interview was with a company recruiter, you may not receive much feedback regarding your chances at this point. However, if you are highly intuitive, you may be able to tell how good your chances are of going on and having further interviews.

After the interview, say "thank you," shake hands, and leave. If the interviewer requests credentials, samples, transcripts, and so on, be sure to provide them as soon as possible. Finally, it is much better to be rejected for a job than to take one that is wrong and that you want to leave two months later. Most people leave their jobs because of personality clashes resulting from mismatched personalities or conditions rather than because of issues concerning money, position, or title.

Preparing for the Interview

Clear thinking is the hallmark of the prepared employee. You can significantly improve your chances of thinking clearly in the interview if you have already thought through answers to questions that almost always come up during an interview. Take the time to study the following questions. Then write down your answers to them and rehearse them out loud. You can save yourself a tense moment at an important interview by calmly and clearly preparing answers to difficult questions beforehand.

SELF-ASSESSMENT

How would you describe yourself?

How do you think a friend or past working associate who knows you well would describe you?

How would a former or present supervisor describe you?

What are your outstanding qualities?

What do you see as your personal shortcomings or weaknesses?

What kinds of situations make you tense or nervous?

What has contributed to your past career successes?

What qualities do you most admire in an immediate supervisor?

What motivates you to bring forth your greatest effort?

WORK EXPERIENCE

What were your most significant accomplishments during the past year?

What skills or capabilities have you developed over the past year?

Which of your past jobs did you enjoy the most? Why?

How have your past jobs prepared you for this position?

When you consider joining an organization, what factors do you take into account?

Why did you leave your past jobs?

In what kind of work environment would you be most comfortable?

What have you learned from your past mistakes?

KNOWLEDGE OF THE JOB

In what area of our company do you think you can make the biggest contribution?

What changes and developments do you anticipate in your field?

Why do you think you would like to work for this company?

What do you see as an advantage to working at our company?
Why should we hire you?
What would you do if . . . ? (imagine situations that test a person's knowledge of the job)

EDUCATIONAL BACKGROUND

What made you decide to attend your college or university?
What determined your choice of major?
Have you had any other schooling or training since college graduation?
Describe your greatest success in college.
How do you think college and other training has contributed to your success?
Do you have plans for continued study? For an advanced degree?

CAREER GOALS

What do you see yourself doing five years from now?
What are your long-range career objectives?
What are the most important rewards you expect in your career?
How would you describe the ideal job?
How would you define success?

MISCELLANEOUS

Do you have any geographical preferences?
Are you willing to travel?
What are your recreational and leisure-time activities?
How do you feel about being relocated?
Do you have recommendations from previous employers?
Is there anything else you would like to tell me about yourself?
Do you have any questions to ask?
When can you begin work?

TIP

For both men and women, navy blue and medium to charcoal gray are considered the best suit colors because they convey an impression of authority. As a rule of thumb, the darker the shade, the more authority the wearer seems to have. However, black clothing can threaten the interviewer by conveying too much authority.

Dressing for the Interview

1. Look professional. First impressions are important because they become lasting impressions. Dress neatly and conservatively—avoid current fads.
2. Always dress one level up from your position. For example, if you are a secretary, dress like an office manager. If you are an office manager, dress like a director; if you are a director, dress like a vice president.
3. Men should wear conservative business suits (navy blue or gray), striped or solid-color ties in subdued colors, white or light blue

shirts, black shoes, over-the-calf black or navy blue socks, and no flashy jewelry. Hair should be neatly groomed; clean shaven is best.

4. Women should wear navy blue or gray tailored suits or conservative dresses with a jacket and dark pumps (no slingbacks, sandals, or boots). Wear sheer pantyhose (no colors or decorations) and carry a briefcase, portfolio, or purse/briefcase combined. Avoid a lot of jewelry; do not wear clunky bracelets or dangling earrings. Hair should be worn away from the face; and if your hair is shoulder length or longer, you should wear it up in a chignon or some similar fashion for a more professional appearance.

♦ Answering Difficult Questions

To some interviewees, all interviews create stress. Most people feel a little uncomfortable being judged and evaluated. It is quite common, for example, for an interviewee to experience sweaty palms, dry mouth, or increased respiration rate. However, stress interviews involve more than these common anxieties. In a stress interview, the interviewer's primary goal is to unnerve you, to challenge you, and to place you in a position where you have to think on your feet.

Sometimes potential employers ask questions that are designed to put you on the defensive. There are certain positions that require the employee to handle interpersonal stress and challenge, and for these reasons certain stress interview techniques are used. Most interviewers will try to bring out an applicant's best qualities, but you must be ready to put your best foot forward when stress questions are introduced.

By nature, interviewers have a certain amount of skepticism regarding job candidates. Many interviewers have made poor hiring decisions before; therefore, they want to know why they should *not* hire you. Although interviewers do not necessarily ask these questions, they think about them nonetheless.

- Will I have any problems with you?
- What are your weaknesses?
- What is it that you really want?
- Why should I hire you?
- Do you really want this job?

These specific objections may underlie the preceding questions:

- You are probably just going to use this job as a stepping stone.
- What can you really do?

- You might be after my job in six months.
- Are you just after a secure job with good benefits?
- What are your *real* weaknesses? How can I bring them out in the open?

Questions and Answers

Now let us consider some questions that could be considered tricky or "double-edged." Look at these questions for what they are, and learn to answer them properly. Do not become defensive. You are being asked these questions because the job you are interviewing for is a stressful one. Can you handle it? You need to prove this to the interviewer.

1. *Why should we hire you? We feel that (teaching/counseling/social work) experience is not the most useful for our business.* Point out the similarities between teaching and training. Show how your experience can be of great value to the employer even if it is from a different field. This is particularly important if you are moving from a nonprofit organization to a profit-making company. You must speak the jargon of the industry interviewing you. If you have a background in education, but are applying for a position in industry, avoid "educationese" and use terms such as training, motivation, incentives, and increased efficiency.

One positive way to respond to this probing question is to clearly communicate your understanding of the objection and then show that you have resolved this issue in a positive way. For example:

> I can understand your hesitation in hiring someone with a teaching background. I also understand that some people cannot make the transition smoothly. However, I do not believe I have that problem because I have researched your company as well as others. I know that being a trainer with your company is exactly what I want to do. I'm very concerned with getting results and increasing efficiency. I'm also experienced in working with people and have no difficulty working on my own.

2. *Don't you think you are overqualified for this position?* This is a chance to really sell yourself. Show your real enthusiasm for the position; emphasize that your so-called overqualification would be an asset to the organization. In other words, play up what you can do for the employer.

3. *Why did you leave your last job? (or: Why are you planning to leave your job?)* You can be sure the interviewer will ask you this question. If you were laid off, simply state that when the

company decided to downsize, a number of people were let go, and you were one of them. For example, you could say, "My position was abolished for budgetary reasons. However, I consider this an opportunity to use my skills in a different organization, such as yours. As a matter of fact, you will benefit from my ten years' experience."

If you are still employed, you might explain that upward mobility is limited and that there is no way for you to advance within the company. Another approach might be to explain that you like to work hard and your present job is not challenging enough or that you feel your company is not using all your talents. For example, you may have completed management training and would like an opportunity to use your managerial skills. You could say something like, "My current position does not allow me to use all my talent. I have just completed a certificate program in business management, and I am eager to put some of my ideas into practice for you."

If you are currently unemployed (in other words, between opportunities), be prepared to discuss it. A good response would be to say that you feel that looking for a job *is* a full-time job and you decided to devote adequate time and energy to attaining that goal; or you could say that you decided to go back to school. (Incidentally, it is much easier to find another job when you are currently employed.)

If you were fired (assuming that it was not for insubordination, nonperformance, or theft), be prepared to discuss it. Most people are fired because of a personality clash with a supervisor, a change in management, or corporate politics. Being fired is more common than you think. Employers know this. The best way to handle this situation is to be *totally honest*. Do not become defensive or speak negatively of your former employer—difficult as it may be. If possible, try to make light of your firing. For example, you might say, "They brought in a new manager who decided to bring in new people," or "My manager suspected I was looking for a new position and asked me to resign."

4. *What do you know about our company?* Here is where your research comes into play. You should have researched the company with reference to its size, income, profits, reputation, products or services, and company structure. (See Chapter Six for sources of information.)

5. *What are some of your weaknesses?* This is tricky! The thing to do here is to answer a negative with a positive. The following answers are all acceptable:

- I tend to be a perfectionist. However, I seem to be hardest on myself.

- I can be impatient at times. That is to say, I am very results-oriented.
- I am not very tolerant of laziness. By that, I mean I value competency on the job.
- I feel that perhaps I am too critical of myself. I try to be too perfect.

Saying "none" or avoiding this question is not recommended.

6. *What are your salary expectations?* This is one of those "Catch-22" questions. The best way to handle it is to simply state that you know what the salary range is for the type of position for which you are applying. (This means you have done your homework.) When the question arises, your first step should be to summarize the responsibilities of the job as you see them. By doing so, you are clarifying the following two points; (1) what the job actually involves, and (2) the skill level or level of responsibility required to do this job. This will help support the salary level that you are seeking. Here is one way you might say this: "As I understand this job, I would report directly to the dean of the school of business and would be in charge of drafting reports and correspondence, scheduling meetings and appointments, and managing a clerical support staff of four."

Such a summary statement clearly establishes for both you and the interviewer that (1) the person in this position reports to upper management, (2) he or she is responsible for making decisions involving scheduling, and (3) he or she will supervise four other employees. Now your conversation could continue like this:

> The salary surveys I have seen indicate that the salary range for the position of Administrative Assistant in a state university setting in this location is between $24,500 and $34,500. I have extensive experience in upper-level management, so I would not need a great deal of orientation for the job. I am sure I could be up and running in this job within a week or two. Taking this into consideration, I believe that a salary nearer the high end of the range would be fair compensation.

Never state a specific dollar amount; you may be selling yourself short.

7. *How do you (or your family) feel about relocating? Do you anticipate having to move again?* If you are the relocating spouse, you must emphasize that although you regretted having to leave your former job, you are always open to new challenges. Familiarity with statistics on local employee turnover may enable you to make a better case for your possibly abbreviated stay. You might say something like this: "You are concerned that I will not be able to o fulfill the requirements of the job. I can understand that. I plan

to fulfill my duties to the very best of my abilities, and I look forward to staying as long as possible."

If you are asked how you might feel about being transferred, be prepared to say that you have thought about it; you have discussed the possibilities with your family, and they are willing and supportive. If you do not wish to relocate, say so. Remember, this could be an "eliminating" question. You might not actually have to move, even if you are willing to do so. Therefore, you would be better off thinking through your priorities. Would you relocate for a better position with a higher salary?

8. *What are some of your strong points?* Here is your chance to shine. Have three or four points "at the tip of your tongue." Relate them to the company and the position you are applying for. For example:

- You are good at motivating others.
- You are a team player.
- You are good at getting others to see your point of view.
- You are well organized and can handle several projects at one time.

9. *What did you like least about your previous (present) job?* Again, never speak negatively of your former employer. Interviewers ask this question to see how you will react. Therefore, speak in general terms and steer the conversation toward your own work ethic and how you are capable of hard work. Convey the message that your previous employer did not fully use all your skills and talents.

If you are looking for a position similar to that of the interviewer (for example, personnel interviewer), you will want to avoid giving the impression that you are out to get the interviewer's position. In other words, do not say, "I would like to have your job."

10. *Where do you see yourself in five years? Ten years?* This can also be a trick question. It is best not to be too specific because it is difficult to know all the job titles within a company until you have worked there. Give a general answer instead: "I would like to be in a middle management position in five years, and in ten years I would hope to be somewhere in top management." Be careful not to seem too upwardly mobile, or you could threaten the interviewer.

Interviewing and the Law

Numerous laws govern what questions are and are not legal to ask in employment interviews, but the general principle that underlies all these laws is simple: questions may not be asked for the purpose of discriminating on the basis of race, color, religion, sex, national origin, or age. According to the Equal Employment Opportunity Commission, an employer cannot use responses to non–job-related questions to discriminate against broad categories of applicants.

When asked what you deem to be an illegal question, you can respond in one of several ways:

1. You can inform the interviewer that you believe the question is irrelevant and politely refuse to answer it.
2. You can make light of it, perhaps in a humorous fashion.
3. You can rephrase the question to respond to what the interviewer really wants to know.
4. You can answer the question directly.

Responses 2 and 3 are perhaps your best bet. For example, if an interviewer asks you how old your children are, you could respond, "My two children are teenagers; actually, don't you think parents of teenagers deserve some type of medal?" Or you could say, "I think what you want to know is whether my children will interfere with my work attendance. I have not missed any days of work in the last two years." If an interviewer's questions become too personal, you might consider whether you really want to work for such an employer.

Federal law restricts employment interview questions to areas clearly related to job requirements. It is generally legal for employers to do the following:

1. Ask an applicant to submit proof of age by supplying a birth certificate or baptismal record. (This is legal only if applicant is subject to verification of legal age requirements.)
2. Ask an applicant if he or she is a citizen of the United States.
3. Ask an applicant to indicate what foreign languages he or she can speak, write, or read fluently.
4. Ask an applicant about past work experience.
5. Request that an applicant provide names of family or relatives who work in the same company.
6. Tell an applicant that he or she must observe prescribed standards (for example, to keep hair short) to obtain a position.
7. Ask an applicant if he or she has reliable transportation to work. (However, an employer cannot ask what type of transportation an applicant has.)
8. Ask an applicant if he or she has ever been under the care of a psychologist or psychiatrist. (*Note:* in some states, employers cannot legally ask this.)
9. Ask an applicant to perform the job on a trial basis before being hired, if the applicant's physical height, weight, or other personal-stamina conditions could affect his or her work performance.

10. Ask an applicant how he or she can be reached if he or she has no phone.
11. Ask an applicant if he or she is a veteran and to state the type of military work performed.
12. Ask an applicant for the names of references.

It is generally illegal for an interviewer to do the following:

1. Ask if an applicant has ever worked under another name.
2. Ask an applicant to name his or her birthplace.
3. Ask about the birthplace of an applicant's parents, spouse, or other close relatives.
4. Ask an obviously older person to submit proof of age.
5. Ask an applicant about religious affiliation, name of church, parish, or religious holidays observed.
6. Ask an applicant if he or she is a naturalized citizen.
7. Ask an applicant for the date he or she acquired citizenship.
8. Ask an applicant if he or she was ever arrested for any crime and to indicate when and where.
9. Ask a veteran what type of military discharge he or she received.
10. Ask an applicant how he or she acquired the ability to read, write, or speak a foreign language.
11. Ask an applicant for his or her weight and height.
12. Ask an applicant if he or she is married, single, divorced, separated, or engaged.
13. Ask a female applicant for her maiden name.
14. Ask an applicant for his or her mother's maiden name.
15. Ask a female applicant if she has children and if she has problems related to child care.
16. Ask for the names of an applicant's brothers and sisters.
17. Ask if the applicant is a member of any clubs, societies, and lodges and to name them.
18. Ask that a photograph be included with application for employment.
19. Ask for addresses of an applicant's relatives, such as cousins, uncles, aunts, nephews, and grandparents, who can be contacted for reference.
20. Ask an applicant to specify the type of transportation he or she will use to travel to work.

Following Up

One way to leave a lasting impression is to be innovative—do something different. This is the premise for follow-up letters and thank-you notes in a job-seeking campaign; therefore, be sure to send a thank-you letter after the interview. Even if you did not get the job, a letter calls attention to your application so that the next time a position is available the chances of your being remembered are greater. It is better to write a letter than it is to telephone. A telephone call takes up the interviewer's valuable time in a business day. A letter, on the other hand, gives an interviewer something tangible to refer to later. (Figure 9.1 is a sample thank-you letter.)

3220 Frontier Avenue
Anaheim, CA 92802
June 25, 1993

Mr. James Earl Wright
District Sales Manager
Southern Pacific Air Freight
2411 La Palma Avenue
Anaheim, CA 92806

Dear Mr. Wright:

Thank you for your time and for the courtesy you showed me during our interview last Thursday afternoon. As a result of our interview, I am even more convinced that the position of sales representative with Southern Pacific Air Freight is exactly the challenge I am seeking.

In consideration of my 15 years of sales and marketing experience, my interest, and my enthusiasm, I feel I am capable of making a real contribution to the continued growth and profit picture of Southern Pacific Air Freight.

You mentioned that the next step would be another interview with one of your executives. I am looking forward to such an interview and will be available at your convenience. Enclosed is my completed employment application.

Sincerely,

Thomas G. Corbin

Thomas G. Corbin

enclosure

Figure 9.1 Sample thank-you letter sent after an interview

2499 East Second Street, #9
Lewisberg, PA 17837
June 10, 1993

Mr. William Walters
Employment Manager
Middlebury and Associates
9422 East Washington Blvd.
Lewisberg, PA 17839

Dear Mr. Walters:

Thank you for your time and consideration throughout our past meetings. I understand the competitive nature of the job market and the difficulty you face in choosing the right person for the job.

Although this has not turned out to be the right time for my employment with you, I remain enthusiastic about Middlebury and Associates and its land development projects. Since we last talked, I have completed another course in computer-aided drafting; this additional education could prove valuable for future openings at your company.

I hope you will keep my application on file for consideration in case another opening occurs in your organization in the near future.

Sincerely,

Charles Newman
Charles Newman

Figure 9.2 Sample letter sent to an interviewer after the job applicant has been rejected for employment

If you have been turned down for a position, you still should write a letter that expresses your continued interest and hope for future openings in the company. After being rejected, naturally you may want to find out why you were not hired. However, the author's research indicates that *very few* employers are willing to go out on a limb and counsel you for your next go-around. A few may simply state something like, "We had several qualified candidates, and we selected someone with extensive experience. . . ." It may be best just to keep in touch by reapplying to the company. Figure 9.2 is a sample letter an applicant would send after being rejected by a company.

If you have the good fortune of being selected for a position, be sure the specifics of the position are in writing. Richard Irish, in his book *Go Hire Yourself An Employer* (1987), advises applicants not to accept a job until the salary and fringe benefits have been agreed upon and clearly stated in a written *employment agreement* that describes the details of your employment. If the employer does not have such an agreement, write your own (see Figure 9.3). This letter will prevent any future misunderstandings in the event that the person who hired you forgets his or her promises or leaves the company. Keep a copy of the letter for your own files.

♦ Summary

This chapter concludes our discussion of marketing yourself. In reality, however, you will refer to Chapters Eight and Nine time and again until you have actually completed your career transition. Be sure to take the time to write your answers to the interview questions in the written exercises that follow. If you prepare, you will be very pleased with the results. Remember, each interview brings you closer to your goal—your new career. Relax and enjoy!

♦ EXERCISE 9.1 Interview Questions

Write your answers to the following questions. This exercise is designed to help you organize your thoughts in preparation for a successful interview.

1. Tell me something about yourself. (A broad "sizing-up" question.) ______________________________

   ____

2. What jobs have you held, and how did you obtain them? (Does it show initiative on your part?) ______________________________

   ____

3. Why did you leave your last job? (Be honest, but be careful not to leave a negative impression.) ______________________________

   ____

9801 East River Road
Ann Arbor, MI 48108
March 16, 1993

Mr. Harvey J. Richards
Vice President, Human Resources
Great American Life Insurance Company
1200 Newport Center Drive
Newport Beach, CA 92660

Dear Mr. Richards:

I am enthusiastic about the prospect of working for Peggy Martin in your organization's Human Resources Division. Before I formally accept the position, I want to confirm some of the points covered in our discussion last Friday.

- I will begin employment as an employment assistant at an annual salary of $21,000. After I have been employed for six months, Ms. Martin will evaluate my performance, and I will have an opportunity for a merit salary increase of up to 5 percent, depending on the quality of my work. Six months after that, or one year from the date of my employment, Ms. Martin will reevaluate my work, and I will have another opportunity for a salary increase of up to 5 percent. At that time the possibility of promotion will also be discussed.

- In addition to merit increases, Great American offers annual cost-of-living increases that have averaged from 1 to 4 percent over the past five years.

- Although Great American generally offers its employees three weeks' paid vacation, I will receive ten days during my first year of employment.

- My fringe benefits include full coverage in the company health insurance plan and an optional low-cost dental plan.

If I have understood you correctly on the preceding points, you may assume I have accepted the position with Great American.

I look forward to working for Ms. Martin beginning April 15. If both you and Ms. Martin are in agreement with all the points listed in this letter, please sign and date at the bottom and return a copy to me. A self-addressed stamped envelope is included for your convenience.

Sincerely,

Patricia O'Reilly
Patricia O'Reilly

____________________ ____________________
Harvey Richards Peggy Martin

Figure 9.3 Sample employment agreement letter

4. Which of your past jobs did you enjoy the most? Why? (Explain fully, but be concise. Be sure to bring out the positive elements.) ____________________________________

____

5. How have your past jobs prepared you for this position? (In other words, how promotable are you?) ________________
____

6. What are your weaknesses? (Make your weaknesses possible strengths; remember, answer a negative with a positive.)
____
____

7. What are your strengths? (You might say something like, "I work well with others on a team basis.") ________________
____

8. Why do you think you would like to work for our company? (Do your homework, and find out all you can about the company.)
____
____

9. How do you think your present supervisor (subordinates, co-workers) would describe you? (Do not be caught off guard on this one; have your response ready.) ________________
____

10. How can you contribute to this job? To our company? (Explain those skills pertinent to the position.) ________________
____

11. Why did you choose the career you are now pursuing? (In other words, How satisfied are you with your career? How long can we expect you to stay with us?) ________________
____

12. How do you work under pressure? (Give some examples; this indicates your working style.) ________________
____

13. What do you see yourself doing five years from now? (What are your long-term goals, and how do they fit in with our company?) ________________
____

14. What motivates you to put forth your greatest effort? (What is important to you? This indicates your work ethic.) ________
____

15. Describe your greatest accomplishments in your past jobs. (Describe those pertinent to the job, but be careful not to ramble.) ______

______

16. What is the biggest mistake you have made in your career? (Be careful on this one: everyone is human. Explain what you learned from a previous mistake.) ______

______

17. How do you feel about working with a younger or older supervisor? (Your concern should be that you do the best possible job for the company; the supervisor is there to help. Age is not a criterion of ability to do this.) ______

______

18. Why do you think we should hire you for this job? (Rehearse this carefully; be clear and concise.) ______

______

19. Do you have any questions about the company or job? (Be prepared to ask some questions.) ______

______

20. Do you have anything you would like to tell me about yourself? (Do you have any additional information the interviewer should be aware of? For example, if you are bilingual, mention it.)

______

______

♦ EXERCISE 9.2 Practicing Your Interviewing Skills

Practice your interviewing skills. This is best done by being videotaped. If videotaping is not possible, arrange for a practice session with a friend, colleague, or career counselor. Use the following critique form for the evaluation.

Interview evaluation form

Name: ______
(Person being interviewed)

	VG	*S*	*F*	*NI*	*COMMENTS*
1. Initial or opening presentation (Impression)					
2. Eye contact					

(continued)

	VG	*S*	*F*	*NI*	*COMMENTS*
3. Sitting position					
4. General appearance and grooming—hair, make-up, shave, beard, mustache, clothing, etc.					
5. Ability to describe past work experience, education, and training					
6. Abiity to explain equipment, tools, and other mechanical aids used					
7. Ability to explain skills, techniques, processes, and procedures; ability to stress how skills relate to job					
8. Ability to explain personal goals, interests, and desires					
9. Ability to explain questionable factors in personal life (functional limitations, frequent job changes, many years since last job)					
10. Ability to answer questions or make statements about company or job being sought					
11. Ability to listen attentively to interviewer's questions and to notice his or her body language					
12. Manner of speech or conversation (voice, tone, pitch, volume, speed)					
13. Physical mannerisms (facial expressions, gestures)					
14. Enthusiasm, interest in job					
15. Attitude (positive?), confidence level					
16. Overall impression: Would you hire this applicant?					

Overall Evaluation: ____________________

VG = Very Good
S = Satisfactory
F = Fair
NI = Needs Improvement

Personal job search progress record

Name ______________________

Employer Contact Person. Title Address/Tel. No.	Method of Contact				Response from Employer		Your Follow-Up			Invitation for Plant/Office Visit				Employer Response		Comments
	Campus Interviews	Letter. Resume	Phone Call	Date	Yes	No	Letter	Phone Call	Date	No	Yes	Date of Visit	Location	Salary Offer	No Offer	Accept or Reject Offer

♦ EXERCISE 9.3 Recording Your Progress

Use the personal job search progress record to record your progress in the job search.

♦ Notes

IRISH, R. (1987). *Go hire yourself an employer.* Garden City, NY: Anchor Press/ Doubleday.

A Vocational History Questionnaire

Writing a complete vocational history can accomplish two important objectives: it can help you summarize your background and experience; and it can provide valuable information that will assist you in making a satisfactory career decision. If this questionnaire is given to a career counselor or other counseling professional, the information you give will be considered confidential.

Name ______________________ Date ____________

Address ______________________________________

Telephone (home) ______________ (office) ____________

Age ______________ Date of birth ______________

Your present job title ______________________________

Year begun ______________ Salary ______________

List several positive and negative aspects of your job:

(+) ____

(−) ____

Outline your advancement history: ______________________

____

____

____

Describe your feelings about your immediate supervisor: ______

____

____

____

What are your possibilities for advancement on this job? ______

____

____

____

List the people who have had the most influence on your career development:

1. ____
2. ____
3. ____
4. ____
5. ____

Which of the following have you done during the last month? (check as many as apply)

___ Talked to a friend about my career
___ Visited a new job site
___ Completed some form of vocational testing
___ Sent out my resume
___ Thought about my career
___ Read information about careers
___ Read a book on careers
___ Read the want ads
___ Talked to a recruiter
___ Went to an employment agency
___ Talked to a career counselor
___ Talked to a person working in a job that interests me

Describe any career failures you have experienced: ____________

____

____

____

Describe any career successes you have experienced: ____________

____

____

____

List all degrees, certificates, licenses, and advanced training you have received: ______________________________________

____

____

____

Degrees/certificates	Year completed
______________________________	______________
______________________________	______________
______________________________	______________
______________________________	______________

List all the jobs (part-time and full-time, paid and nonpaid) that you have held during each of the following periods of your life; be specific.

YOUNG ADULT (AGES 16 TO 21)

Job title ______________________________ Years ____________

How obtained ____

Positive and negative aspects _________________________________

____

Job title ______________________________ Years ____________

How obtained ____

Positive and negative aspects _________________________________

____

ADULT (AGES 22 TO PRESENT)

Job title ______________________ Years __________

How obtained ______________________________

Positive and negative aspects ______________________

Job title ______________________ Years __________

How obtained ______________________________

Positive and negative aspects ______________________

____

____

Job title ______________________ Years __________

How obtained ______________________________

Positive and negative aspects ______________________

____

____

List any other information that would assist your career counselor in understanding your situation.

____

____

____

____

____

____

____

B Financial Planning Guide

The following is a composite of information gleaned from several financial planners. It is intended to help you put your financial affairs in order while you are in career transition. It can help you identify expenses that could be reduced if your job search takes longer than anticipated. If you have been unemployed for a while, it may be wise to talk to your creditors before you fall too far behind in your payments. You may be able to work something out, and you will probably receive much better consideration from your creditors in the long run.

Although this guide can assist you in analyzing your own situation, you should not use it in lieu of consulting a certified financial planner. As a matter of fact, you may want to use these data when you consult a financial professional. You may also want to discuss such things as borrowing against your life insurance policy rather than cashing it in; your policy may offer a lower interest rate than is currently available. You might also consider a single-source loan to consolidate smaller debts. Finally, as stated earlier in this book, you may need to work at a part-time job while you conduct your job search.

When you analyze your finances, you will want to examine three basic areas: your projected current expenses, your present cash position and projected income, and sources of additional income or cash. The latter is necessary in case you decide to extend your transition time.

♦ Estimated Expenses

The following are types of expenses common to most households. This list is a very general guide. However, while completing this exercise, you may uncover hidden expenses or hidden income that could make a difference in your planning. Also, keep in mind that if you are undergoing a complete career change, you may incur extra expenses for gasoline, telephone, postage, and printing; be sure to budget for these expenditures.

Months

	1	*2*	*3*	*4*	*5*	*6*
Food						
Mortgage or rent						
Clothing						
Automotive expenses: Gas						
Maintenance						
Household operations: Heating						
Electricity						
Water						
Telephone						
Property taxes						
Automobile insurance premiums						
Medical insurance premiums						
Life insurance premiums						
Other installment payments						
Bills and debts outstanding						
Interest on debts						
Local transportation (taxi, bus)						
College tuition						

(continued)

Months

	1	2	3	4	5	6
Other travel						
Laundry and dry cleaning						
Barber/beauty salon expenses						
Entertainment						
Drugs and medical supplies						
Personal items (cosmetics, etc.)						
Contributions/gifts						
Other/miscellaneous						
TOTAL (All the above)						
Estimated job search costs						
GRAND TOTAL (Estimated cash outflow)						

♦ Estimated Income

The following are categories for assessing your present income and anticipated future cash inflow. If you are now on a monthly salary or severance pay, you obviously can just list it. However, if your income fluctuates (as in the case of sales), or if you receive dividends or other payments on an irregular basis, divide the total amount evenly into six months. After you have listed all your sources of income and anticipated cash inflow, you will be in a better position to make decisions based on the comparison of these amounts with your calculated expenses.

Months

	1	2	3	4	5	6
Monthly salary or severance pay						
Unused vacation pay						
Unemployment compensation						
Retirement funds						
Pay in lieu of stock plan						
Interest from savings account						
Dividends from stocks						

(continued)

	Months					
	1	2	3	4	5	6
Interest from bonds						
Tax refund						
Collectable debts owed to you						
Income generated by spouse						
Income generated by part-time job						
Other						
TOTAL (Anticipated cash position)						

♦ Sources of Additional Income or Cash

In case you are unemployed for a long period, you should have a plan for generating additional income or cash. The following is merely a guide for you to brainstorm such a plan. Of course, no one wants to have to take these measures. However, having a contingency plan can provide you with a sense of security in case of unforeseen events. At this point, you have no doubt thought about holding down extra expenses, such as entertainment, gifts, contributions, lessons for the children, extra telephones, and so on.

	Months					
	1	2	3	4	5	6
Secondary properties						
Automobiles (second car)						
Sporting equipment (boats, planes, campers)						
Expensive hobby equipment (cameras, guns, etc.)						
Jewelry						
Furs						
Musical equipment						
Works of art						
Other equipment (unused appliances, etc.)						
Other						
TOTAL (Supplemental income)						

C Supplemental Reading

♦ Sources for Career Change

ALLEN, J. G., & GORKIN, J. (1985). *Finding the right job at midlife.* New York: Simon & Schuster.

BASTRESS, F. (1989). *The relocating spouse's guide to employment.* Chevy Chase, MD: Woodley.

BLOCHER, D. H. (1989). *Career actualization and life planning.* Denver, CO: Love.

BOLLES, R. N. (1992). *What color is your parachute?* Berkeley, CA: Ten Speed Press.

BRIDGES, W. (1984). *Transitions.* Reading, MA: Addison-Wesley.

COVEY, S. R. (1989). *The seven habits of highly effective people.* New York: Simon & Schuster.

COXFORD, L. M. (1991). *Résumé writing made easy* (4th ed.). Scottsdale, AZ: Gorsuch Scarisbrick.

DAIL, H. L. (1989). *The lotus and the pool: How to create your own career.* Boston: Shambhala.

DAVIS, M., ESHELMAN, E. R., & McKAY, M. (1991). *The relaxation and stress reduction workbook* (4th ed.). Oakland, CA: New Harbinger.

DOWD, M. E. (1987). *A consumer's guide to financial planning: How to get the best plan for your money.* New York: Watts.

FALVEY, J. (1987). *What next? Career strategies after 35.* Charlotte, VT: Williamson.

FEDER, M. E. (1989). *Money minder: Simplify, organize, and manage your personal financial records.* Blue Ridge Summit, PA: Liberty House.

FIGLER, H. (1988). *The complete job-search handbook.* New York: Holt.

FITZPATRICK, W. G. (1990). *Does your resume wear combat boots? Successful transition from military to civilian life: A job seeking guide.* Charlottesville, VA: Blue Jeans Press.

HOOVER, G., CAMPBELL, A., & SPAIN, P. J. (1990). *Hoover's handbook: Profiles of over 500 major corporations.* Austin, TX: Reference Press.

IRISH, R. (1987). *Go hire yourself an employer.* Garden City, NY: Anchor Press/Doubleday.

JAFFE, D. T., & SCOTT, C. D. (1984). *From burnout to balance: A workbook for peak performance and self-renewal.* New York: McGraw-Hill.

KRANNICH, R. L. (1989). *Careering and re-careering for the 1990's.* Manassas, VA: Impact.

LAKEIN, A. (1989). *How to get control of your time and your life.* New York: NAL/Dutton.

LEWIN, E. (1989). *Financial fitness for new families.* New York: Facts on File.

MASON, J. W. (1990). *The easy family budget.* Boston: Houghton Mifflin.

MAYER, N. (1978). *The male mid-life crisis: Fresh starts after 40.* Garden City, NY: Doubleday.

MEDLEY, H. A. (1984). *Sweaty palms: The neglected art of being interviewed.* Belmont, CA: Lifetime Learning.

MOLLOY, J. T. (1987). *John T. Molloy's new dress for success.* New York: Warner Books.

NADEL, L., HAIMS, J., & STEMPSON, R. (1990). *Sixth sense.* New York: Prentice Hall Press (Simon & Schuster, Inc.).

NAISBITT, J., & ABURDENE, P. (1990). *Megatrends 2000.* New York: Morrow.

PINES, A., & ARONSON, E. (1988). *Career burnout: Causes and cures.* New York: Free Press.

PORTER, S. (1990). *Sylvia Porter's your finances in the 1990's.* New York: Prentice-Hall.

ROBBINS, P. I. (1978). *Successful midlife career change.* New York: AMACOM.

SHER, B. (1983). *Wishcraft: How to get what you really want.* New York: Ballantine Books.

SINETAR, M. (1987). *Do what you love, the money will follow.* New York: Dell.

STUDNER, P. K. (1990). *Super job search: The complete manual for job-seekers and career-changers.* Los Angeles: Jamenair.

VANCASPEL, V. (1988). *Money dynamics for the 1990's.* New York: Simon & Schuster.

VAN HOOSE, W. H. (1985). *Midlife myths and realities.* Atlanta, GA: Humanics.

WOODMAN, B. E. (1987). *Personal financial planning.* Andover, MA: Brick House.

♦ Sources for Entrepreneurs

AASENG, NATHAN. *From rags to riches: People who started businesses from scratch.* Minneapolis, MN: Lerner.

BANGS, D. H. (1989). *Start up guide: A one-year plan for entrepreneurs.* Portsmouth, NH: Upstart.

BERMONT, H. (1989). *How to become a successful consultant in your own field.* Rocklin, CA: Prima.

BREITBARD, S., & CARPENTER, D. S. (1990). *The Price Waterhouse book of personal financial planning* (rev. ed.). New York: Holt.

BROWN, D. (1990). *The entrepreneur's guide.* New York: Ballantine Books.

DESSAUER, J. P. (1991). *Passport to profits: Opportunities in international investing.* Chicago: Dearborn Financial Publications.

DRUCKER, P. F. (1985). *Innovation and entrepreneurship: Practice and principles.* New York: Harper & Row.

EYLER, D. R. (1990). *Starting and operating a home-based business.* New York: Wiley.

FALLEK, M. (1990). *How to set up your own small business.* Minneapolis, MN: American Institute of Small Business.

FEINGOLD, S. N. (1987). *Making it on your own.* Washington, DC; Acropolis Books.

FROHBIETER-MUELLER, J. (1987). *Stay home and mind your own business: How to manage your time, space, personal obligations, money, business, and yourself while working at home.* White Hall, VA: Betterway.

FUCINI, J. J. (1987). *Experience, Inc.: Men and women who founded famous companies after the age of 40.* New York: Free Press.

GIVENS, C. J. (1990). *Financial self defense: How to stop getting taken and start making money.* New York: Simon & Schuster.

GOLDSTEIN, A. S. (1984). *Starting on a shoestring: Building a business without a bankroll.* (2nd ed.). New York: Wiley.

GOULD, J. S. (1987). *Starting from scratch: Fifty profitable business opportunities.* New York: Wiley.

HOLTZ, H. (1989). *How to make money with your desktop computer.* New York: Wiley.

HOLTZ, H. (1990). *The complete work-at-home companion.* Rocklin, CA: Prima.

JONES, C., & THE P. LIEF GROUP. (1987). *The 220 best franchises to buy.* New York: Bantam Books.

JONES, S., COHEN, M. B., & COPPOLA, V. V. (1988). *The Coopers & Lybrand guide to growing your own business.* New York: Wiley.

KAHN, S., & THE P. LIEF GROUP. (1988). *One-hundred and one best businesses to start.* New York: Doubleday.

KLEIN, F. (1990). *Building a profitable business.* Seattle, WA: Entrepreneurial Workshops.

LASSER, J. K. (1989). *How to run a small business* (6th ed.). New York: McGraw-Hill.

MANCUSO, J. R. (1984). *How to start, finance, and manage your own small business.* Englewood Cliffs, NJ: Prentice-Hall.

MUCCIOLO, L. (1987). *Make it yours! How to own your own business, buy a business, start a business, franchise a business.* New York: Wiley.

SCHREIBER, N. (1991). *Your home office.* New York: Harper & Row.

SERVICE CORPS OF RETIRED EXECUTIVES (SCORE). *Preliminary points to consider in planning a business of your own.* Washington D.C.: U.S. Small Business Administration.

STEVENS, M. (1988). *The Macmillan small business handbook.* New York: Macmillan.

WHITMYER, C., RASBERRY, S., & PHILLIPS, M. (1989). *Running a one-person business.* Berkeley, CA: Ten Speed Press.

♦ Sources for Women

GARDENSWARTZ, L. (1987). *What it takes: Good news from 100 of America's top professional and business women.* New York: Doubleday.

HYATT, C. (1980). *The woman's selling game: How to sell yourself . . . and anything else.* New York: Warner Books.

INGRAM, S. (1978). *A woman's guide to personal and business credit.* New York: Pilot Books.

JACKSON, C. (1987). *Color me beautiful.* New York: Ballantine Books.

JENNINGS, D. (1987). *Self-made women: Twelve of America's leading entrepreneurs talk about success, self-image, and the superwoman.* Dallas, TX: Taylor.

JENSEN, M. (1987). *Women who want to be boss: Business revelations and success strategies from America's top female executives.* Garden City, NJ: Doubleday.

JESSUP, C., & CHIPPS, G. (1991). *The woman's guide to starting a business.* New York: Holt.

LESTER, M. (1989). *A woman's guide to starting a small business.* Babylon, NY: Pilot Books.

MACKOFF, B. (1990). *What Mona Lisa knew: A woman's guide to getting ahead in business by lightening up.* Los Angeles: Lowell House.

MITCHELL, J. S. (1982). *I can be anything: A career book for women.* (3rd ed.). New York: College Entrance Examination Board.

PERKINS, G. (1980). *The women's financial survival handbook.* New York: American Library.

ROGERS, H. C. (1988). *Rogers' rules for businesswomen: How to start a career and move up the ladder.* New York: St. Martin's Press.

SCOLLARD, J. R. (1985). *The self-employed woman: How to start your own business and gain control of your life.* New York: Simon & Schuster.

SENTER, S. (1982). *Women at work: A psychologist's secrets to getting ahead in business.* New York: Coward, McCann & Geoghegan.

WILKENS, J. (1987). *Her own business: Success secrets of entrepreneurial women.* New York: McGraw-Hill.

WISELY, R. (1981). *The independent woman: How to start and succeed in your own business.* Los Angeles: Tarcher.

ZEITZ, B. (1988). *The best companies for women.* New York: Simon & Schuster.

D Bibliography and Resource List for Older Workers

Bibliography

ADLER, J. (1975). *The retirement book: A complete early-planning guide to finances, new activities, and where to live.* New York: Morrow.

ASQUITH, G. H. (1975). *Living creatively as an older adult.* Scottsdale, PA: Herald Press.

BADDELEY, A. D. (1976). *The psychology of memory.* New York: Basic Books.

BADDELEY, A. D. (1982). *Your memory, a user's guide.* New York: Macmillan.

BARNES, J. (1978). *More money for your retirement.* New York: Harper & Row.

BIRSNER, E. P. (1991). *The 40+ job hunting guide: Official handbook of the 40+ club.* New York: Facts on File.

BOLLES, R. N. (1978). *The three boxes of life: And how to get out of them.* Berkeley, CA: Ten Speed Press.

CARLSON, A. D. (1979). *In the fullness of time.* South Yarmouth, MA: Curley.

COMFORT, A. (1976). *A good age.* New York: Crown.

DOUD, M. E. (1987). *A consumer's guide to financial planning: How to get the best plan for your money.* New York: Watts.

GALLANT, R. A. (1980). *Memory: How it works and how to improve it.* New York: Four Winds Press.

KINZEL, R. K. (1979). *Retirement: Creating promise out of threat.* New York: AMACOM.

LEVINSON, D. (1978). *The seasons of a man's life.* New York: Knopf.

LOCKERBIE, J. W. (1976). *Fifty plus: How recycling your potential now can mean a joyous and fulfilled tomorrow.* Old Tappan, NJ: Revell.

MAYER, N. (1978). *The male mid-life crisis: Fresh starts after forty.* New York: Doubleday.

MITCHELL, J. (1986). *Making more money: Fifty-five special job hunt strategies for retirees.* New York: Prentice-Hall.

MONEY MAGAZINE. (1989). *Guide to a secure retirement.* Boulder, CO: Oxmoor House.

MORGAN, J. S. (1987). *Getting a job after 50.* Princeton, NJ: Petrocelli Books.

MYERS, A., & ANDERSON, C. P. (1984). *Success over sixty.* New York: Summit Books.

OLSEN, N. (1986). *Starting a mini-business: A guidebook for seniors and others who dream of having their own part-time, home-based business.* Sunnyvale, CA: Bear Flag Books.

Price waterhouse retirement planning advisor, 1992–93. (1992). New York: Simon & Schuster.

ROSENFIELD, I. (1988). *The invention of memory: A new view of the brain.* New York: Basic Books.

SHANE, D. (1989). *Finances after 50: Financial planning for the rest of your life.* New York: Perennial Library.

SHEPPARD, H. L. (1977). *The graying of working America: The coming crisis in retirement-age policy.* New York: Free Press.

TEGELER, D. (1990). *Retiring in Arizona: Your onestop guide to living, loving, and lounging under the sun.* Phoenix, AZ: Fiesta Books.

URIS, A. (1979). *Over 50: The definitive guide to retirement.* Radnor, PA: Chilton.

WALTON, W. R. (1978). *The retirement decision: How the new social security and retirement age laws affect you.* Kansas City, MO: Sheed Andres and McMeel.

WEAVER, P. (1980). *Strategies for the second half of life.* New York: Watts.

♦ Resource List

AARP Books Catalog 1991/AARP Books
Scott, Foresman and Company
1865 Miner Street, Dept. OF10
Des Plaines, IA 60016
1-800-627-6565

American Association of Retired Persons
Worker Equity Department
1909 K Street, NW
Washington, DC 20049
(202) 662-4956

American Civil Liberties Union
132 West 43rd Street
New York, NY 10036
(212) 944-9800

EEO Institute
4801 Massachusetts Avenue, NW
Washington, DC 20016
(202) 364-8710

Equal Employment Opportunity Commission
2401 East Street, NW
Washington, DC 20506
1-800-USA-EEOC

Forty Plus
15 Park Row
New York, NY 10038
(212) 233-6086

Forty Plus
23172 Plaza Point
Laguna Hills, CA 92653
(714) 581-7990

Legal Services for the Elderly
132 West 43rd Street
New York, NY 10036
(212) 595-1340

National Association for Human Development
1750 Pennsylvania Avenue, NW
Washington, DC 20006
(202) 393-1881

National Association of Area Agencies on Aging
2033 K Street, NW
Suite 208, West Wing
Washington, DC 20024
(202) 484-7520

National Association of State Units on Aging
2033 K Street, NW, Suite 304
Washington, DC 20006
(202) 785-0707

National Caucus and Center on Black Aged
1414 K Street, NW, Suite 500
Washington, DC 20005
(202) 637-8400

National Clearinghouse on Aging
Department of Health and Human Services
Washington, DC 20201
(202) 245-0188

National Commission For Employment Policy
1522 K Street, NW, Suite 300
Washington, DC 20005
(202) 724-1545

National Council of Senior Citizens
925 15th Street, NW
Washington, DC 20005
(202) 347-8800

National Council on the Aging
600 Maryland Avenue, SW
West Wing 100
Washington, DC 20024
(202) 479-1200

National Senior Citizens Law Center
1424 16th Street, NW, Suite 300
Washington, DC 20036
(202) 232-6570

Select Committee on Aging
U.S. House of Representatives
300 New Jersey Avenue, SE
Room 712, HOB Annex 1
Washington, DC 20515
(202) 226-3375

Special Committee on Aging
U.S. Senate
SD-G41
Washington, DC 20510
(202) 224-5364

Index

TO THE OWNER OF THIS BOOK:

I hope that you have been significantly influenced by *Changing Careers: Steps to Success*. I'd like to know as much about your experiences with the book as you care to offer. Your comments can help me make it a better book for future readers.

School: ______________________ Instructor's name: ____________________

Address of school (city, state, and zip code): ______________________________

1. What I like most about this book is: ______________________________

____

____

2. What I like least about this book is: ______________________________

____

____

3. Of how much interest and value were the exercises? ____________________

____

4. Specific topics in the book I thought were most relevant and important: ___________

____

____

5. Specific suggestions for improving the book: __________________________

____

____

6. The name of the course in which I used this book: _____________________

____

7. In the space below—or in a separate letter, if you care to write one—please let me know what other comments about the book you'd like to make. I welcome your suggestions!

Optional:

Your name: ______________________________ Date: ____________________

May Brooks/Cole quote you, either in promotion for *Changing Careers: Steps to Success* or in future publishing ventures?

Yes: _______ No: _______

Sincerely,
Lola Sikula

FOLD HERE

NO POSTAGE NECESSARY IF MAILED IN THE UNITED STATES

BUSINESS REPLY MAIL

FIRST CLASS PERMIT NO. 358 PACIFIC GROVE, CA

POSTAGE WILL BE PAID BY ADDRESSEE

ATT: *Lola Sikula*

Brooks/Cole Publishing Company
511 Forest Lodge Road
Pacific Grove, California 93950-9968

FOLD HERE

Brooks/Cole is dedicated to publishing quality publications for education in the human services fields. If you are interested in learning more about our publications, please fill in your name and address an request our latest catalogue.

Name ________________________________

Street Address ________________________________

City, State, and Zip ________________________________

FOLD HERE

BUSINESS REPLY MAIL

FIRST CLASS PERMIT NO. 358 PACIFIC GROVE, CA

POSTAGE WILL BE PAID BY ADDRESSEE

ATT: *Human Services Catalogue*

Brooks/Cole Publishing Company
511 Forest Lodge Road
Pacific Grove, California 93950-9968

FOLD HERE